Muslims, Scholars, Soldiers

AAR
AMERICAN ACADEMY OF RELIGION

ACADEMY SERIES

SERIES EDITOR
Kimberly Rae Connor, University of San Francisco

A Publication Series of
The American Academy of Religion
and
Oxford University Press

CREATIVE DWELLING
Empathy and Clarity in God and Self
Lucinda A. Stark Huffaker

HOSPITALITY TO STRANGERS
Empathy and the Physician-Patient Relationship
Dorothy M. Owens

THE BONDS OF FREEDOM
Feminist Theology and Christian Realism
Rebekah L. Miles

THE SPECTER OF SPECIESISM
Buddhist and Christian Views of Animals
Paul Waldau

INCARNATION AND PHYSICS
Natural Science in the Theology of Thomas F. Torrance
Tapio Luoma

OF BORDERS AND MARGINS
Hispanic Disciples in Texas, 1888–1945
Daisy L. Machado

YVES CONGAR'S THEOLOGY OF THE HOLY SPIRIT
Elizabeth Teresa Groppe

HSIEH LIANG-TSO AND THE *ANALECTS* OF CONFUCIUS
Humane Learning as a Religious Quest
Thomas W. Selover

GREGORY OF NYSSA AND THE CONCEPT OF DIVINE PERSONS
Lucian Turcescu

GRAHAM GREENE'S CATHOLIC IMAGINATION
Mark Bosco, S.J.

COMING TO THE EDGE OF THE CIRCLE
A Wiccan Initiation Ritual
Nikki Bado-Fralick

THE ETHICS OF ANIMAL EXPERIMENTATION
A Critical Analysis and Constructive Christian Proposal
Donna Yarri

PAUL IN ISRAEL'S STORY
Self and Community at the Cross
John L. Meech

CROSSING THE ETHNIC DIVIDE
The Multiethnic Church on a Mission
Kathleen Garces-Foley

GOD AND THE VICTIM
Traumatic Intrusions on Grace and Freedom
Jennifer Erin Beste

THE CREATIVE SUFFERING OF THE TRIUNE GOD
An Evolutionary Theology
Gloria L. Schaab

A THEOLOGY OF CRITICISM
Balthasar, Postmodernism, and the Catholic Imagination
Michael P. Murphy

DISABILITY AND CHRISTIAN THEOLOGY
Embodied Limits and Constructive Possibilities
Deborah Beth Creamer

MEETING ON THE CROSS
Christ, the Cross, and the Feminist Critique
Arnfridur Gudmundsdottir

MUSLIMS, SCHOLARS, SOLDIERS
The Origin and Elaboration of the Ibāḍī Imāmate Traditions
Adam R. Gaiser

AAR
AMERICAN ACADEMY OF RELIGION

Muslims, Scholars, Soldiers

The Origin and Elaboration of the Ibāḍī Imāmate Traditions

ADAM R. GAISER

OXFORD
UNIVERSITY PRESS
2010

OXFORD
UNIVERSITY PRESS

Oxford University Press, Inc., publishes works that further
Oxford University's objective of excellence
in research, scholarship, and education.

Oxford New York
Auckland Cape Town Dar es Salaam Hong Kong Karachi
Kuala Lumpur Madrid Melbourne Mexico City Nairobi
New Delhi Shanghai Taipei Toronto

With offices in
Argentina Austria Brazil Chile Czech Republic France Greece
Guatemala Hungary Italy Japan Poland Portugal Singapore
South Korea Switzerland Thailand Turkey Ukraine Vietnam

Published by Oxford University Press, Inc.
198 Madison Avenue, New York, New York 10016
www.oup.com

Library of Congress Cataloging-in-Publication Data
Gaiser, Adam R., 1971–
Muslims, scholars, soldiers: the origin and elaboration of the Ibadi imamate traditions /
Adam R. Gaiser.
p. cm.
Includes bibliographical references and index.
ISBN 978-0-19-973893-9
1. Ibadites—History. 2. Imamate—History. I. Title.
BP195.I3G35 2010
297.8'33—dc22 2009042620

9 8 7 6 5 4 3 2 1

Printed in the United States of America
on acid-free paper

For Shirley Russell

Acknowledgments

Many have assisted me with my research, and deserve thanks. I would like to express gratitude to my advisor at the University of Virginia, Abdulaziz Sachedina, and to Cynthia Hoehler-Fatton, Elizabeth Thompson, and Robert Wilken, for their guidance, patience, and efforts on my behalf. Thanks to Dr. Romanella for his part in the completion of this work. I also thank Gordon and Robin Gaiser, and Shirley Russell for their encouragement and support. At Florida State University, John Kelsay read several drafts of this manuscript and offered his comments and guidance. Similarly, John Corrigan pointed me in the right direction too many times to count. My thanks go to the both of them for their leadership and wise counsel, and also to my colleagues at FSU who offered constant encouragement. I am grateful to Kim Conner for her steadfast work on my behalf, and to the anonymous readers of the manuscript for their comments. Finally, my thanks to Cynthia Read and the editorial board at the AAR/Oxford University Academy Series for their suggestions, and for seeing the work through.

The original research for this manuscript began in Amman, Jordan, with a Fulbright-Hays doctoral dissertation fellowship; my gratitude goes to Alain McNamara and the staff at the Fulbright Commission for their assistance. Many other scholars helped me during my year of research in Jordan; of special mention are ʻAbd al-ʻAzīz al-Dūrī and Muḥammad Khraysāt of the University of Jordan History Department, and Farūq ʻUmar Fawzī of the Omani Studies Department at Āl al-Bayt University. My appreciation goes to Ahmad Obeidat, Islam Dayeh, and

Nihad Khedair, my research assistants at the time (and now accomplished scholars of their own), for our many hours spent together in translation and discussion. I also thank the Omani Student Union in Amman, Āl al-Bayt University, and the University of Jordan, all of whom granted me unlimited use of their library and access to their manuscript collections. Further research took me to Muscat, Oman; thanks to Michael Bos, Shaykh ʿAbd al-Raḥmān al-Sālimī, Shaykh Kahlān b. Nahbān al-Kharūsī, Shaykh Mahmūd b. Zāhir al-Hināʾī, Dr. Khalfān al-Madūrī, Aḥmad al-Siyābī, Shaykh Ziyād b. Ṭālib al-Maʿāwalī of the *Maʿhad al-ʿUlūm al-Sharʿiyya*, and to the students who shared their research and excitement.

And finally, thanks go to Carolina Gonzalez for accompanying me on the way.

Contents

Abbreviations

BSOAS	*Bulletin of the School of Oriental and African Studies*
EI2	*Encyclopedia of Islam*, second edition
IJMES	*International Journal of Middle Eastern Studies*
JAOS	*Journal of the American Oriental Society*
SI	*Studia Islamica*
WTQwTh	*Wizārat al-Turāth al-Qawmī wa al-Thaqāfa*

Note on Transliteration, Dates, and Qur`ānic Citations

Transliterations from Arabic follow the *IJMES* system, which has become the standard system in the United States. I dispense in my chapters with diacritical marks over commonly used words or names (i.e., Sunni, Shi'a, Muhammad), but keep them in the bibliography. Dates are given as *hijri* year or century first, followed by a slash and then common-era year or century. For Qur`ānic citations, I use the 1923 Egyptian printed recension of Ḥafs from 'Aṣim, which has also become the standard.

Muslims, Scholars, Soldiers

Introduction

In their ascendancy during the late first/seventh through the early fourth/tenth centuries, the *khawārij* (sing. *khārijī*, also known by its Anglicized form, the Khārijites) represented a third column in Islamic history, an interpretation of Islam as promising as the proto-Sunni and pro-ʿAlid groupings that survived into the modern era as Sunni and Shiʿa Muslims. Islamic history, written in large part by the victorious Sunnis, remembers them chiefly as lawless brigands, theological deviants, and opponents of the rightful Caliphs—those who numbered among the seventy-two erring sects for whom the Prophet predicted damnation.[1] However, the distribution of Khārijite subsects throughout the Islamic world—from Spain to Afghanistan—testifies to their widespread popularity in early Islamic history. Likewise, the longevity of the Khārijite sects confirms their long-lasting appeal in the early Islamic world. Despite the rapid demise of the extremist Khārijites, as a result of their militancy, quietist Khārijite subsects persisted until the sixth/twelfth century before falling into obscurity. One group, the Ibāḍiyya, successfully established political dynasties in Oman and North Africa and survive to the present day in Oman, the Mzab region of Algeria, the Jabal Nafūsa area of Libya, Tunisia, and the east coast of Africa.

As the sole remaining Khārijite subsect, the Ibāḍiyya are the last representatives of the opposition movement that was Khārijism, and the inheritors of its narrative and legal traditions. When compared with other Islamic sects such as the Muʿtazilites or Murjiʾites, the endurance of Khārijism in its Ibāḍī form, even in the small numbers in which they survive, is a testament to their resourcefulness, and to the resilience of Ibāḍī thought. Although the connection between the Ibāḍiyya and the early Khārijites should not be overstated—centuries of change have transformed the modern Ibāḍiyya into a unique Islamic sect—nevertheless, they remain irrevocably linked to the early Khārijites. Just as certain species of modern birds are related to their evolutionary ancestors, the dinosaurs, so the religious thought of the Ibāḍiyya reveals a unique connection with classical Khārijism.

Of the subjects that comprise the religious thought of the Ibāḍiyya, no issue illustrates their relationship with early Khārijism more than the notion of authority as it was institutionalized in the Ibāḍī *imāma*—the institution of the Imām. The distinctive features of the Ibāḍī imāmate are an inheritance from the Khārijite era, and one that differentiates the Ibāḍiyya from their Sunni and Shi'a counterparts in the Islamic world. This is not surprising, for as Madelung rightly observes, "no event in history has divided Islam more profoundly and durably than the succession to Muhammad."[2] From the death of the Prophet, embryonic schisms involving the nature of legitimate succession existed within the Islamic community, and eventually fragmented the *umma* into sects. These different views toward legitimate authority became permanently embedded in the institutions of leadership that developed around the nascent Islamic sectarian groups. The Ibāḍī *imāma*, as heir to the Khārijite understanding of rightful succession, retained much of the uniquely Khārijite interpretation of authority.

At the same time, the Ibāḍī *imāma*, as it is preserved in the North African and Omani Ibāḍī legal and historical corpus, is an elaborate institution, and one that continued to develop long after the demise of other Khārijite subsects. Nevertheless, given the Ibāḍī relationship to Khārijism, the complexity of imāmate structures suggests an intricate debt to Khārijite notions of legitimate authority, which were themselves rooted in early Islamic conceptions of leadership. It is the aim of the present study to illuminate the foundations and subsequent elaboration of the Ibāḍī imāmate institutions by investigating their inheritance from Khārijite, early Islamic, and pre-Islamic traditions.

The Present Study: Scope and Methodology

Whereas scholars—contemporary and medieval alike—commonly associate the Ibāḍiyya with the constellation of groups collectively known as the Khārijites, and often posit continuity between them, it is less common to consider connections between the Khārijites and other near contemporaries, such as the early Islamic state as it existed under the so-called *rāshidūn* (rightly guided) Caliphs, the Umayyads, or members of what has been called the "pious opposition." Indeed, it is more often the case that treatments of the Khārijites isolate them as exceptional cases in early Islamic history. Although there are several reasons for such an approach—ranging from textual to scholarly prejudices—the perceived uniqueness of the Khārijites obscures the ways that the early Khārijites received traditions of religious and political authority, manipulated them according to their needs in specific historical conditions, and thus made them available to those who survived them, such as the Ibāḍiyya. Consequently, the intellectual continuity of the Ibāḍī *imāma* has not been sufficiently appreciated due, in part, to scholarly failure in considering the continuity of the Khārijite imāmate structures with non-Khārijite institutions and models of authority.

There are several reasons for such a failure. To begin with, until recently most researchers did not have sufficient access to Ibāḍī texts, and were therefore unable, first, to adequately assess the history and development of the Ibāḍite sect in relation to the Khārijites, and second, to use Ibāḍī sources as a means to illuminate early Islamic history from a quasi-Khārijite viewpoint.[3] Fortunately, recent publications by the Omani Ministry of Heritage and Culture (*Wizarat al-Turāth al-Qawmī wa al-Thaqāfa*) of much of the Ibāḍī historical and legal corpus have made hundreds of works accessible to the researcher. In addition, the Libyan scholar 'Amr Ennami collected and published several rare North African legal and theological works before his death,[4] while Crone and Zimmerman, working from a document provided by Ennami, completed a translation of an Ibāḍī manuscript—the epistle of Sālim Ibn Dhakwān—that dates from the second/eighth century.[5] These edited texts offer an important new resource for studies of the Ibāḍiyya, as well as, by extension, the Khārijites, and they have only just begun to be appreciated.

A second hurdle facing scholarship on the Ibāḍiyya and the Khārijites is the way that some scholars read and interpret the texts that they possess. One problem plaguing the study of the Ibāḍiyya and Khārijites is the uncritical reliance on either Sunni or Ibāḍī sources for historical narratives. Such an approach ignores the fact that these accounts were, to varying degrees, tailored to serve the polemical and self-serving interests of the sect.[6] Similarly, this same uncritical reliance on principally Sunni texts has directed other researchers to oversimplified and distorted conclusions about the Khārijites, in spite of caveats from scholars such as Watt and Lewinstein on the overall limitations of historical and heresiographical sources.[7] A common example of this mistake is to attribute to all Khārijite subsects the late Najdite belief that under certain circumstances the community did not require an Imām.[8] However, such a generalization, while appropriate to later manifestations of the Najdāt Khārijite subsect, cannot be applied to all Khārijite groups uniformly. It certainly cannot be applied to the Ibāḍiyya.

Yet another flawed method of viewing the Khārijites is to interpret their activities through the lens of their most extreme or militant subsects. It is not uncommon to find, for example, a focus on the Azāriqa (or Najdāt), whose core activities lasted a mere fourteen years, as representatives of "the original Khārijite position."[9] This statement grossly overestimates the importance of the Azraqite subsect to the general history of Khārijism, and relegates the Ibāḍiyya, who have survived for thirteen centuries (and, incidentally, opposed the Azāriqa from the outset) to an undeserved historical footnote that does not reflect their longevity. Such distortions prevent an accurate appreciation of the role of Khārijite thought in shaping the Ibāḍiyya.

Neglect of or overreliance on Ibāḍī and Sunni sources, overgeneralization, and a misguided telescopic focus on one Khārijite subsect or sects represent some of the more general failings of studies on the Khārijites and Ibāḍiyya.[10] Such misconceptions impede the overall appreciation of sectarian development, and complicate any attempt to understand the connections between Khārijite sectarian groups with other Muslims of their era. Although these fallacies represent broad failings in scholarship, there also exist several specifically misguided concepts about Khārijite notions of leadership. One of the most common impediments facing any attempt to contextualize the Ibāḍī imāmate is that many treatments of the Khārijite *imāma* dismiss its Islamic and pre-Islamic precedents, thus effectively cutting off inquiry into the possible connections between Khārijites, Ibāḍites, and others. Such scholarship has two main methods of explaining the conceptual history of the Khārijite imāmate (and, often by implication, the Ibāḍī imāmate): the first posits no historical precedents for the Khārijite imāmate, while the other finds parallels mainly in the pre-Islamic history of the Arabs. The first type of treatment remains problematic because it automatically precludes the possibility of continuity by defining the Khārijites as sui generis groups that appear seemingly out of nowhere. This exceptionalism is not only antihistorical but also relies too heavily on polemical sources that wish to show the Khārijites as disconnected to any "acceptable" form of Islam.

The second conceptualization of Khārijite and Ibāḍite imāmate history locates the roots of the Khārijite institutions of authority in the pre-Islamic era. This approach finds a spirit of nomadic egalitarianism, akin to the original desert ethos of the Arabs before Islam, which pervades the Khārijite notion of leadership. In attempting to reconstruct the tribal groups with which they had been familiar in the desert, the Khārijites imported the desert (that is, tribal) ideal of leadership. Thus, it is argued, the authority of the Khārijite Imām becomes "primus inter pares like the Arab *sayyid*."[11] While scholars who subscribe to this thesis acknowledge the importance of Islamic justifications to the Khārijite imāmate (that is, its "Islamic basis"), this theory ultimately posits the source of the Khārijite *imāma* in the pre-Islamic heritage of the Arabs and does not comment on how the Khārijite process of "Islamicizing" pre-Islamic norms of authority differed significantly from the ways that the early Caliphs justified and envisioned caliphal authority. And although this treatment of the Khārijite precedents for the imāmate remains slightly less anti-historical than the first method of ignoring historical precedent altogether, both theses ultimately dismiss the possibility that the Khārijites and Ibāḍiyya found justifications for their particular views toward leadership in the Qur'ān or early traditions of the Caliphs.

The implications of an exceptionalist view of the Khārijite imāmate traditions may readily be seen in the scholarship on the Khārijite Imām. In assuming little or no continuity with earlier Islamic or pre-Islamic institutions of authority, several scholars imagine the Khārijites as inherently unstable, even anarchist. These scholars see a clash between the authority of the Imām and that of the Khārijite community, with the Imām ultimately bowing to the community, his role and importance thereby reduced. Khārijite institutions of authority appear contradictory. On the one hand, historical texts emphasize the military struggle of the various Khārijite subsects with the dominant Islamic powers. Such struggles required strong leadership, and accordingly, scholarly studies portray the Khārijite Imāms as figures of limited authority. On the other hand, theological sources accentuate the Khārijite practice of excluding sinners from the Islamic community by treating them as *kuffār* (unbelievers). This practice (known as *takfīr*), according to the heresiographers, extended also to the leaders of the Khārijites, who could be deposed for committing an infraction of the divine law. Thus, it is argued, the Khārijite community enjoyed final authority by reserving the right to depose their leader. For some scholars, positing the Khārijite community as the "true" authority solves the apparent contradiction between the existence of an authority figure, the Khārijite Imām, and the possession of actual authority by the community. By so doing, these scholars envisioned the Khārijite political system as inherently antiauthoritarian, a type of theocratic anarchism or democratic puritanism.[12]

Conceiving the Khārijite political system as overbalanced in favor of the power of the community drastically reduced the importance of the Khārijite Imām in the eyes of scholars. Nevertheless, these scholars explain the existence of the Khārijite Imāms, and the nature of their authority, by citing the "practical" need of the Khārijite community for leadership.[13] Others rely on the "democratization of legitimacy," whereby the community's recognition of the Imām became the basis of his legitimacy, rather than the consequence of his legitimacy.[14]

As a corollary to this conceptualization of the Khārijite *imāma* whereby the Imām's practical authority was overshadowed by the ultimate authority of the Khārijite community, some scholars postulate an inherent instability in Khārijite institutions of authority.[15] According to these scholars, it is the nature of the

Khārijite approach to authority that, lacking meaningful connection to any previous system of authority, allows the puritanical urges of the Khārijites to run amok, destabilize the sect, and make impossible the establishment of a lasting institution of authority. Absent from such treatments of early Khārijite (and Ibāḍite) history is any connection to earlier conceptions of Islamic political organization. Equally absent is the notion that the relentless pursuit, incarceration, killing, and general persecution of every Khārijite subsect by the Umayyads, and later 'Abbasids—not an inherent instability of Khārijite political thought itself—might have contributed to their political volatility.

The unwillingness to view Khārijite institutions of political authority as a continuation of certain earlier modes of religious and political authority impedes the appreciation of the roots of the Ibāḍī imāmate institution. Not only have many scholars underestimated the importance of different types of legitimate authority in Khārijite Islamic thought, but they have consequently misrepresented the history and composition of Khārijite institutions of authority. This general misunderstanding, combined with the general lack of critical scholarship on the Ibāḍiyya, has led to an impoverished view of the history of Ibāḍī political thought in relation to its Khārijite and pre-Khārijite predecessors.

Not all scholars of the Khārijites subscribe to the thesis that views the Khārijites as separated from earlier trends in Islamic history. Crone's recent publications on the Khārijites and Ibāḍites, in addition to advancing the study of Khārijism immensely, represent a scholarly reassessment of the nature of Khārijite authority that challenges an antihistorical treatment of the nature of their authority. Crone argues that the Khārijites viewed eligibility for the imāmate in terms of merit, with the criterions of a meritorious leader being piety and knowledge.[16] Accordingly, she argues, the Imām was envisioned as a political leader and religious guide. Crone rightly notes how the Ibāḍiyya attempted to mitigate the power of the Ibāḍī community (represented by the scholars) by requiring absolute obedience to the Imām—a situation undermined by the fact that Ibāḍī *'ulamā'* retained the right to install and depose him. In addition, Crone observes that the Khārijites believed they were "systematizing the principles behind the early caliphate in Medina."[17]

The brevity of Crone's observation leaves much work to be done. A reexamination of the Ibāḍī imāmate structure in light of its historical precedents presents an opportunity to challenge the antihistorical view of Khārijite institutions of authority, and to trace how the institutions of the Ibāḍī imāmate came into being. This study takes up Crone's insight into the early Islamic roots of Khārijite notions of authority and traces them to the formulation and systematization of the Ibāḍī *imāma*.

As a starting point from which to work back to the connections between the Ibāḍī *imāma* and its intellectual predecessors, it will be instructive to provide a brief overview of the Ibāḍī imāmate. This is, however, no mean feat, as the medieval Ibāḍī imāmate ideal as it was preserved in the Ibāḍī legal and historical corpus of the seventh/eleventh through eleventh/fifteenth centuries presents itself as a highly complex institution. It consists of different subinstitutions of authority, which were believed to be appropriate to certain contexts (called *masālik al-dīn*, stages of religion), and thereby to supply a suitable type of leader for the distinct situations in which the Ibāḍī community found itself. In other words, different conditions of the community required different types of authority and therefore necessitated different kinds of leaders. Each institution of authority possesses a unique history stretching back, in many cases, to the pre-Islamic era. An evaluation of the different institutions comprising the Ibāḍī *imāma* will show that the particularities of each institution is based on precedents located in earlier Khārijite, early Islamic, and pre-Islamic institutions of authority. As a historical study, the chapters will elucidate, for each piece of the imāmate under consideration, a progression of development that begins with conceptual and institutional precedents in the pre-Islamic era and ends with specific configurations in the medieval Ibāḍī theory of the *imāma*.

In the interests of historical accuracy, a distinction will be maintained between the medieval Ibāḍī institution of the Imām and its early or "formative" predecessor. That is, the medieval Ibāḍī *imāma* will be defined as the *imāma* as it appears in the (predominantly legal) tradition that postdates the dissolution of the initial Ibāḍī imāmates of Oman and North Africa—after the mid-third/ninth to fourth/tenth century up to the eighth/fourteenth century. The formative Ibāḍī *imāma* will be defined as the institution that developed from the era of the first political leader of the Basran Ibāḍiyya (Abū ʻUbayda Muslim b. Abī Karīma, d. mid-second/eighth century) up to and including the founders of the Ibāḍī dynasties in North Africa (ʻAbd al-Raḥmān b. Rustum, d. 171/788) and Oman (al-Wārith b. Kaʻb al-Khārūṣī, d. 193/808). In other words, the formative and medieval Ibāḍī imāmates will be defined by a temporal distinction based upon the existence or nonexistence of a formal Ibāḍī polity—a premodern state. This distinction can be justified with reference to the fact that the absence of a state made it unlikely that the process of institutionalization was completed during the formative *imāma*. Indeed, some of the early Imāms functioned as precedents for certain aspects of the medieval imāmate structure. In addition, the few Ibāḍī sources that survive from the early Ibāḍī era contain unique interpretations of the role of the Imām—descriptions that obviously functioned as precedents for certain aspects of the later medieval imāmate. For these reasons, the formative period of the imāmate will be kept distinct from the medieval imāmate so that the early precedents may be investigated.

Another reality that significantly complicates the attempt to locate historical precedents for the Ibāḍī *imāma* is that differences do exist between the ways in which the medieval North African and Omani Ibāḍī communities configured and described their imāmate institutions. These differences can be attributed to the divergent historical paths of these two communities; the Ibāḍīs in North Africa and Oman began to pursue dissimilar solutions to the question of leadership after the establishment of their respective polities. The North African Ibāḍiyya modified their imāmate tradition after the death of the first Rustumid Imām, ʿAbd al-Raḥmān b. Rustum. His son, ʿAbd al-Wahhāb b. ʿAbd al-Raḥmān, while formally acknowledging the Ibāḍī imāmate ideal, established a hereditary dynasty based upon his absolute authority.[18] After the dissolution of the Rustumid dynasty in 296/909, North African Ibāḍism, while preserving the original ideal of the imāmate, eventually established communal councils (called *ḥalqa*, and later *ʿazzāba*) of *ʿulamāʾ* to oversee the affairs of the community in the permanent absence of their Imām. While the official structure of the imāmate was preserved in theory, in reality the North African Ibāḍiyya functioned without an Imām. They continue to do so up to the present day.

Omani Ibāḍīs also modified the institution of the Imām after the establishment of their Ibāḍī polity in Nizwa in 180/796. In particular, tribal alliances and the realities of political authority necessitated certain adaptations to the imāmate as it was practically implemented. Some of these changes were formally rationalized into the medieval Ibāḍī *imāma*, while others remained implicit in its functioning.[19] Unlike their North African cousins, however, the Omani Ibāḍiyya maintained an operative imāmate tradition after the dissolution of the first Omani Ibāḍī state in 280/893, and periodically reestablished Ibāḍī imāmates throughout their history. The last Omani Ibāḍī Imām, for example, ruled in the interior of Oman until his expulsion in 1958, when Sultan Saʿīd b. Taymur unified Muscat and Oman with help from the British.

Both the theoretical character of the North African Ibāḍī imāmate traditions and the practical nature of the Omani *imāma* lent distinctive qualities to their respective imāmate traditions. Medieval North African Ibāḍī theories of the imāmate postulated four possible types of recognized Imāms who corresponded with four situations (that is, the stages of religion, *masālik al-dīn*) in which the Ibāḍī community existed. These collective situations, in turn, were based upon reified historical conditions in which the Ibāḍī community (imagined as an unchanged entity stretching back to the era of the early Khārijites) found (or imagined) itself. The first systematic statement of the four stages is attributed to the Maghribī Ibāḍī scholar Abū Zakariyya:

> The stages of religion are four: Secrecy (*al-kitmān*), and this was the previous state of the Prophet when he was in Makka; then Manifestation (*al-ẓuhūr*), like when he was in Madīna, and then [the

> Prophet] ordered the *jihād*; then Defense (*al-difā'*) like the defense of the people of Nahrawān against those who were satisfied with the arbitration of Ibn al-'Āṣ and 'Abdullāh b. Qays; then Selling [one's soul to God in order to fight] (*al-shirā'*), like Abū Bilāl, may God be pleased with him.[20]

This North African configuration of the imāmate represents a theoretical arrangement of the imāmate that does not correspond to a temporal North African institution of authority. The North African Ibāḍiyya created the four "stages" of religion and their equivalent Imāms to create the fiction of an unbroken chain of Imāms stretching back to the Prophet Muhammad, and to link the transmission of knowledge (*'ilm*) and authority to the earliest periods of Islam.

The Omani Ibāḍiyya, on the other hand, did not conceive of the stages of religion or their Imāms in the same manner as their North African counterparts until after the Ibāḍī renaissance of the tenth/sixteenth century. Prior to this time, there were only two stages of religion: *ẓuhūr* and *kitmān*.[21] Likewise, Omani Ibāḍī jurists recognized two types of Imāms, the *shārī* (the Imām who "sells" his soul in order to fight) and *difā'ī* (defensive) Imāms, respectively.[22] These Imāms did not necessarily correspond (as they did in North Africa) to the stages of the community: both *shārī* and *difā'ī* Imāms could rule during the state of *ẓuhūr*. Moreover, Omani jurisprudence recognized no distinct type of Imām appropriate to the state of *kitmān*, but later associated an Imām dubbed the *muḥtasib* Imām with that state.[23] Finally, both *shārī* and *difā'ī* Imāms could be further classed as "weak" (*ḍa'īf*) Imāms if they did not possess sufficient knowledge.[24] This configuration of the Omani *imāma* reflects the practical considerations of the Omani Ibāḍī *'ulamā'*, who attempted to create a working institution of the Imām that remained relevant to their needs.

While acknowledging the important differences between the North African and Omani imāmate traditions, a central assumption of this study is that Ibāḍī institutions of authority preserve references to a conceptual past as a means of bolstering their claims to legitimacy because they are themselves the products of a conceptual heritage that is conceived as legitimate. That is, the Ibāḍī imāmate as it is preserved in the medieval legal-theological corpus was profoundly shaped by their formative experiences in Basra, the memory of the early Khārijites and the earliest Caliphs, all of whom the Ibāḍiyya regard as pious forerunners. As Wolf notes, legitimacy is of paramount importance to institutions of authority: "if [authority] is not perceived as legitimate by the object of authority, then there is little chance of the authority being exercised effectively."[25] Wansbrough characterizes legitimate authority in Islamic thought as apostolic; that is, as based upon the belief in an unbroken line of transmission reaching back to the original sources of authority.[26] Indeed, the Ibāḍiyya viewed themselves as the unchanging and unchanged successors to the Prophet Muhammad, and the preservers of the authentic form of Islam. A conceptual history of the medieval Ibāḍī institutions of authority benefits from this need for legitimacy insofar as the Ibāḍī *imāma* traditions were believed to reflect the institutions that composed the apostolic sources of transmission—especially, but not limited to, the Qur'ān, the Prophet Muhammad, the early Madīnan caliphate, the early Khārijites, and the earliest Ibāḍīs; the pre-Islamic era presents another important, yet unacknowledged, precedent. The Ibāḍī imāmate tradition, therefore, must be viewed as the accumulation of such influences, which—in each specific time and place where Ibāḍīs find themselves—are put to the task of articulating a legitimate structure of authority. Thus, despite the differences between the North African and Omani conceptions of the imāmate, medieval North African and Omani traditions' common origin in the formative Ibāḍī imāmate of Basra provided them with a core conceptual vocabulary and practice of the *imāma*.

The advantage of tracing a line of development from the earliest sources of Islamic legitimacy to the Ibāḍiyya lies in its ability to supply continuity between distinct institutions of authority across a wide swath of history and allow for the discovery of "family resemblances" between classical Ibāḍī, early Ibāḍī, Khārijite and pre-Khārijite institutions in doctrines, practices, technical vocabularies, or shared interpretations of history. A potential hazard of this method is contained in its presentation of conceptual progression. A conceptual history necessarily searches for similarities between institutions through time; it is a technique that can make the succession of institutions appear static and unaffected by historical forces. Yet the process of institutional development was dynamic precisely because historical changes motivated Islamic groups to constantly reinterpret the institutional norms of earlier systems in terms of the novel circumstances in which they found themselves. Thus, for example, the experience of the first Islamic *fitna* prompted the early Khārijites to incorporate particular aspects of the early Madīnan caliphate of Abū Bakr and 'Umar (itself an original interpretation—driven by the death of the Prophet Muhammad—of certain Islamic and pre-Islamic notions of legitimate authority) into the early Khārijite institutions of authority. In order to preserve an accurate perspective of the conceptual development of institutions of authority, reference must constantly be made to the particular historical contexts in which these institutions operated.

The four "stages of religion" and the Imāms who properly govern the Ibāḍī community during those respective conditions will provide an organizing principle for this study and a means to investigate the conceptual and institutional history of the medieval Ibāḍī imāmate. Indeed, although their usages differ slightly, the notions of *ẓuhūr*, *difāʿ*, *kitmān*, and *shirāʾ* remain common to both Ibāḍī imāmate traditions and possess significant institutional similarities. This shared institutional terminology of the imāmate will function as the starting point for tracing the shared institutional precedents of authority in the medieval Ibāḍī imāmate.

Chapter 1 begins with the notion of *ẓuhūr*, for of the four medieval Ibāḍī Imām-types, the *imām al-ẓuhūr* most resembled the Sunni Caliph in function. The state of *ẓuhūr* denoted an independent Ibāḍī imāmate, with a leader capable of fulfilling the duties incumbent upon him. The *imām al-ẓuhūr*, as the head of the sect believed to be the truest expression of Islam, epitomized the just and righteous leader (*al-imām al-ʿādil*). Ibāḍī historiography, for example, posited Abū Bakr and ʿUmar as examples of Imāms of *ẓuhūr*. During their reigns, the righteous Islamic (that is, Ibāḍī) community was held to openly exist and properly function. Piety and moral probity, encompassing the notions of justice (*ʿadl*), asceticism (*zuhd*), and religiosity(*warʿ*), were the salient (though not the only) legitimating characteristics of the Ibāḍī *imām al-ẓuhūr*. The so-called *rāshidūn* Caliphs, especially Abū Bakr and ʿUmar, as well as being the pre-Islamic models upon which the first two "rightly-guided" Caliphs modeled their own caliphates, serve as the conceptual precursor, via the early Khārijites, to Ibāḍī notion of the *ẓuhūr* Imām. Likewise, the Caliphs ʿUthmān and ʿAlī function in Ibāḍī literature as negative models for the imāmate.

Chapter 2 takes up the notion of *kitmān* and the institution of the *imām al-kitmān* (the Imām of secrecy). This Imām ruled when the Ibāḍī community could not openly proclaim an imāmate. Although no comparable institution existed in medieval Oman, Omani Ibāḍī texts identify as Imāms the same individuals who in North African texts are labeled Imāms of *kitmān* while simultaneously describing the state of the community during their reigns as one of secrecy (*kitmān*) and prudent concealment (*taqiyya*). In reality, it seems that the *imām al-kitmān* was a theoretical construct established in order to retroactively create Imāms out of the *ʿulamāʾ* who led the early quietist Khārijite movement in Basra (and who eventually established the Ibāḍiyya as a distinct Khārijite subsect).[27] Nevertheless, the hypothetical institution of the *imām al-kitmān* illustrates how the predominant trait of authority for the *imām al-kitmān* was knowledge (*ʿilm*). The formative period in Basra thus serves as a starting point for the investigation of the *imām al-kitmān*, as well as setting the stage for the importance of the community in regulating the Imāms who did not possess knowledge.

Chapter 3 deals with the *shārī* Imām, or the Imām who "exchanges" or "sells" his soul to God for the promise of the afterlife, and fights for the establishment of the Ibāḍī state. Although the concept of the *imām al-shārī* existed in both Oman and North African imāmate theories, the conception of the *shārī*

Imām differed slightly in the two regions. In North Africa, the *imām al-shārī* was a purely theoretical institution. He was conceived as a military leader whose sole purpose was to expand or establish the Ibāḍī *dār al-islām* or perish in the attempt. Hypothetically, he could exist simultaneously with other Imāms so long as he prosecuted the struggle (*shirā'*) against the enemies of the Ibāḍiyya, although technically he had to either become the Imām or step down if he succeeded.[28] In Oman, the *imām al-shārī* remained a practical institution: a *shārī* Imām was an Imām with full powers—an Imām who possessed all the necessary traits of leadership—whose primary responsibility lay in fighting to establish or maintain a condition of *ẓuhūr*. In both North Africa and Oman, the operative characteristic of the *shārī* Imām's authority was his bravery and willingness to sacrifice himself for the good of the sect—a concept known to the early Khārijites and and Ibāḍites as *shirā'*. Stories of the early Khārijite heroes thus present the basis upon which the imāmate of *shirā'* was founded, while the later history of Ibāḍism transformed the concept of *shirā'* into an institution of leadership.

The last chapter addresses the role of the community, using the example of the "defensive" Imām. As a distinguishing feature of the medieval Ibāḍī *imāma*, the formal role established for the community (represented by the *'ulamā'*) in choosing, monitoring, and deposing the Imām remained common responsibilities to both North African and Omani imāmate traditions. In fact, the North Afican Ibāḍī *'ulamā'* assumed full control of the Ibāḍī community after the dissolution of the Rustumid dynasty. However, they maintained the imāmate ideal in their literature. In Oman, the institutional features of the *imām al-difā'* (the Imām of defense, also known as the *imām 'alā al-difā'* or the *imām al-mudāfi'*) and the Omani concept of the "weak" (*ḍa'īf*) Imām illustrate the authority of the community in relation to their leader. The *difā'ī* Imām could be required to consult with the *'ulamā'* before making any decisions, and to relinquish the office of Imām after an appointed time. Moreover, *shārī* and *difā'ī* Imāms who did not possess knowledge were simultaneously known in Omani legal texts as "weak" (*ḍa'īf*) Imāms, though the exact usage of this term in often obscure.[29] As a result of their deficiency in knowledge, the *'ulamā'* could impose certain conditions (*shurūṭ*) upon their rule. Thus, in addition to the duties of selecting, monitoring, and deposing the Imām, the Omani Ibāḍī community occasionally assumed extra responsibilities in relation to their Imām. These features of the Ibāḍī imāmate make it appropriate to speak of the Ibāḍī community as an integral aspect of the *imāma*—a dependent institution with its own rules governing how it should operate. This authority is likewise rooted in the early Islamic period of the *rāshidūn* Caliphs.

Sources

Examining the conceptual precedents of the Ibāḍī *imāma* will require sources that can provide the "family resemblances" among various historical institutions of authority from the different historical eras under consideration. Specifically, the doctrines, practices, technical vocabularies, interpretations of events, and biographies will provide the textual discussions in which historical portraits of institutions are preserved. A variety of genres of texts from both the mainstream Islamic and Ibāḍī traditions are used here. They include the standard histories, biographical works (*sīra*) on the Prophet and his early Companions, as well as in innumerable other shorter works that have become the customary references for early Islamic history. Many of these texts date from several decades to several centuries after the events and personalities they describe, but preserve reports from earlier sources within them. In addition, the Qur'ān and the *ḥadīth* corpus, insofar as they are historically based texts, also serve as resources of information on the early Islamic institutions of authority.

One type of text—heresiography—deserves special mention as a source of information on the early Khārijites. Heresiography is a genre dedicated to promoting a certain sect's claim to authenticity through the explication of the "heretical" beliefs and practices of other groups. As such, the heresiographical tradition presents a rich, but polemical, source for information on the Khārijites and Ibāḍites. Although heresiographers quote and utilize the works of earlier authors in their texts, their works date from many years after the formative period of the Khārijite subsects. Caution should therefore be exercised when dealing with heresiographical texts, as the predilections of their authors, the structure of their texts, and reliability of their information are not always clear.

Although relevant primary and secondary source materials will be evaluated in their appropriate chapters, certain general comments should be made, by way of overview, regarding Ibāḍī sources. These sources are not well known, even to scholars of Islamic studies. The Ibāḍī textual corpus is a massive body of works that span the thirteen centuries of Ibāḍī presence in Oman, Basra, Ḥaḍramawt, and North and East Africa. Ibāḍī authors pursued the same genres as their non-Ibāḍī Muslim counterparts: histories, biographical dictionaries (*ṭabaqāt*), legal works (*fiqh*), theological works (*'ilm al-kalām*), and heresiography.[30] However, in general, North African texts relevant to the imāmate tend to be histories and biographical dictionaries, while Omani sources on the *imāma* incline toward the legal genre. Although exceptions to this rule abound, this situation reflects the historical particularity of the North African and Omani communities, respectively: the North African community existed without an

Imām, and so the texts relating to the Imām are primarily historical in nature. The Omani Ibāḍīs, on the other hand, maintained the imāmate as a living tradition, and thus their sources are legal—reflecting the practical concerns of a functioning imāmate.

A chronological list of the major Ibāḍī sources, along with a brief description of their significance to this study, will help the reader to navigate the grand and often confusing textual geography of the Ibāḍiyya. The chronology of Ibāḍī sources may be broken down into early (that is, formative) works that date from before the establishment of Ibāḍī states, early medieval works (from the period of the first Ibāḍī states), and later medieval works (from the late-third/ninth centuries and after).[31] Like the other Islamic sources mentioned above, most of the Ibāḍī works date from the late-third/ninth century or later, that is, after the dissolution of the original Ibāḍī states in North Africa and Oman. Very little material survives from the formative Ibāḍī era: these sources include some early legal opinions and letters of Jābir b. Zayd (d. 94 or 104/712 or 722);[32] the (probably late-second/eighth century) epistle of Sālim b. Dhakwān; a collection of Ibāḍī *ḥadīth* attributed to the Basran Imām al-Rabīʿ b. Ḥabīb al-Farāhidī (d. 170/786);[33] a letter on *zakāt* attributed to Abū ʿUbayda Muslim b. Abī Karīma (d. mid-second/eighth century);[34] and two early (probably early-second/eighth century) epistles attributed to the postulated founder of Ibāḍism, Ibn Ibāḍ.[35] Of this material, the epistle of Sālim b. Dhakwān remains important as an example of early heresiography and formative Ibāḍī doctrine. Similarly, the letters of Ibn Ibāḍ and select *ḥadīth* from the collection of al-Rabīʿ represent early examples of Ibāḍī doctrines during the formative period of Ibāḍī thought.

Examples of Ibāḍī sources from the early medieval period (that is, from the era of the Ibāḍī states) are slightly less rare. The early biographical work of Abū Sufyān Maḥbūb b. al-Raḥīl (d. second/eighth century) survives in quotations in the later North African biographical sources of al-Shammākhī, al-Darjīnī, and the histories of al-Barrādī and Abū Zakariyya. Abū Sufyān's quotations provide an important glimpse into the development of the early biographical traditions of the Ibāḍī sect. Likewise, the early epistle (*sīra*) from Shabīb b. ʿAṭiyya (d. late-second/eighth century) contains some relevant references to the imāmate.[36] The epistle of Munīr b. al-Nayyar al-Jaʿlānī (d. second/eighth century), a Basran "bearer of learning" (*ḥāmil al-ʿilm*) in Oman, to the second Omani Imām Ghassān b. ʿAbdullāh al-Yaḥmadī (d. 208/823) provides an invaluable perspective on the early personalities of the Ibāḍī movement as well as the concept of *shirāʾ*.[37] Likewise, the epistle of the Omani scholar Abū ʿAbdullāh Muḥammad b. Maḥbūb (d. 260/873) provides a similar view on the early medieval Omani Ibāḍī imāmate.[38] An exception to the usual silence of North African texts on the early imāmate tradition comes from the epistle of an unknown Abū ʿUbayda al-Maghribī to the Rustumid

Imām ʿAbd al-Wahhāb b. ʿAbd al-Raḥmān b. Rustum (r. 168–188/785–804). In addition, two historical works from North Africa—Ibn Salām's *Kitāb Ibn Salām* (written after 273/886)[39] and Ibn al-Ṣaghīr's (d. late-third/ninth century) *Kitāb Akhbār al-Āʾimma al-Rustumiyyīn*—offer late-third/ninth century views on the Ibāḍī Rustumid dynasty in North Africa.[40]

The transition from the early to the later medieval periods in Oman is represented by two Omani scholars who witnessed and wrote about the dissolution of the first Omani Ibāḍī imāmate: Abū Mu'thir al-Ṣalt b. Khamīs (d. late-third/ninth century) and Abū Qaḥṭān Khālid b. Qaḥṭān (d. early-fourth/tenth century). Of particular interest to this study are their epistles (*siyar*), which mention some of the early Basran personalities associated with the Ibāḍī movement.[41] Later classical Omani Ibāḍī thought on the imāmate comes primarily from jurists; Abū Jābir Muḥammad Ibn Jaʿfar (d. third/ninth century) and Abū al-Ḥawārī Muḥammad b. al-Ḥawārī (d. early-fourth/tenth century) wrote important early compendiums of legal opinions, although their thought on the imāmate survived primarily in the form of quotations in later Omani legal sources. Abū Saʿīd Muḥammad b. Saʿīd al-Kudamī's (d. fourth/tenth century) works—*al-Muʿtabar*, *al-Istiqāma*, and *al-Jāmiʿ al-Mufīd min Aḥkām Abī Saʿīd*—contain chapters on different aspects of the imāmate, as well as quotations from earlier Ibāḍī thinkers. The fifth/eleventh century Ḥaḍramawtī Ibāḍī scholar Abū Isḥāq Ibrāhīm b. Qays's digest of legal opinions (*Mukhtaṣar al-Khiṣāl*) likewise provides valuable information on the legal aspects of the imāmate, as do the opinions (preserved primarily in quotations located in other works) of the two fifth/eleventh century jurists Abū Muḥammad ʿAbdullāh b. Muḥammad Ibn Baraka and Abū al-Ḥasan ʿAlī b. Muḥammad al-Bisyānī (sometimes given as al-Bisyawī).

The fifth/eleventh century in Oman witnessed the compilation of the multivolume legal compendium known as the *Bayān al-Sharʿ* of Muḥammad b. Ibrāhīm al-Kindī. This enormous work collected numerous legal opinions on a variety of subjects, including the imāmate and the early personalities of Ibāḍism. Similarly, the sixth/twelfth-century legal scholar (and relative of Muḥammad al-Kindī), Abū Bakr Aḥmad b. ʿAbdullāh b. Mūsā al-Kindī (d. 558/1162) created a legal compendium, known as the *Muṣannaf*, and devoted an entire volume to questions surrounding the imāmate. This source, along with al-Kindī's shorter works the *Kitāb al-Ihtidāʾ* and the *al-Jawhar al-Muqtaṣir*, present the range of legal opinions regarding the imāmate, and remain invaluable sources for the study of the medieval Ibāḍī *imāma*. Finally, the eleventh/seventeenth-century Omani historical tract the *Kashf al-Ghumma al-Jāmiʿ Akhbār al-Āʾimma*, attributed to the Omani historian Sirḥān b. Saʿīd al-Izkawī (d. eleventh/seventeenth century), contains important historical information regarding the early Imāms of Oman, as does Nūr al-Dīn ʿAbdullāh al-Sālimī's (d. 1333/1914) *Tuḥfat al-ʿAyān bī-Sirat Ahl*

'Umān. Although both of these works date from well after the medieval era, they quote sources from earlier periods.

In North Africa, the fifth/eleventh and sixth/twelfth centuries produced numerous historians and theologians of note. Yaḥya b. Abī Bakr al-Warjlānī (Abū Zakariyya) (d. 472/1079) wrote his *Kitāb al-Sīra wa Akhbār al-Ā'imma* concerning the Rustumid imāmate and its dissolution; and Tabghurīn b. Dawūd b. 'Īsā al-Malshūṭī (d. early-sixth/twelfth century) composed his *Kitāb Usūl al-Dīn* on the theological underpinnings of Ibāḍī religious thought. Likewise, Abū 'Ammār 'Abd al-Kāfī b. Abī Ya'qūb al-Tanwātī's (d. mid-sixth/twelfth century) *al-Mūjaz*, Abū Ya'qūb al-Warjlānī's (d. 570/1174) *al-Dalīl wa al-Burhān*, and his *al-'Adl wa al-Inṣāf*, became important theological works that dealt, in part, with the question of the imāmate. The eighth/fourteenth-century theological-legal tract *Kitāb Qawā'id al-Islām*, by Abū Ṭāhir Ismā'īl b. Mūsā al-Jiṭālī (d. 750/1349), contains scattered references to the imāmate, as does Abū Sulaymān b. Dawūd b. Ibrāhīm al-Talāti's (d. 968/1560) commentary (*sharḥ*) on Abū al-'Abbās Aḥmad b. Abī 'Uthmān Sa'īd al-Shammākhī's (d. 928/1521) *Muqaddimat al-Tawḥīd*. Al-Shammākhī also wrote an important biographical dictionary, the *Kitāb al-Siyar*, which, along with Abū al-'Abbās Aḥmad b. Sa'īd al-Darjīnī's (d. 670/1271) biographical dictionary the *Kitāb Ṭabaqāt al-Mashāyikh bī al-Maghrib* and Abū al-Faḍl b. Ibrāhīm al-Barrādī's (d. early to mid-ninth/fifteenth century) historical work the *Kitāb al-Jawāhir*, constitute the primary historical works of the later North African Ibāḍī period.

1

Imām al-Ẓuhūr

One of the institutions constituting the medieval Ibāḍī *imāma* was the Imām known in North Africa as the *imām al-ẓuhūr*, and in Oman simply as the Imām who reigned when the Ibāḍiyya fully controlled the territory in which they were located; this was a state called *'alāniyya* (openness) or *ẓuhūr* (manifestation).[1] This condition of *ẓuhūr* represented the most favorable state for the community, for in these circumstances the Ibāḍiyya openly practiced their form of Islam without fear of persecution. In it, a competent Imām ruled without conditions placed upon him by the *'ulamā'*, and performed all duties incumbent upon the office of the Imām.[2] According to the medieval Ibāḍiyya, *'alāniyya* was the state of affairs bequeathed to the Islamic community after the death of the Prophet Muhammad, and sustained by Abū Bakr and 'Umar.[3] *Ẓuhūr* thus illustrated the representative state of affairs for the Ibāḍī community, and the state to which the Ibāḍiyya aspired.

Just as the state of *ẓuhūr* symbolized the optimal conditions for the Ibāḍī community, the *imām al-ẓuhūr* epitomized the ideal leader of the Ibāḍiyya. In North Africa, the *imām al-ẓuhūr* represented the prototypical Imām: the Imām who ruled during ordinary conditions (that is, not during a state of defense, expansion, or secrecy). In Oman, the term *imām al-ẓuhūr* was not used; Imāms were either *difā'ī* Imāms or *shārī* Imāms, or simply Imāms who, it was implied, ruled during a state of *ẓuhūr*.[4] Nevertheless, a typical Imām was one who was not weak (*ḍa'īf*), not contracted for a specified period of time or for a specific purpose (like some kinds of *difā'ī* Imāms), and not necessarily exceptional like an *imām al-shārī*.[5]

As the prototypical Imām, the characteristics of the *ẓuhūr* Imām exemplified the traits that the Ibāḍiyya expected of leaders during the ideal state of affairs. Conceptually, what epitomized the medieval Ibāḍī Imām of *ẓuhūr* was his demonstrated moral qualities—what may be summarized as merit in the form of piety—as the paramount legitimating quality of the his authority.[6] The Ibāḍī Imām was, foremost, a moral Imām, and the Ibāḍiyya incorporated this quality into the institution that became the *imām al-ẓuhūr*. Piety, conceived as justice (*'adl*), asceticism (*zuhd*), or religiosity (*war'*), formed a common denominator among the *ẓuhūr* Imāms in the medieval imāmate. This concern for moral rectitude in leadership made the institution of the Ibāḍī imāmate unique in three ways: in the level to which it preferred piety over other legitimate qualities of leadership, in the exclusion on the basis of piety of characteristics accepted as legitimate traits of leadership by other Islamic groups, and in the extent to which the Ibāḍiyya formalized the rules for enforcing piety among their leaders. These institutional traits embodied the Ibāḍī conception of piety as legitimate authority in institutional forms. This concern with piety as a demonstrated moral quality of leaders, and the subsequent institutionalization of piety in certain structures of the classical Ibāḍī *imāma*, reflect the conceptual and historical heritage of the Ibāḍiyya from their many predecessors, pre-Islamic and otherwise. That is, the distinctive features of the Ibāḍī institution of the *ẓuhūr* Imām developed from a systematization of the principles of moral rectitude and piety (variously appreciated) insofar as they animated earlier institutions of authority: specifically, the pre-Islamic *sayyid*, the Prophet, the early caliphate, the first Imāms of the Muḥakkima, and the early Khārijite leaders, including the early Ibāḍī leaders in Basra.

It should be noted that the Islamic concepts of piety and moral rectitude were not "fixed" types of authority, and the Qur'ānic elevation of piety as the marker of authority and excellence among human beings did not easily replace pre-Islamic attitudes toward legitimate political authority. Although Islam made strong universal claims on its followers, the first Muslims maintained a complex relationship with the pre-Islamic milieu into which they were born. Consequently, what might be called early Islamic norms of authority simultaneously mixed with, replaced, and were sometimes superceded by pre-Islamic notions of authority. Concurrent with this process, the notion of what constituted Islamic behavior and virtue developed as the Muslim experience grew, and as the Muslims conquered and assimilated new peoples.

The Authority of the Pre-Islamic *Sayyid*

Although the Ibāḍiyya do not acknowledge the pre-Islamic era as a genuine source for their religious and political thought, the *jāhiliyya* provided the initial context from which Islam sprung. Certain aspects of pre-Islamic thought were inevitably reinterpreted and incorporated into early Islamic patterns of reasoning, so that they became integrated with it. Accordingly, the personal characteristics valued in the pre-Islamic institution of the *sayyid* function as an unacknowledged precedent—via the early Islamic Caliphs and then the Khārijites—for the later Ibāḍī conviction in demonstrated personal qualities (merit) as the paramount legitimating factor of authority. Failure to appreciate some of the underlying principles of pre-Islamic Arabian authority, which led in early Islamic history to the ascendancy of the Quraysh and the pretensions of Arab superiority, has resulted in a misunderstanding of the pre-Islamic antecedents to Khārijite modes of authority. While it is true that the Khārijites absolutely rejected the exclusive claims of the Quraysh (and the Arabs in general) to the candidacy of leadership, they did not reject the principle on which Qurayshī excellence was founded. Personal merit, even if expressed within the framework of a tribal system that glorified ancestral deeds over the achievements of an individual, nonetheless legitimized leadership within the sphere of those considered "noble" on the basis of personal qualities. Thus, the pre-Islamic office of the *sayyid* offers a partial, if abstract, precedent for the Ibāḍī elevation of piety as the meritorious quality that legitimated political leadership.

"Piety," as such, did not belong to the pre-Islamic vocabulary, and was not a recognized category of thought in the pre-Islamic era. However, personal qualities relevant to leadership—what might be considered the equivalent of "moral virtues" in pre-Islamic Arabia—did exist. The personal qualities admired by the Arabs have been categorized under the rubric of *murūwwa* (manliness), which included the traits of bravery, patience, the willingness to exact revenge, protect the weak, and defy the strong.[7] To these might also be added generosity and hospitality (*karam*), and loyalty to one's tribe (*al-'aṣabiyya*). In particular, the pre-Islamic term *karīm* was an important concept denoting nobility of lineage, which had secondarily acquired the notion of "extravagant generosity." Generosity remained a visible means by which a pre-Islamic Arab might show his nobility and quality.[8] Especially relevant to the moral virtues of leaders in pre-Islamic Arabia was the quality of *ḥilm* (self-restrained authority). *Ḥilm* originally denoted control over one's passions, the ability to calmly assess a situation and remain unprovoked.[9] As such, it remained one of the most essential qualities of an Arab tribal chief, as it allowed the chief to govern other people through cool tact and skillful manipulation. Such qualities (especially *ḥilm*) constituted the core traits acknowledged in pre-Islamic leaders.

However, the Arabs did not believe noble qualities, and thus leadership, to be generally obtainable exclusively on the basis of their demonstration. As important as the manifestation of the ability to lead was the notion that noble qualities—including the qualities of leadership—were passed down genetically from the tribal ancestors through certain families.[10] Thus, the Arabs judged the relative nobility (*sharaf*) of a tribe according to the accumulated deeds of their ancestors and gauged the relative superiority of tribes with reference to genealogy (*nasab*).[11] No honor was accorded to those without honorable ancestors. Among the Arabian tribes, a type of loose aristocracy developed out of the system of honor and ancestry. Within tribes, a particular clan claimed greater glory, and thereby greater right to leadership, if its line of ancestors was more distinguished by their achievements than other clans of the same tribe.

Inherited tribal qualities limited the weight of personal achievements for those without honor, while simultaneously imposing on those who claimed exalted ancestry a duty to demonstrate their noble qualities. As Jafri claims:

> the Arabs made a clear distinction between inherited nobility and nobility claimed only on account of personal merit, the former being a source of great social prestige while the latter was of little consequence. In other words, personal fame and merit counted for little in securing for oneself an exalted position: it was inherited fame and inherited merit which confirmed proper estimation in society.[12]

For those who possessed *ḥasab* (honor based upon genealogy) strong incentive existed to emulate the glorious deeds of their ancestors. The tribal system required the demonstration of personal merits from those claiming nobility of ancestry, but held personal merit to be the result of that ancestry.

The choice of a leader (*sayyid* or *shaykh*) in pre-Islamic Arabia reflected the Arabs' esteem for inherited traits of nobility, and the leader was chosen in part for his genealogy and in part for his leadership qualities. The death of a tribal chief instigated a succession of leadership to the most qualified person within those clans already considered noble.[13] The Arabs maintained their practical attitude toward leadership to the extent that the authority of the *sayyid* was not guaranteed by his status as such. The ability to command, as measured by the perceived wisdom of the *sayyid*'s command, determined whether or not the *sayyid*'s opinion would be consulted and respected.

Such demonstrated virtues of leadership, even when understood as the consequence of inherited traits restricted to certain "noble" tribes, determined the leadership of the Quraysh within the political system of sixth-century Makka. That the

Quraysh may have enjoyed preeminence as leaders in Makka, and perhaps in the whole of the Arabian Peninsula, must be attributed to socioeconomic factors peculiar to Makka at that time. Although Makka stood off of the north-south (Syria-Yemen) and east-west (Abyssinia-Iraq, India) trade routes, it has recently been argued that the leather trade may have connected Makka to the wider economic geography of the Arabian Peninsula.[14] Compounding the importance of Makka as an economic center for leather production were the disastrous wars between the Sāsānian and Byzantine empires, whose armies required an enormous amount of raw leather for their outfitting. In addition, disruption of the regular trade routes through the northern Middle East diverted more commerce to the Arabian Peninsula, indirectly benefiting the Quraysh in Makka.

The existence of the *ka'ba* in Makka would have further added to the position of the Quraysh in Arabia. Pilgrims converged on the sacred precinct, bringing business and animals for sacrifice with them. In addition to the accommodation of merchants, the Quraysh set up different idols in the *ka'ba* to attract pilgrims from all over Arabia. The prospect of mutual benefits from the economic prosperity of Makka attracted tribes to form relationships of confederacy (*ḥilf*) with the Quraysh. Confederates (*ḥulafā'*) meant greater military strength and the ability to protect themselves and their clients, and to exact revenge—traits that would have contributed to the fame of the Quraysh in the whole of Arabia.

Although influence within the Quraysh tribe depended, as it did throughout Arabia, on the qualifications of clan and demonstrated ability, the accumulation of wealth had begun to challenge this system. Prosperity became a means to power that supplanted, to a certain extent, the traits of inherited nobility. By the time of Muhammad, the wealthy clans of 'Abd Shams and Makhzūm dominated Makkan politics, while Muhammad's clan of Hāshim occupied a relatively modest position. Although the Banū Hāshim enjoyed status as caretakers of the *ka'ba*, the real power of 'Abd Shams and Makhzūm was demonstrated by their ability to organize the boycott of the Hāshimites during the early years of the Prophet's mission in Makka. Nevertheless, personal qualities were of paramount importance to the acceptance of a leader within the Quraysh, as shown by the example of Abū Sufyān, whose financial acumen, diplomatic skill, and ability to lead insured that he would remain a powerful figure among the Makkans.[15] Additionally, the Quraysh as a whole were famous for their *ḥilm*, that is, their ability to gain control over their neighbors through patient statesmanship. Although *ḥilm* was thought to be an inherited trait, neither hereditary qualities nor wealth could ever replace the practical importance of demonstrated ability to the leadership of the Quraysh.

As the Arabs recognized confirmed traits of leadership within those tribes known for their noble ancestry, they generally mistrusted other forms of leadership that did not involve a hereditary notion of verifiable tribal virtues. Dynastic succession, or kingship, was not alien to the pre-Islamic Arabs, and the pre-Islamic kingdoms of al-Ḥīra, the Banū Ghassān, and al-Kinda were well known among them. Kingship (*mulk*) originated as a metaphor of space and possession. Ibn Sa'd wrote of "kings" who presented gifts to the Prophet: "they were called kings because each of them was in possession of a valley and everything therein."[16] Likewise, the Arabs would have known of the concept of divine kingship from trading with their Sāsānian and Byzantine neighbors. The Sāsanian notion of authority revolved around the notion of a divinely appointed king, the *shāh*, whose legitimacy and authority were unquestioned and absolute. However, divine kingship and the kingly metaphor of space and possession remained alien to the Arabs, who valued personal qualities and breeding in their leaders. This aversion to kingship is reflected in early Islamic literature. The Qur'ān describes the Queen of Sheba telling her council (*malā'*): "kings, when they enter a township, ruin it and make the honor of its people shame."[17] This attitude may have reflected the Arab attitude toward kingship in general.

Moral Authority in the Qur'ān and the Example of the Prophet Muhammad

The second historical precedent for the Khārijite's particular interpretation of piety as the fundamental aspect of legitimate authority comes from the Qur'ān and the example of the Prophet Muhammad, insofar as his example can be reconstructed with any certainty. With the advent of the Qur'ān and the leadership of the Prophet Muhammad, Islamic piety was defined as a desirable personal quality that distinguished excellence in human beings, and the example of the Prophet Muhammad as a moral-political authority quickly became embedded in the religious thought of the Muslims.

In the Islamic context, the Qur'ān conceptualized the notion of morality and thereby provided a basis for the Khārijite and Ibāḍite equation of piety and leadership. The Qur'ān connects the principles of right and wrong, and the impetuous for human beings to act in a moral manner, to the nature of God and to God's purpose for humanity. Among the numerous adjectives describing God, several refer to specifically moral attributes: merciful, compassionate,[18] forgiving,[19] and just,[20] to name but a few. These theological attributes of God have definite consequences for human beings. As a moral Being, God creates the universe with a moral purpose, and places humanity on earth so that they may perfect their personalities and create a just social order. The Qur'ān describes human beings' role in the creation of such an order as that of vice-regency (*khilāfa*) on earth, stemming from a primordial covenant established between God and humankind.[21] Because human beings accepted a primordial "trust" (*amāna*), God entrusted them to be the caretakers or vice-regents (*khalīfa*) of His creation.

The primordial trust has several important consequences for human beings. By consenting to the responsibility for being God's vice-regents on earth, human beings accept accountability for the realization of God's moral plan. Consequently, they accept that they will be judged according to their success or failure in achieving God's purpose. At the most fundamental level, then, human beings have a reason to be moral, if only to escape the dire punishment that God promises for failure.

However, the weakness and ignorance of human beings frustrates the fulfillment of their duty to God. The Qur'ān describes the human being as "a tyrant (*ẓalūm*) and a fool (*jahūl*)";[22] "they have hearts but cannot understand, they have eyes but cannot see, they have ears but cannot hear."[23] These basic human weaknesses are, in some respects, the consequence of a dual human nature that endows them with the capacity to understand and pursue both good and evil: "Surely We created man of the best constitution, but then We reduced him to the lowest of the low";[24] "[I swear by] the soul and by that whereby it was formed, and God has inspired it [with consciousness of] what is right and what is wrong."[25] Additionally, the devil, Iblīs, tempts human beings to sin, luring them away from their duties toward God.[26] Thus, despite the capacity for human beings to do good, their weak and sinful natures and the predations of the Devil make them largely unable to discharge their responsibilities toward God.

Without some form of assistance, human beings remain morally enfeebled and incapable of creating a just society on earth. For this reason, God sends His Prophets to bear divine guidance, which will steer human beings toward the path of moral and social perfection: "And We have revealed the scripture (*al-kitāb*) to you only that you may explain to them that wherein they differ, and [as] as guidance and mercy (*hudan wa raḥmatan*) for a people who believe."[27] This guidance is a fundamentally moral guidance, whose aim is to create a just society whereby "good will be commanded, and evil prohibited."[28]

Being moral involves active participation in the normative system of action implied in and demanded by the fundamental act of *islām* ("submission" of the individual will to the will of God). The term in the Qur'ān for morality, or more accurately "piety," is *taqwā*.[29] Notoriously difficult to translate, *taqwā* is defined by Izutsu as an awareness of the "absolute earnestness" of life that comes from "the consciousness of the impending Day of Judgment."[30] Similarly, Rahman sees *taqwā* as a type of active awareness in action: when people are fully aware of the consequences of their actions, they conduct themselves with true *taqwā*.[31] Additionally, insofar as "piety" is an awareness of the consequences of one's actions and the fear that comes from the knowledge of the Judgment, *taqwā* then refers to "fear" of God. *Taqwā*, thus, appears as a type of consciousness—even fear—that enables a human being to become a more moral being.

As the moral aspect of the Islamic system of action, the concept of *taqwā* involves the performance of the obligations inherent in being a Muslim: "Help one another to righteousness and piety (*'alā al-birri wa al-taqwā*); do not encourage one another to sin and transgression, but keep your duty to God (*wa ittaqū Allāh*)."[32] Similarly, the Qur'ān defines the *muttaqūn* (those who have *taqwā*) as those who "believe in the unseen, and establish worship, and spend of that which We have bestowed on them; and who believe in that which is revealed unto you [Muhammad] and that which was revealed before you, and are certain of the hereafter; who depend on guidance from their Lord."[33] As such, the definition of the *muttaqūn* is nearly equivalent to that of the *muslimūn* (muslims) or *mu'minūn* (believers). Indeed, the concept of *taqwā* involves the performance of the Islamic duties as well as the moral consciousness that should simultaneously pervade the performance of these duties.

The Qur'ān unambiguously makes *taqwā*, "piety," the criterion of excellence between human beings: "Surely the most noble among you (*akramakum*) is the most pious (*atqākum*)."[34] Here the Qur'ān employs the word *karīm* (in the superlative *akram*), which indicated in pre-Islamic times a nobility of character. However, the Qur'ān redefines what it means to be noble by associating the concept of nobility with the moral concept of *taqwā* (also in the superlative form *atqā*). The Qur'ānic use of the superlative forms of the adjectives for *karam* and *taqwā* makes it clear that the Qur'ānic concept of *taqwā* is to supercede all other means of distinction between human beings. The moral qualities and actions of a person (their *taqwā*) become the standard by which human beings may be distinguished.

Along with the revelation of the Qur'ān came the concept of prophecy. Unsurprisingly, moral excellence was believed to be an essential aspect of the Prophetic office. As the living embodiment of the Prophetic institution, the Qur'ān presents Muhammad as exemplifying to a very high degree—if not to perfection—moral virtue: "Surely in the messenger of God you have a good example for him who looks to God and the Last Day, and remembers God much."[35] Muhammad's moral traits were considered a fundamental and integrated side of his prophethood: that is, the essentially moral message of the Qur'ān presupposed an essentially moral messenger. Another verse implies that Muhammad was guided away from errant behavior toward proper action: "Did [God] not find you erring (*ḍālan*) and guide you (*fa-hadā*)?"[36] This verse implies that moral behavior, conceived in terms of right guidance, was synonymous with the office of Prophet. Likewise, certain *ḥadīth* (probably of later origin) express a conviction in the absence of negative moral traits in Muhammad's character: when asked about the *shayṭān*, the base faculties of the human personality, Muhammad commented: "My *shayṭān* has submitted completely, and does only what I order him."[37] Although later writers elevated the piety of the Prophet Muhammad for their own purposes, the conviction in the moral excellence of the Prophet Muhammad echoes similar sentiments in the Qur'ān and undoubtedly existed in some form among early Muslims.

Belief in the moral excellence of the Prophetic office became a standard feature of later Islamic literature. For example, the *Sanūsiyya*, a well known medieval handbook of Sunni doctrine, expresses the moral qualities that were considered fundamental to the institution of the Prophet:

> A Prophet has four necessary attributes: he must be truthful (*ṣidq*) and trustworthy (*amāna*); he has definitely to proclaim the Divine word (*tablīgh*) and has to be sagacious and intelligent (*faṭāna*). It is impossible that he should lie (*kidhb*), be faithless or treacherous (*khiyāna*), should conceal the Divine message (*katmān*) or be stupid (*badāla*).[38]

This later systematization of Prophetic attributes reflects what was implied in an unsystematic fashion in the Qur'ān and *ḥadīth* literature.

Another later means of expressing the moral excellence of a Prophet was through the doctrine of *'iṣma*. As a consequence of his moral superiority, Muhammad was believed to have the quality of *'iṣma*, a term defined by Schimmel as "protection or freedom (from moral depravity)."[39] However, there are no records of the doctrine of *'iṣma* from the earliest sources, and later commentators are divided as to the exact level of the Prophet's *'iṣma* (whether, for example, he was perfectly free of moral defects, or was prone to minor human weaknesses). Nevertheless, *ḥadīth* and *sīra* literature, for example, mention an incident during the time before the prophetic calling of Muhammad, when supernatural beings miraculously opened Muhammad's chest, and cleansed his heart of impurities and "Satan's part."[40] Similarly, there are accounts of Muhammad's wet nurse, Ḥalīma, being purified so that her milk would be cleansed for Muhammad to drink.[41] Like the "guidance" mentioned above, Muhammad's moral preeminence was later believed to be the consequence of divine intervention: the quality of *'iṣma* was believed to be God-given, and the "opening" and purification of Muhammad's breast completed by angelic beings. These somewhat earlier convictions about the institution of prophethood as a moral institution prefigure the formal statement in the doctrine of *'iṣma* about the "moral protection" of the Prophets.

Another fundamental aspect of the office of Prophet included the Prophet's authority: concurrent with Muhammad's possession of a high level of moral perfection was his enjoyment of comprehensive authority over his followers. The Qur'ān clearly established this authority in numerous verses: "Say: obey God and the Messenger";[42] "And obey God and the messenger, that you may find mercy."[43] Just as the moral preeminence of the Prophet was believed to be a divine gift, so

Muhammad's authority also resulted from his status as a Prophet. That is, as one "sent" (*rasūl*) by the ultimate source of authority (that is, God), Muhammad's authority derived from his "possession" of the Revelation (*al-risāla*; literally "that which is sent"). The contingency of Muhammad's authority on God's authority, and its connection with the notion of messengership is made clear in 7:158:

> Say [oh Muhammad]. Oh Mankind! I am the messenger of God (*rasūl Allāh*) to you all—[the messenger of Him] unto Whom belongs the sovereignty of the heavens and the earth. There is no God save Him. He quickens and he gives death. So believe in God and His messenger (*rasūluhu*), the unlettered Prophet, and follow him that haply you may be guided.

Thus, Muhammad's authority was presented as an integral element of the office of Prophet.

Insofar as the moral superiority and complete authority of the Prophet Muhammad were associated with the institution of the Prophet, their specific forms remained associated with Muhammad, and ceased with his death. However, the exclusivity of Muhammad's prophetic traits must be understood with reference to what aspects, exactly, remained restricted to Muhammad, and in what manner they remained limited to him. As "seal of the Prophets," Muhammad's status as *rasūl* quickly came to be unattainable to any other human being after him. His prophethood, it was believed, remained exclusive in a way that precluded participation in it. Similarly, the level of Muhammad's moral superiority—the character trait of being *ma'ṣūm*—was later thought to be unattainable to ordinary human beings.[44] However, moral excellence as such was not only possible but was encouraged by Muhammad and the Qur'ān as an essential practice of religion. Ordinary Muslims were expected to develop their moral faculties as part of the divine plan to establish a just society on earth. The moral perfection of the Prophet, while never accessible to the average believer, could nonetheless be imitated, if only in an imperfect way. Thus, some of the moral qualities of the Prophet could be reproduced and shared by the average believer.

It was precisely the accessibility and desirability of moral development to the essence of the Islamic endeavor, combined with the Qur'ānic proclamation that moral qualities were the sole basis for distinguishing excellence in human beings, that provided the Khārijites with a precedent for making moral qualities the criterion for political leadership. Moreover, the example of Muhammad provided the preeminent exemplar of a moral-political leader, and it did not require a great leap for the Khārijites to equate political leadership with the possession of highly developed moral qualities. Indeed, the Muslim community never abandoned the idea that religion and governance should reflect one another, just as they had during the exemplary era of the Prophet Muhammad.[45] For the Khārijites and Ibāḍites, the moral aspects of the Prophetic office only strengthened their belief that an Islamic government, as the heir to the Prophet, should be a moral government, necessarily led by a moral leader.

Moral Authority in Islam after the Death of the Prophet Muhammad

The early Madīnan caliphate provided the third precedent for the Khārijites' conception of legitimate authority as piety insofar as the institutionalization of a specific view toward legitimate succession was broad enough to accommodate what later became systematized into the Khārijite and Ibāḍite interpretations of legitimate authority. The actual authority of the first Caliphs was only partially based upon piety as the legitimating factor of their leadership; other factors, such as membership in the Quraysh tribe, also played a role in justifying their authority. However, although the partial reliance of Abū Bakr and 'Umar on their Qurayshī credentials stood in tension with the spirit of the Qur'ān, their demonstrated piety kept the inherent tension between these two qualifications of authority in check. The caliphate of 'Uthmān brought these mutually antagonistic interpretations of legitimate authority to the fore, and established a precedent whereby those who became the first Khārijites preferred moral rectitude as the legitimating trait of authority above all other qualifications.

The caliphate that arose in Madīna after the death of the Prophet Muhammad provided a solution to the problem of his succession insofar as significant portions of the Muslim community accepted the selection of Abū Bakr as leader (*khalīfa*—literally "successor") of the *umma*, and later recognized Abū Bakr's designation of 'Umar.[46] However, the concepts of legitimate authority underlying the choice of Abū Bakr and 'Umar as successors remained complex and, in certain respects, contradictory. The first Caliphs and their supporters reintroduced significant pre-Islamic norms to the process of establishing legitimate succession. Specifically, they established the precedent that the leader be an Arab, from the Quraysh tribe, as a criterion for recruitment to the office. This norm, based on the actions of Abū Bakr and 'Umar, became a standard feature of the later Sunni doctrine of the Caliph.[47] The argument for Islamic unity made by Abū Bakr and 'Umar on the porch (*saqīfa*) of the Banū Sā'ida was based on the conviction that the Quraysh tribe was the most noble of the Arabian tribes, and therefore no other group would be able to assert dominance over the whole of Arabia.[48] By invoking pre-Islamic principles of nobility and lineage, Abū Bakr affirmed the primacy of the Quraysh in Arab affairs, and established the precedent whereby they maintained it.

At the same time, the exclusive right of the Quraysh to lead the Muslims existed in tension with the spirit of Qur'ānic meritocracy, and the specifically tribal qualifications of Abū Bakr were not the qualities indicated by the Qur'ān as the basis for determining excellence.[49] While Qurayshī leadership, especially during the time following the death of the Prophet, insured the unity of the Islamic community, its exclusivity challenged the Qur'ānic notion that the "most noble" among the Muslims "is the most pious." Furthermore, Muhammad reportedly ordered the believers to obey even "a mutilated Ethiopian slave... so long as he leads you in accord with the Book of God" (according to Ibn Sa'd's wording of this *ḥadīth*).[50] Although temporarily eclipsed by the need for unity in the Islamic polity, piety (*taqwā*), as measured by the visible adherence to the moral precepts of Islam, ideally superseded all tribal considerations as the norm of human excellence. As such, reliance on tribal credentials stood in direct contradiction to the implications of piety as the legitimate basis for political authority.

The potential for tension between the reemerging tribal norms of leadership and the Qur'ānic and Islamic standards for pious authority was apparently resolved, at least temporarily, by the conduct of Abū Bakr and 'Umar as Caliphs. So far as the early sources can be trusted, Abū Bakr and 'Umar possessed all the necessary Islamic and pre-Islamic qualifications. In addition to the pre-Islamic characteristics mentioned above, Abū Bakr was an early convert to Islam, and a close Companion of the Prophet. He was numbered among those Companions who were promised paradise (*al-mubāshara*).[51] His piety and earnest devotion to the fulfillment of the Qur'ānic message was beyond question. Similarly, although 'Umar owed his position as Caliph to his membership in the Quraysh, Abū Bakr's designation, and the backing of the Makkan elite, 'Umar's devotion to the moral tenets of the Qur'ān and the mission of Muhammad were well known, and his policies sought to establish an Arab-Islamic meritocracy. For example, 'Umar limited the power of Makkan aristocracy by establishing the *diwān*, whereby Muslim soldiers received their share of the wealth from the conquests, on the principle of precedence (*sābiqa*) in the service of Islam. Actions such as the establishment of the *diwān* demonstrated 'Umar's commitment to the moral vision of Islam, even while his authority was partially based on his tribal qualifications. Abū Bakr and 'Umar thus embodied all the pre-Islamic and Islamic traits that made them eligible for leadership, and as long as the Muslim community enjoyed the headship of Caliphs like Abū Bakr and 'Umar, the tension inherent between the pre-Islamic and Islamic norms of authority was rendered invisible.

However, during the caliphate of 'Uthmān, the tension between the requirement of moral rectitude and the need for unity based upon an Arab-Quraysh monopoly on power materialized as the result of 'Uthmān's transgression of the norms of Islamic conduct and consequent failure to meet, in the eyes of many Muslims, the criterion for eligibility for leadership. Following the precedent established by Abū Bakr and ʿUmar, ʿUthmān hailed from the circle of Companions of the Prophet, and was a member of the Quraysh. His credentials, by both Islamic and pre-Islamic standards, were genuine, but not as impressive as other contemporary candidates for the caliphate. For example, although ʿUthmān had been a wealthy merchant before the advent of Islam, and was credited with the virtue (*faḍl*) of having selflessly devoted his wealth to the Islamic cause, he lacked military ability and was frequently excused from battle by the Prophet himself.[52] ʿUthmān enjoyed none of the traits prized by the pre-Islamic Arabs in their leaders, and was chosen, according to Madelung, with the strong backing of the Makkan aristocracy as the "strong counter-candidate to ʿAlī."[53]

Despite ʿUthmān's credentials as an early convert to and supporter of Islam, his conduct as Caliph quickly turned many Muslims against him. His transgressions (*aḥdāth*), which eventually led to his death at the hands of Muslim rebels in 36/656, illuminate the nature of the anti-ʿUthmān group's grievances.[54] In essence, this group held that ʿUthmān had failed to live up to the standards of piety and moral rectitude, as defined by adherence to the Book of God, the *sunna* of Muhammad, and the actions of Abū Bakr and ʿUmar. For example, ʿUthmān bestowed money and land from the "fifth" of the war spoils (*khums*) on his close relatives, arrogating the Qur'ānic right reserved for the family of the Prophet to his own family (Abū Bakr and ʿUmar had left the *khums* to the *bayt al-māl*, the treasury).[55] ʿUthmān's land policy, in which he allowed former Byzantine and Sāsānian crown lands (*ṣawāfī*), previously regarded as communal property (*fay'*), to go to his administrators and to some Companions, provoked serious displeasure among pious Muslims such as ʿAlī, who accused him of appropriating money belonging to the Muslim collectivity.[56] When the prominent Companion Abū Dharr al-Ghifārī loudly criticized ʿUthmān's land policies, ʿUthmān had him exiled.[57] Similarly, ʿUthmān had the Companion ʿAmmār b. Yāsir beaten unconscious for his part in censuring ʿUthmān's land policy.[58] Discontent with ʿUthmān's nepotism was so high that a comment by the Kūfan governor Saʿīd b. al-ʿĀṣ, to the effect that the cultivatable land (*sawād*) was for the Quraysh, provoked a riot by the Kūfan Qur'ān readers (*qurrā'*) who demanded the governor's removal.[59] ʿUthmān's refusal to punish his uterine brother al-Walīd b. ʿUqba for his drunkenness or his dabbling in witchcraft (*ṣiḥr*) further alienated pious Muslims.[60]

Although later Sunni tradition regards ʿUthmān as one of the "rightly guided" Caliphs, and therefore does not wish to accuse him of sin, it is clear that many Muslims of the time regarded his actions as impious. ʿUthmān's sermons in the mosque were frequently interrupted with calls for him to "act in accordance with the Book of God."[61] ʿAlī was able, on one occasion, to persuade ʿUthmān to publicly renounce his actions and to repent of them, an action that clearly demonstrates the depth to which "piety" was regarded as an informal requirement for leadership of the Islamic community.[62] Despite 'Uthmān's qualifications as a member of the Quraysh, and regardless of the backing of the Makkan aristocracy, the issue of 'Uthmān's piety and moral rectitude ultimately decided his fate as leader of the Muslims. 'Uthmān's continued abuses led to widespread frustration with his actions, and ultimately provoked his murder. His actions induced a group of Egyptians to make the trip to Madīna with the hope of securing improvement. Having received what they believed was assurance that 'Uthmān would reform his behavior, the Egyptians intercepted on their return a messenger bearing note with the Caliph's seal. The note contained instructions that their party should be imprisoned upon their return. Incensed, the Egyptians returned to Madīna, confronted 'Uthmān, and surrounded his residence. After a number of days, the standoff turned violent, and 'Uthmān was killed.[63]

In the turmoil following 'Uthmān's death, 'Alī accepted in Madīna the allegiance of a portion of the Islamic community. However, 'Alī's power was far from secure, as 'Ā'isha, the youngest wife of the Prophet, Ṭalḥa b. 'Ubaydullāh, and al-Zubayr b. al-'Awwām were planning to oppose him from Makka, and Mu'āwiya b. Abī Sufyān waited in Damascus for the proper time to assert his claims to authority. This period later became known as the Islamic first civil war: in Arabic, the *fitna*.[64]

The caliphate of 'Alī presents a special case when it comes to the institutionalization of the Prophet's authority, and the qualifications for leadership as understood by the later Sunnis, Shi'ites, Khārijīs, and Ibāḍīs. Like Abū Bakr, 'Umar, and 'Uthmān, 'Alī was an early Companion of the Prophet, and possessed the necessary traits of membership in the Quraysh and moral rectitude. Later Sunni tradition regards 'Alī as a "rightly guided" Caliph, and implicitly accepts him on the basis of these qualifications. 'Alī and his supporters (*shī'a*), however, never relied on the same paradigm of legitimacy that bolstered Abū Bakr, 'Umar, and 'Uthmān's claim to succession. Consequently, a different model of legitimate succession applies to their situation, as well as different norms and proofs of eligibility for leadership. What became the Shi'ite answer to the problem of Muhammad's succession authority combined two solutions. First, the supporters of 'Alī accentuated the long-held belief that character traits and qualities were passed on to the offspring, and that therefore certain families and tribes were known to possess the qualities of bravery, generosity, or leadership. Based on this belief, some Arabs held that the family of the Prophet (the *ahl al-bayt*)—and especially his cousin 'Alī—were entitled to authority over the Muslim community as a consequence of their familial relationship to Muhammad. Additionally, the Qur'ān had shown the families of Prophets as their inheritors and successors upon their deaths. Thus, Hārūn (Aaron) assumed the mantle of prophethood after Mūsā

(Moses), and Sulaymān (Solomon) succeeded Dawūd (David) as leaders of their respective communities.[65] An exclusively Shi'ite norm for leadership, thereby, became descent from the Prophet's clan of Hāshim, and piety and moral rectitude were assumed as characteristics inherited genealogically from membership in the Prophet's family.[66]

Second, 'Alī's supporters came to believe in his designation (*naṣṣ*) as successor by Muhammad. As proof, the supporters of 'Alī evoked an instance during the lifetime of Muhammad when, at a well called Ghadīr al-Khum, the Prophet had said that to whomever he was a *mawlā*, 'Alī was also his *mawlā* (*man kuntu mawlāhu fa-hādha 'Alīun mawlāhu*).[67] The term *mawlā* (from the root *w-l-y*) admits to many possible meanings; among them "friend," "leader" and "master." To the supporters of 'Alī, the word denoted the designation of political authority: "To whomever I am a leader, 'Alī is his leader."[68] Thus, in the *ḥadīth* of Ghadīr al-Khum the supporters of 'Alī found a mandate for 'Alī's right to rule. Beyond the Prophet's designation of 'Alī as his successor, no further proof of eligibility was needed. However, as was the case with Abū Bakr and 'Umar, 'Alī's credentials as a member of the Quraysh, his companionship with the Prophet, and his obvious piety made his legitimacy such that all parties (aside from those who accused 'Alī of harboring 'Uthmān's killers) were satisfied with him as leader of the Muslims. Among those who accepted the leadership of 'Alī were those who would become the first Khārijites.

In summary, although piety was not the only consideration for legitimacy among early Islamic leaders, notions of moral rectitude served as one among other norms for determining genuine authority during the early caliphal period. Piety functioned to a certain extent to justify the reigns of Abū Bakr, 'Umar, and 'Alī, just as the popular interpretation of 'Uthmān's actions (*aḥdāth*) in terms of sin illegitimated his rule in the eyes of some Muslims. Nevertheless, it is entirely possible, even likely, that certain individuals held piety as the paramount quality of legitimate leadership even before such a position was fully articulated by the early Khārijites. The speed with which the first Khārijites—beginning with the Muḥakkima—articulated their opposition to 'Alī in terms of impiety, and established the counter-imāmate of 'Abdullāh b. Wahb al-Rāsibī along the lines of their own interpretation of legitimacy in leadership suggests that those who would become the Khārijites had previously attached a certain significance to the idea of piety as the validating characteristic of leadership. This added importance that was placed upon Qur'ānic means of establishing human excellence may have come from affiliation with a group of individuals known as the *qurrā'*.[69] Although obscure, the term *qurrā'* may refer to individuals who specialized in reciting the Qur'ān for inspiration before the battle lines of the Muslim armies.[70] These individuals, whose dedication to the Qur'ān lent them an air of piety, may have insisted on a more "Islamic" interpretation of authority, that is, one that did not necessarily rely on Qurayshī or Hāshimite credentials, and took demonstrated piety as the legitimating factor of leadership.

Moreover, the tribal affiliations of the proto-Khārijites, many of whom came from the tribes of Tamīm, Bakr, Ḥanīfa, and Shaybān, suggests that those who became the first Khārijites were outsiders to the Makkan-Quraysh power structure. Although the majority of Muslims tacitly accepted the Qurayshī leadership of the Muslims, there is no evidence that they necessarily knew of it as a *requirement*. Outside the circle of those who chose the Caliphs (that is, the Companions of the Prophet) and their Makkan and Madīnan affiliates, there was no need for the average Muslim to ponder details of leadership over which he had no real influence in the first place. In other words, recognition of the Caliph by the community did not necessarily imply that the community was aware of the norms and proofs of eligibility by which the Companions chose and designated the Caliph (and indeed, they were not formalized until much later). As such, the proto-Khārijites among the Muslim community could have "accepted" the Caliphs according to their own understanding of legitimate leadership. Similarly, they could have accepted (and rejected) the first four Caliphs on the basis of their demonstrated piety, without reference to hereditary traits, or membership in the Quraysh tribe or the Hāshimite clan.

Moral Authority in Khārijite Islamic Thought

That the convictions and actions of the early Khārijites functioned as a precedent for later Khārijite—and by extension Ibāḍite—doctrine and practice seems obvious until it is recalled that over one hundred years separates the birth of the *khawārij* from their specific expression in the Ibāḍiyya at the beginning of the formative Ibāḍī period. The first Khārijites—known as the Muḥakkima after their use of the slogan *lā ḥukm illā li-lāh*, "No judgment but God's"—emerged at the Battle of Ṣiffīn in 35–36/656. The next major upsurge of Khārijite activity occurred during the second *fitna* in 61/680, and the Ibāḍiyya materialized as a recognizable sect in the period 102–124/720–740. They established independent political states only in the late half of the second/eighth century. Given the gap of time separating the first Khārijites from their subsequent subsects and offshoots, the changing historical contexts in which these groups operated inevitably resulted in a wealth of practical and doctrinal expressions of Khārijī and Ibāḍī religious thought.

At the same time, certain deeply held convictions provided continuity between the Khārijite subsects throughout the evolution of their history, and afforded an underlying connection between different Khārijite groups. With the appearance of the Muḥakkima after the Battle of Ṣiffīn, the pre-Islamic, Qur'ānic, and early Madīnan precedents for the notion of piety as the underlying characteristic of legitimate authority culminated in the way in which the Muḥakkima seceded from 'Alī and then designated their first leaders. These concrete expressions of the conception of legitimate authority among the first Khārijites became paradigmatic for all subsequent Khārijite subsects, as well as the Ibāḍiyya.

Due to the paucity of sources and the inherent bias of Sunni heresiographers, much material on the Khārijite subsects is lost or unrelated to the question of leadership. Nonetheless, significant evidence can be amassed from the mainstream historical and heresiographical traditions to examine how the belief in piety and moral rectitude (with impiety/sin as its opposite) as the legitimating conception of authority shaped the actions of the Muḥakkima in relation to 'Alī and the first Khārijite leaders. Among others, al-Ṭabarī, al-Mubarrad, and al-Balādhurī preserve much material relevant to the Khārijites. Al-Ṭabarī and al-Balādhurī use the work of earlier authors, such as Abū Mikhnaf and Wahb b. Jarīr, in their presentation of the Khārijites. Abū Mikhnaf probably used some Khārijite sources for his account, but this source is not acknowledged, and is mixed in with other materials. Likewise, Wahb b. Jarīr probably based his accounts on Khārijite sources, but does not acknowledge those sources. Al-Mubarrad's accounts likewise tend toward the anonymous, though there are significant exceptions to this rule.[71]

Muslim historians and heresiographers date the genesis of the Khārijites, distinguished from the later Khārijite subsects by the term Muḥakkima, to the Battle of Ṣiffīn and its aftermath.[72] The name Muḥakkima is derived from those who voiced the *taḥkīm*: that is, the phrase *lā ḥukm illā lil-lāh*—"No judgment but God's." This slogan made its appearance in the context of opposition to 'Alī's arbitration agreement (*ḥakam al-ḥākimayn*, *ḥukūma*) with Mu'āwiya.[73] It became the catchphrase of the early Khārijites, and summed up their objection with the arbitration, and with 'Alī's acceptance of it.

Implicit in the *taḥkīm* was a complex view toward the limits of human judgment in relation to God's judgment, and thereby of the proper character of human authority in relation to the divine authority. On one level, the *taḥkīm* expressed a belief in the restrictions of human judgment: the Qur'ān had declared, in a phrase reminiscent of the *taḥkīm* itself: "judgment rests only with God" (*inna al-ḥukma illā lil-lāhi*).[74] The sense of what exactly constituted these divine decisions differed according to the different verses in which this phrase appeared. In 6:57, the phrase *inna al-ḥukma illā lil-lāhi* indicates the divine ability (and consequently, the human inability) to decree the Final Judgment (that is, to decide when it should happen and bring it about). In 12:40, the phrase *inna al-ḥukma* is used to underscore God's ability to command worship (that is, to decree whom human beings should worship), just as its use in 12:67 highlights God's ability to control the destiny of human beings (that is, to arrange events to help or hinder their actions). Simultaneously, these verses express the impropriety of human beings' attempt to contravene the decree of God: in 6:57, human beings do not have the ability to bring about the Day of Judgment, yet the verse ironically describes the Makkans as impatient (*tasta'jilūn*) for it. Similarly, in 12:40 the *innā al-ḥukma* phrase is couched in a criticism of polytheism as disobedience to the command of God. In other verses, the Qur'ān expressed the idea, using the word *ḥukm*, that human beings were expected to observe God's decrees: the Qur'ān commanded Muhammad to "wait for the decision of your Lord," just as it ordered the believers to "abide patiently by the decision (*li-ḥukm*) of your Lord."[75] Obedience to the "judgments" of God, therefore, became a mark of submission to the divine will—an act of *islām* and, therefore, an act of piety. Although the Qur'ān did not offer a systematic exposition of God's decrees, it can be assumed by their connection with the notions of command and obedience that the "decree" of God was synonymous with the totality of the specific content that made up the action of *islām*. Thus, the phrase *inna al-ḥukm illā lil-lāh* in the Qur'ān expressed the limits of human ability in relation to God's decrees, as well as the impropriety of human beings to go against (or to presume that they can go against) those decrees.

In the context of the Battle of Ṣiffīn, the phrase *lā ḥukm illā lil-lāh* did not express a belief in the inability of human beings to arbitrate the battle, but rather a conviction in the impropriety of human beings doing so. According to many different sources, 'Urwa b. Udaya was credited with being the first individual to utter the *taḥkīm*.[76] Upon hearing of the arbitration agreement, he exclaimed "You have set up men to judge God's commands?! There is no judgment except God's!" Implicit in 'Urwa's statement was the idea that God had already made his command regarding Mu'āwiya's army clear: they should be fought, and it was therefore improper for 'Alī to allow human beings to arbitrate the outcome of the battle. A variant in al-Shahrastānī credits 'Urwa with the words: "Are the conditions (*sharṭ*) of [any] one of you more reliable (*awthaq*) than the conditions of God?"[77] Like the previous statement, 'Urwa's words in al-Shahrastānī's account imply the unseemliness of the *taḥkīm*. In the words of the early Ibāḍī heresiographer Sālim b. Dhakwān, by accepting arbitration 'Alī "abandoned the path the Muslims followed in the past by making somebody other than God the judge in a case already settled by God."[78] According the Khārijites, 'Alī's persistent acceptance of the arbitration violated a clear Qur'ānic verse ordering the Muslims to fight.[79] For this reason, two early Khārijites, Zur'a b. Burj al-Ṭā'ī and Ḥurqūs b. Zuhayr al-Sa'adī, approached 'Alī demanding that he resume the fight against Mu'āwiya. When 'Alī refused, Zur'a declared: "[I swear] by God Oh 'Alī! If you do not cease making human beings judges over the Book of God, I will fight you!"[80] Again, it is the inappropriateness of judging, not the inability to judge, that rankles the Khārijites. Finally, in a version of the verbal contest (*munāẓara*) at Ḥarūrā' between the Khārijites and Ibn 'Abbās, the Muḥakkima express the notion that God had made his judgment on Mu'āwiya clear, and it was therefore unsuitable for human beings to impose their judgment (in the form of arbitration) over that of God's: "As for what God has decreed, it is final, and it is not for [His] servants to meddle in it; for God has concluded his judgment of Mu'āwiya and his party such that they should be killed or return [to obedience]."[81]

Belief in the impropriety of the arbitration led the Muḥakkima to declare its acceptance a sin.[82] Arbitration, according to a report on the Khārijites in Ibn Qutayba, would result in "disunion, sin before God, and disgrace in this world."[83] Likewise, Ḥurqūs b. Zuhayr al-Sa'adī and Zur'a b. al-Burj al-Ṭā'ī demanded that 'Alī repeal the arbitration and return to battle with Mu'āwiya, ordering 'Alī to "repent your sin (*khaṭī'atak*)."[84] In some cases, the acceptance of the arbitration is described in terms of unbelief (*kufr*). When 'Alī accused the Khārijites who gathered at Ḥarūrā'[85] of forcing him into arbitration, they replied to 'Alī: "you have spoken the truth—we were as you recalled and we acted as you described; but that was an act of disbelief (*kufr*) on our part, and we have repented to God for it."[86] Although different terms are employed for the concept of "sin" (*ma'ṣiya*, *khaṭī'a*, and *kufr*), a general consensus exists among the sources that the Muḥakkima regarded acceptance of the arbitration with Mu'āwiya as a transgression of a clear Qur'ānic decree to fight.

Moreover, the conviction that 'Alī had sinned by accepting the arbitration subsequently resulted in the secession of the Khārijites from 'Alī's army, and their rejection of his authority.[87] As the Muḥakkima stated in a letter to 'Alī: "We cannot take you as our Imām, for you have become an unbeliever (*kāfir*)."[88] Similarly, the Muḥakkima at Ḥarūrā' demanded of 'Alī: "So repent as we have repented and we will pledge allegiance to you, but if not we will continue to oppose you."[89] Early Ibāḍī sources simply state that the Khārijites "deposed him" (*khala'hu*) after 'Alī made "a mockery of God's judgment."[90] This rejection of 'Alī on the basis of his sin/disbelief represents the initial manifestation of the Khārijite conception of legitimate authority as demonstrated merit, in its negative form (that is, sin disqualifies). Their action illustrated the extent to which the belief in piety as the legitimating issue of leadership made the Muḥakkima willing to abandon their Imām on the basis of demonstrated sin.

The first expression in the positive sense of the Khārijite notion of piety as the legitimating factor of leadership came from the accounts of the appointment of the first Imām of the Khārijites. Al-Ṭabarī, using Abū Mikhnaf's account, reports that the Muḥakkima, after becoming convinced of 'Alī's illegitimacy as leader, gathered in the house of 'Abdullāh b. Wahb al-Rāsibī and there agreed to flee Kūfa.[91]

A man named Hamza b. Sinān al-Asadī encouraged them to "grant authority of your affairs to one among you, for you cannot do without a support, a prop, and a banner around which you can rally and to which you can return." After those present rejected the offer of authority, ʿAbdullāh b. Wahb al-Rāsibī accepted the oath of allegiance (*bayʿa*) and became the first Imām of the Khārijites. Upon receiving the oath of allegiance, al-Rāsibī reportedly stated, "By God I do not take it wishing [for reward] in this world (*raghbatan fī al-dunyā*)."[92] He was said to have the nickname *dhū al-thafināt*—"he of the calluses"—because of the calluses on his forehead and hands from his excessive praying.[93] As these reports illustrate, the outward signs of al-Rāsibī's ascetic piety contributed to his candidacy for leader insofar as his piety was exceptional and exemplary.

Another aspect of the appointment of al-Rāsibī as the Imām of the Muḥakkima involved characteristics that were rejected by the Muḥakkima as legitimate traits of authority. Specifically, al-Rāsibī did not come from the Quraysh: thus his appointment as leader flouted the (probably not yet formally established) "precedent" that the Imām be from this tribe.[94] Concurrently, his assumption of power disregarded the pro-ʿAlīd notions of legitimacy based on designation or membership in the Prophet's clan of Hāshim. Although no comments of the Muḥakkima have been preserved regarding their disregard for Qurayshī credentials, their overt rejection of proto-Shiʿite notions of legitimacy are reiterated in a letter in which the Muḥakkima accused ʿAlī of relying on his kinship (*qarāba*) with the Prophet to justify acceptance of the arbitration: "You [ʿAlī] thought, 'I have kinship with the Prophet of God...and therefore the people will not place me on the same level as Muʿāwiya.'"[95] In addition, implicit criticism of the notion of hereditary authority was echoed in the Muḥakkima's criticism of the pledge of allegiance (*bayʿa*) offered by ʿAlī's supporters after the desertion of the Khārijites:

> When ʿAlī approached Kūfa, and the Muḥakkima—and they are the Khārijites—had deserted him, ʿAlī's supporters rushed to him saying: We are bound by your allegiance and we are friends of those you befriend, and enemies of your enemies. The Khārijites said: These people and the people of Syria are competing with one another in unbelief (*kufr*) like betting horses: The people of Syria pledged allegiance to Muʿāwiya according to their likes and dislikes, and these people pledged allegiance to ʿAlī on the condition that they will befriend who he befriends, and take as enemies those he takes as enemies.[96]

Thus, the first Khārijites absolutely rejected allegiance to the person of the leader, no matter who that person happened to be. For them, legitimate authority depended on the demonstrated piety of a leader, regardless of kinship ties or its implied hereditary traits.

So formative were the events of the first *fitna*, and the reactions of the first Muḥakkima to it, that they became paradigmatic for all subsequent Khārijite subsects. This debt to the Muḥakkima can be seen in heresiographical definitions of what is common to all Khārijite subsects. Al-Shahrastānī, for example, characterized a common tenet of the Khārijites by explaining how all Khārijites "declare grave sinners to be unbelievers and view rising against an Imām who transgresses the *sunna* as a required duty."[97] Other heresiographers make the connection between the Muḥakkima and later Khārijite groups more explicit: al-Baghdādī paraphrased al-Ash'arī's definition of what typifies the Khārijites as "the declaration of 'Alī, 'Uthmān, the People of the Camel [that is, those who participated in the Battle of the Camel], the two arbiters, those who were satisfied with the arbitration, or who sanctioned the two arbiters, or [those who sanctioned] one of them as infidels; and rising (*khurūj*) against an unjust ruler (*al-sulṭān al-jā'ir*)."[98] This pairing in heresiographical definitions of Khārijism of the Khārijite doctrine of sin as infidelity and the necessity to resist an impious or unjust ruler is not accidental or random, but rather represents the implications of the Khārijite's insistence on piety and moral rectitude as the legitimating qualities of a leader. In this particular case, sin represents the demonstrated lack of the virtues of piety and moral rectitude that legitimate leadership, and, therefore, it debars an individual from positions of authority. This particular view toward sin and legitimate authority owes an obvious debt to the Muḥakkima's treatment of 'Alī on the basis of his acceptance of the arbitration agreement.

The specific example of the Muḥakkima's attribution of sin to 'Alī as the result of his agreement to arbitrate the Battle of Ṣiffīn became the basis for the general Khārijite belief that sin makes a person an unbeliever (*kāfir*)—the Khārijite doctrine of sin. Although it is not explicitly stated in the sources, it is safe to assume that the attribution of sin/infidelity to an individual immediately disqualified that person from a position of authority over the Muslims, and thus, the connection between sin and ineligibility in leadership can be generalized to all Khārijite subsects. As a distinguishing mark of Khārijism, all Khārijite subsects upheld the doctrine of the grave sinner to some degree. At the extreme end of the spectrum, the Azāriqa and Najdāt believed that anyone who did not make a *hijra* their camp—any non-Khārijite Muslim—was an unbeliever (*kāfir*) or polytheist (*mushrik*) along with their wives and children, and could therefore be legally killed and plundered. In other words, all sinners were considered collectively *kāfirūn* and *mushrikūn*.[99] At the other end of the spectrum, the early Ibāḍiyya, as the most moderate development from the pre-Azraqite Khārijites, reserved the term *mushrik* for those who denied God's existence.[100] Although the Ibāḍīs still referred to sinners as *kuffār*,[101] they considered them "people of the *qibla*," "monotheists" (*muwāḥidūn*), and members of their *qawm* (a term that refers to non-Khārijite Muslims).[102] As such, sinners among the *qawm* were *kuffār* in the sense of hypocrites (*munāfiqūn*), rather than unbelievers (*mushrikūn*).[103] Thus, given that the most moderate of the early Khārijite subsects, the early Ibāḍiyya, nonetheless considered a sinner a *kāfir-munāfiq*, and that a *kāfir* is by definition disqualified from positions of authority over the Muslims, it is safe to assume that all Khārijite groups—from the moderate Ibāḍiyya to the extremist Azāriqa and Najdāt—shared similar views regarding the illegitimacy of sinners as leaders as a consequence of the doctrine of sin. Although this view is not explicitly stated in either early Ibāḍī literature or heresiographical materials, it is strongly implied by the doctrine of sin.

Certain evidence in heresiographical materials corroborates the application of the doctrine of sin to the Khārijite Imāms. It is reported, for example, that a faction of the Najdāt forced their leader, Najda b. ʿĀmir al-Ḥanafī, to recant and repent for his opinion that a person is excused from sin if he is ignorant of the fact that the action is a sin.[104] A smaller section of the Najdāt then decided that it was not their place to question the *ijtihād* of their Imām, and forced Najda to repent his original repentance—which Najda did. As a result of this second repentance, the majority of the Najdāt deposed (*khalaʿūhu*) Najda and forced him to choose the next Imām.[105] Thus, for some early Najdites, the doctrine of sin directly related to the legitimacy or illegitimacy of their leader. Despite the fact that this is the only clear instance of the application of the doctrine of sin to a Khārijī leader, the potential nonetheless existed, as it was implied in the widely accepted Khārijite doctrine of sin.

The Khārijites, of course, had no qualms in applying the doctrine of sin, and thereby the notion that sin disqualifies an individual from ruling over the Muslims, to the Umayyad Caliphs. Abū Ḥamza al-Khārijī, a moderate Khārijite associated with an Ibāḍī-inspired rebellion of ʿAbdullāh b. Yaḥyā (known as Ṭālib al-Ḥaqq) in the Ḥijāz that briefly captured and controlled Makka and Madīna in 129–130/746–747, expressly connected the sinfulness of the Umayyads to the justification for their removal.[106] In an oration (*khuṭba*) to the people of Makka, Abū Ḥamza characterizes the Umayyad Caliphs as a corrupt dynasty: "Then there took charge Muʿāwiya b. Abī Sufyān, who was cursed by the Messenger of God and the son of who so cursed. He made the servants of God slaves (*khawl*), and the property of God something to be taken in turns, and His religion a cause of corruption."[107] Abū Ḥamza likewise censures Yazīd b. Muʿāwiya and Yazīd b. ʿAbd al-Malik as sinners (*fāsiq*), and labels the Banū Umayya collectively as the party of misguidance (*firqat al-ḍalāla*). Abū Ḥamza's examples, from which he illustrates the impiety of the Umayyad Caliphs, include: wine drinking, lasciviousness, arbitrary arrests, failure to judge or punish crimes consistently, and improper collection and distribution of the alms. The implication of Abū Ḥamza's oration is that these sins have justified Abū Ḥamza and Ṭālib al-Ḥaqq's rebellion against the Umayyads. Abū Ḥamza's speech is thus an illustration of the Khārijite belief in moral considerations—the notion that legitimate authority was associated with pious behavior—as the ultimate validation for authority. This pattern of thought is a direct continuation of the Muḥakkima's conviction that sin expressly disqualifies (and moral rectitude qualifies) a leader from a position of authority.

In light of later juridical developments in Sunni Islam, the deposing of a Caliph on the grounds that he has sinned appears to be an affront to caliphal authority. In general, Sunni Muslim jurists viewed a Caliph as legitimate if he was capable of maintaining order and stability in the realm.[108] Substantive issues of justice or morality were practically irrelevant to the legitimacy of the Caliph, so long as his actions did not provoke *fitna*. For this reason, Sunni historians and heresiographers focused primarily on the Khārijite doctrine of the grave sinner, and the consequent notion that sin (as unbelief—*kufr* or *shirk*) disqualified an Imām from rule as a means of portraying the Khārijites as deviant or heretical. In other words, Sunni historians were interested mainly in the negative connotations of the doctrine of sin. However, a positive flipside to this Khārijite doctrine was implied, but was not made explicit in the Sunni sources: namely, that the exceptionally pious individual possessed an especially strong mandate to rule. Some evidence for the positive expression of piety as a legitimating factor of leadership comes from one line of the early Ibāḍī *sīra* of Sālim b. Dhakwān. In general, Sālim's epistle is heresiographical in nature, and therefore prefers to describe "heretical" doctrines rather than directly speak of Ibāḍī (that is, "correct") doctrine. Nonetheless, Sālim advises the Muslims to "appoint to the command their most excellent men, and those among them who understand [religion]."[109] Although the term *faḍl* is not explicitly associated with moral excellence, Sālim encourages dissociation (*barā'a*) from "the Imāms of wrongdoing" (*ā'immat al-ẓulm*). The Ibāḍī Imām would presumably be, thereby, an Imām of correct action, or, a pious Imām. Similarly, Ibn al-Jawzī states: "And of the opinions of the Khārijites is that they do not give the imāmate to a person unless knowledge and asceticism (*zuhd*) are combined in him."[110] In this case, piety, envisioned as ascetic qualities, was essential to the Imām. Thus, while systematic evidence for the expression of the positive aspects of the doctrine of sin would have to wait until the medieval Ibāḍī *imāma*, the implications of this doctrine existed in earlier conceptions of the doctrine of the grave sinner, as well as in the early Ibāḍī epistle of Sālim b. Dhakwān and others.

Just as the Muḥakkima's rejection of 'Alī on the basis of the sin of accommodating the arbitration of Ṣiffīn formed the basis for later Khārijite doctrines of sin, so the acceptance of 'Abdullāh b. Wahb al-Rāsibī further entrenched the precedent whereby piety became the main criterion for legitimate leadership. This straightforward acceptance of piety over the requirement for Qurayshī descent is borne out by early Ibāḍī *ḥadīth*, which are probably from the formative period of Ibāḍism. Although these *ḥadīth* were preserved in an arrangement (*tartīb*) of Abū Ya'qūb al-Warjlānī dating to the sixth/twelfth century, the entire collection is attributed to the fourth Basran Ibāḍī Imām, al-Rabī' b. Ḥabīb al-Farāhidī, who is said to have died in 170/786. In fact, al-Warjlānī probably organized a wide variety of sources, including some materials from Jābir b. Zayd, al-Rabī' b. Ḥabīb as well as the last Basran Imām, Abū Sufyān Maḥbūb b. al-Rāhil (d. early-third/ninth century), who edited some of the materials.[111] Nevertheless, the *aḥadīth* of al-Warjlānī's collection that have a direct bearing on the issue of the exclusive claims of the Quraysh or Hāshimites to the leadership of the Muslims bear the *isnād* of Jābir b. Zayd on the authority of Ibn 'Abbās. Thus, they almost certainly come from the strata of materials taken from the *athār* of Jābir b. Zayd, which are likely to be some of the earliest materials in the collection.

The *ḥadīth* in question contain a straightforward rejection of Qurayshī claims to authority in favor of piety as the final legitimating criterion of leadership: the Quraysh will remain leaders of the community "as long as they refrain from reproachable deeds."[112] Another *ḥadīth* warns against the temptations of kingship (*mulk*) with the familiar connotation that the Umayyads have usurped legitimate leadership of the Muslim community while simultaneously transforming it into kingship. By adding qualifying conditions of piety to the leadership of the Quraysh, their exclusive claim to rule is superseded by the conditions of moral probity expected of the Imām. Moreover, another *ḥadīth* (worded differently from Ibn Sa'd's version above) commands the believers to obey "an Ethiopian slave with a mutilated nose" so long as he upheld the book of God. This *ḥadīth* expresses the contra-positive of the others: so long as the leader is pious, he can be anyone (including the most unlikely of persons, an Ethiopian slave).

The sentiment is echoed in the statement of a follower of Shabīb al-Khārijī, Muṭarraf b. Mughīra, who argued:

> We do not see that the Quraysh have more right to this matter [the caliphate] than any other Arab... for surely they know that the best people in God's sight are the most pious, and the most deserving of them for [the caliphate] is the one who is most pious and virtuous among them.[113]

Shabīb's rebellion began, according to the reports of Abū Mikhnaf in al-Ṭabarī, around 85/704. Al-Ṭabarī records Muṭarraf's comments as being from the year 87/706. Thus, the conviction that piety outweighed all other considerations, including Qurayshī credentials, dates from the earliest period of Khārijite activity, and can be directly linked to the original actions of the Muḥakkima with regard to their first Imām, ʻAbdullāh b. Wahb al-Rāsibī.

Medieval Ibāḍī Articulation of Piety as Legitimate Authority

The medieval Ibāḍī *imāma* ideal, the direct inheritor of the early Khārijite concept of demonstrated merit as the legitimating quality of authority, succeeded to earlier, pre-Khārijite (and even pre-Islamic) notions of moral rectitude as legitimate authority. As the final inheritors of Khārijite notions of authority, the medieval Ibāḍī imāmate subsequently took the inspiration for its specific institutional structure from the preceding institutions of authority in pre-Islamic, Prophetic, Madīnan, and early Khārijite eras. This claim is strengthened by the existence of Ibāḍī "apostolic" lines of legitimacy that parallel the historical and conceptual lines of transmission for the notion of piety as the legitimate mode of authority.

These apostolic lines of legitimacy exist in numerous Ibāḍī sources. Their purpose was to provide the sense of legitimacy that comes from the belief in an unbroken chain of authoritative transmitters of Ibāḍī doctrine and practice. Al-Jiṭālī, a eighth/fourteenth-century North African theologian and jurist, provides a short list of those Imāms about whom ignorance is not possible; his list includes, among others, Abū Bakr, ʻUmar, the first North African Imām ʻAbd al-Raḥmān b. Rustum, and his progeny. This North African list offers, in brief, a synopsis of the chains of legitimacy accepted by North African Ibāḍīs.[114] Omani lists tend to be more extensive: al-Kudamī states that those persons who maintain the ways of the people of Nahrawān—especially those of ʻAbdullāh b. Wahb al-Rāsibī—are the authoritative sources (*al-ḥujja al-tāma*) of the ways practiced by the Prophet, Abū Bakr, ʻUmar, and those who fought against ʻUthmān, Ṭalḥa, Zubayr, ʻAlī, and Muʻāwiya.[115] The implication, of course, is that legitimacy derives from the line of persons extending from the first Khārijites back to the Prophet, and illegitimacy resides with those who supported ʻUthmān, ʻAlī, and Muʻāwiya. Likewise, al-Kindī traces the preservation of the "true religion" to the Prophet Muhammad through Abū Bakr, ʻUmar, and ʻAbdullāh b. Wahb al-Rāsibī.[116] Muḥammad b. Ibrāhīm al-Kindī, the fifth/eleventh-century jurist, traces the "genealogy of Islam" (*nasab al-islām*) from Muhammad to Abū Bakr and ʻUmar through ʻAbdullāh b. Wahb al-Rāsibī to the Imāms of Oman.[117] Al-Sālimī, a fourteenth/twentieth-century scholar, quoting Abū Mu'thir, an early third/ninth-century jurist, adds Ḥurqūs b. Zuhayr al-Saʻadī and Zayd b. Ḥiṣn al-Ṭā'ī, two prominent early Muḥakkima, to the list.[118] While the parallels between the "apostolic" lines of transmission and the historical and conceptual precedents of the Ibāḍī *imāma* reflect the chronological path of development that led to the formation of the medieval Ibāḍiyya, the links of transmission do not provide details as to the specific contributions of each individual link to Ibāḍī religious thought as a whole. Moreover, the Ibāḍī line of transmission noticeably rejects any link with the pre-Islamic era. Nonetheless, the Prophetic, early Madīnan caliphate, and the early Khārijite eras are all acknowledged as predecessors to the medieval Ibāḍiyya, and the figures of the Prophet, Abū Bakr, 'Umar, 'Abdullāh b. Wahb al-Rāsibī, Ḥurqūs b. Zuhayr al-Sa'adī, and Zayd b. Ḥiṣn al-Ṭā'ī are mentioned as individuals from whom the Ibāḍīs inherited the true religion.[119]

The debt of the medieval Ibāḍī *imāma* to earlier conceptions and institutions of authority can also be seen in the distinctive features that make up the medieval Ibāḍī institution of the Imām. In terms of what the North African Ibāḍiyya referred to as the *imām al-ẓuhūr*, the preference attached to the personal qualities of piety distinguishes the Ibāḍiyya from other Islamic groups. In Omani legal texts, the moral trait often citied by Ibāḍī legal texts as necessary for a leader is the quality of *'adāla*, justice, and Omani Ibāḍī sources consistently note that the only legitimate form of leadership is that of the just leader (*sulṭān* or *imām 'ādil*).[120] Al-Kudamī defines the just Imām as one who "obeys God and His messenger, and acts by the Book of God and the *sunna* of His Prophet."[121] Al-Bisyānī, a fifth/eleventh-century Omani jurist, quotes the Prophetic *ḥadīth* that states: "Do not disobey a just ruler."[122] Justice thus forms one of the primary attributes of a legitimate leader. As al-Kudamī states, "the main proof (*al-ḥujja al-qā'ima*) for the people regarding their Imām and for their obedience to his authority is his just conduct (*'adl sīratihi*) with his subjects." He continues: "Likewise, the main proof for the people regarding the deposing of the Imām is his unjust conduct (*jawr sīratihi*) with his subjects."[123] So important was the quality of justice to the legitimate authority of the Ibāḍī Imām that al-Kindī allows even a ruler who is not an Ibāḍī to be tolerated as Imām so long as he is just; obedience to such a leader is due in the same manner as if he were an Ibāḍī.[124]

Although paramount, the quality of justice is not the only necessary characteristic of the Imām. Abū Isḥāq Ibrāhīm b. Qays, a fifth/eleventh-century Ḥaḍramawtī jurist and Imām, wrote of the necessary traits (*khiṣāl*) for establishing the imāmate, stipulating that the imāmate be given to "the best of [the Ibāḍīs] in religion (*dīn*), knowledge (*'ilm*), and demonstrated religiosity (*war'*)."[125] Indeed, as al-Bisyānī explains, the *imām al-difā'* and the *imām al-shārī* may lack knowledge (*'ilm*), but they cannot lack in religiosity (*war'*);[126] piety, envisioned as religiosity, thus forms the minimum requirement for all Omani (and Yemeni) Ibāḍī Imāms.

As noted above, the North African Ibāḍiyya tended not to preserve as detailed a legal tradition as their Omani counterparts, due in part to the fact that their imāmate effectively ended after the fall of the Rustumid dynasty to the Fātimids.

Nevertheless, North African Ibāḍīs preserved a rich biographical and historical tradition from which an idealized portrait of leadership may be gleaned. In North African historical texts, the notion of piety as the legitimating quality of the Imām is expressed in the idealization of the first North African Ibāḍī Imām, 'Abd al-Raḥmān b. Rustum, as the prototype of the perfect Imām.[127] Savage notes that historical reasons surround the creation of this image for 'Abd al-Raḥmān b. Rustum, notably the need to bolster the credibility of 'Abd al-Raḥmān's son 'Abd al-Wahhāb. 'Abd al-Wahhāb's reign witnessed two major schisms: the Nukkāriyya and the Khalafiyya. Both challenged the legitimacy of 'Abd al-Wahhāb's right to succession, but the Khalafīyya claimed to be the direct descendents of the first Ibāḍī Imām of Qayrawān, Abū al-Khattāb. By idealizing the life and rule of 'Abd al-Raḥmān, the authors diminished the importance of Abū al-Khattāb. For our purposes, it is important to remember that the picture of 'Abd al-Raḥmān as the ideal just ruler was ultimately motivated by political considerations.

Although ascetic piety and moral rectitude were by no means the only legitimating factors of 'Abd al-Raḥmān's imāmate, they nonetheless remained among his most important qualities as an Imām.[128] In an anecdotal story related by Abū Zakariyya and Ibn al-Ṣaghīr, when Ibāḍī visitors from Basra called on the Imām 'Abd al-Raḥmān, they found him engaged in constructing a ceiling with his servant.[129] In the same story, Ibn al-Ṣaghīr describes 'Abd al-Raḥmān's house as simply furnished with only a leather mat, a pillow, sword, and lance.[130] Similarly, the meal eaten by the visitors is described as simple.[131] Ibn al-Ṣaghīr and Abū Zakariyya depict 'Abd al-Raḥmān's humility and ascetic practices (*zuhd*) as exceptional, and his accentuated qualities are intended to bolster his claim to authority over the Muslims by their uniqueness.

In addition to the personal qualities of ascetic piety, 'Abd al-Raḥmān's official actions as Imām are celebrated as just (*'ādil*). Specifically, 'Abd al-Raḥmān is described as always accessible to his people when sitting in his mosque.[132] Abū Zakariyya notes how no person found fault with 'Abd al-Raḥmān during his reign as Imām,[133] and Ibn al-Ṣaghīr mentions that 'Abd al-Raḥmān's justice as a legal judge was renowned, and his *qāḍī*s were also considered just.[134] During his reign, the treasury was always full, the poor were fed, and the police force (*shurṭa*) and military were well disciplined and effective.[135] As the public aspect of moral rectitude, the aspect most commonly associated with political power, 'Abd al-Raḥmān's *'adāla* is presented as unusually grand, a quality that further justifies his rule. Later North African jurisprudence considered 'Abd al-Raḥmān a prime example of the *imām al-ẓuhūr*, and included the Omani Imāms of the first Omani dynasty along with him.[136] In such a way, the figure of 'Abd al-Raḥmān, as the prototypical North African Imām during the state of *ẓuhūr*, exemplified the qualities of piety and moral rectitude.

Piety and moral rectitude in both Omani and North African Ibāḍī texts were specifically associated with the qualities of religious piety (*war'*), asceticism (*zuhd*), and justice (*'adl*), with the characteristic of justice being favored above the others. These personal qualities legitimated the authority of the Ibāḍī Imāms above all other qualities, even to the extent that moral rectitude (as *'adl*) justified the rule of a non-Ibāḍī. The opposite situation is also institutionalized in medieval Ibāḍī jurisprudence: namely, that sin and immoral behavior specifically disqualify a leader from rule. So widespread is this notion in Ibāḍī thought that virtually every Ibāḍī legal text (both Omani and North African) has a section devoted to dissociation (*barā'a*) from a sinning Imām.[137] However, an Imām who sinned or behaved in a way that was improper did not immediately become an illegitimate Imām. The Ibāḍī community gave him the opportunity to repent and make amends, such as the opportunity given to 'Uthmān before his killing.[138] If the Imām repented, he regained his proper place as leader of the Muslims. If he persisted in his sinful behavior, dissociation from him and active opposition to him then became a duty.[139]

The Ibāḍiyya openly trace the formalization of the rules regarding a sinning Imām to the actions of 'Uthmān and 'Alī. Ibāḍī sources depict 'Uthmān as a depraved sinner, portraying the proto-Ibāḍiyya as the very people who killed him.[140] Although there is no evidence that the Egyptians who killed 'Uthmān later became Khārijites, there can be no doubt that the later Ibāḍī portrayal of 'Uthmān as an unjust (*ẓālim*) ruler was part of the Ibāḍī inheritance from the Khārijites, and specifically justified the Ibāḍī stance toward unjust rulers. Similarly, Ibāḍī texts depict 'Alī's acceptance of the arbitration as a sin that disqualified him from rule over the Muslims. According to the Ibāḍīs, God commanded the Muslims to fight Mu'āwiya's army as the "rebellious party" (*al-fi'a al-bāghiya*) that should "return to the command of God."[141] There was, therefore, "no judgment but God's" in the matter and consequently, no need for arbitration.[142] Ibāḍī sources unequivocally state that the sin of arbitration disqualified 'Alī from the position of Imām: by his sin he "removed himself" (*khāl' nafsahu*) from rule.[143] 'Alī thus became another prototype for the medieval Ibāḍī rules regarding the deposition of a sinning Imām.[144]

Additionally, as was the case with the early Khārijites, the qualities of piety and moral rectitude legitimated the *imāma* to the exclusion of other characteristics of authority. Ibāḍī jurisprudence specifically rejected membership in the Quraysh, relation with the Prophet, and designation (*naṣṣ*) as criterion for authority; the sixth/twelfth-century Omani jurist and heresiographer al-Qalhātī explicitly disallows the notion that the imāmate was "designated for 'Alī and his progeny."[145] Likewise, al-Kindī views the Prophet's command to "obey even a mutilated Ethiopian slave if he upholds the Book of God and my *sunna*" (according to the wording of this *ḥadīth* in al-Kindī's *Muṣannaf*) as nullifying the exclusive claim of the Quraysh to the caliphate.[146] In fact, the Ibāḍiyya did not reject the notion of Qurayshī leadership, but viewed the conditions of piety as eclipsing the exclusive claim of the Quraysh to authority. Therefore, al-Kindī claims, the imāmate of a Qurayshī and non-Qurayshī are both valid, and the final criterion for their legitimacy remained the "justice of their decisions, the fairness of their decrees, and their perpetuation of the Book of God and *sunna* of the Prophet."[147]

Conceptions of piety and moral rectitude as the personal characteristics that legitimated authority, and their institutionalization in the later Ibāḍī legal and historical corpus, became an integral aspect of the Ibāḍī imāmate, especially of the imāmate in a state of *ẓuhūr*. The unacknowledged debt of Ibāḍī thought to pre-Islamic notions of authority as personal traits, as well as the Qur'ānic concept of piety (*taqwā*) as the demonstrated actions that come from an awareness of human accountability before God, both became precedents for the peculiar Ibāḍī ideas about piety as a type of legitimate authority. In addition, the paradigm of the Prophet Muhammad as a moral-political leader, and the examples of Abū Bakr, 'Umar, and the Imām of the Muḥakkima—'Abdullah b. Wahb al-Rāsibī—provided models for the institutionalization of moral rectitude as the paramount and exclusive characteristic of leadership, just as 'Uthmān, 'Alī, and the Umayyad Caliphs offered precedents for the institutionalization of the rules regarding the deposition of or resistance to sinning Imāms. The medieval Ibāḍī conception of moral rectitude as a type of legitimate authority, and its consequent institutionalization in the Ibāḍī *imāma*, thus possessed a history in the preceding eras of Islamic history.

However, piety and moral rectitude were not the only legitimate kinds of authority that were recognized and institutionalized by the Ibāḍiyya. The medieval Ibāḍī imāmate incorporated different kinds of legitimate authority and acknowledged other types of Imāms. Just as the notion of piety in the medieval Ibāḍī *imāma* was the product of numerous precedents in pre-Islamic, Prophetic, early Madīnan, and early Khārijite history, so the other types of authority, and their specific institutional configurations in the Ibāḍī imāmate, possessed their own distinct history.

2

Imām al-Kitmān

In addition to piety and moral rectitude, the medieval Ibāḍiyya valued the possession of knowledge (*'ilm*) in their leaders, and made it an integral aspect of the Ibāḍī *imāma*.[1] *'Ilm* in Islamic thought is a concept with many nuances and synonyms, as well as a long linguistic history. In the early Islamic period, the word denoted "knowledge" or "learning" in the general sense of the term, and specifically referred to intuitive or inferential knowledge (that is, knowledge based on something beyond itself). In contrast to *ma'rifa*, ordinary knowledge,[2] or *adab*, knowledge obtained from literature or professional training, *'ilm* related to knowledge of a religious nature.[3] Another concept for knowledge, and an early synonym for *'ilm*, was *ḥikma*, which denoted "that which prevents ignorant behavior," and came to mean wisdom and intellectual knowledge. With the passage of time, *'ilm* as religious learning became associated with specialized disciplines, such as theology (*'ilm al-kalām*), philosophy (*falsafa*), and law (*fiqh*). Of these disciplines, law and legal reasoning occupied a special place in early Islamic history. In fact, the word *fiqh* originally denoted "understanding," and is thus very close to the concept of *'ilm* itself.[4]

The possessors of specialized religious knowledge (that is, *'ilm* and *fiqh*) came to be known as the *'ulamā'* and *fuqahā'*. To a certain extent, being an *'ālim* or a *faqīh* involved holding a title (which is to say, being "in" authority as well as being "an" authority), but this title remained informal; it was earned by the demonstration of the *'ālim*'s knowledge rather than by any type of official designation.[5] At the same time, the early Islamic state created official roles for the *'ulamā'*. The early Caliphs, and later the Umayyads, assigned judges (*quḍā'*) to the provincial towns to assist the governors with the application of Islamic law. These positions, however, were not necessarily positions of political authority.

This chapter examines the interplay between knowledgeable persons as authorities and knowledgeable persons in authority as leaders to determine the extent to which those in authority (that is, Imāms) were expected to be authorities (that is, *'ulamā'* or *fuqahā'*), as well as how political authority devolved upon the *'ulamā'* in the absence of an Imām. By examining the ways in which the relationship between political and juristic institutions of authority functioned from the pre-Islamic period through the early Islamic era, this chapter will illuminate the precedents for *'ilm* as an aspect of the medieval Ibāḍī institution of the Imām, as well as the precedents for the *'ulamā'* as the advisors of the Imām and as the deputies of the community during *kitmān*.

Like their Sunni counterparts, yet unlike the Shi'a, the medieval Ibāḍiyya preferred but did not require knowledge as a trait of their Imāms. If a prospective leader lacked *'ilm*, he could nonetheless become an Imām. In Oman, for example, where the imāmate remained a living tradition after the dissolution of the first Ibāḍī state, Ibāḍī jurisprudence accommodated Imāms without knowledge: they were called "weak" (*ḍa'īf*) Imāms. Such Imāms were permissible on the condition (*sharṭ*) of consultation (*mashwara*) with the *'ulamā'*.[6] Although Ibāḍī jurisprudence did not officially recognize the *'ulamā'* as the deputies of the *ḍa'īf* Imām, they functioned as such by substituting their *'ilm* for the Imām's lack of knowledge. In this way, *'ilm* remained an essential characteristic of the medieval Ibāḍī *imāma* through the *'ulamā'*, even though it was not a trait of the *ḍa'īf* Imām himself. Such a relationship points to a complex rapport between Imām and *'ulamā'*, and to a more formalized relationship between the two.

Moreover, during a state of *kitmān* ("secrecy"), the partial deputyship of the Ibāḍī *'ulamā'* over the *ḍa'īf* Imām gave way to a full deputyship in the absence of the Imām, and the *'ulamā'* assumed all or most of the Imām's duties. The medieval Ibāḍiyya conceived of the state opposite that of *ẓuhūr* as that of *kitmān*. As the converse of *ẓuhūr*, *kitmān* represented the worst of all possible situations for the Ibāḍī community. During it, the Ibāḍiyya were forced to hide their beliefs and practices, and to dispense with the imāmate.[7] The unique historical situations of the North African and Omani communities after the breakup of their first imāmates resulted in different applications of the rule of the *'ulamā'* during the condition of *kitmān*. The North African Ibāḍī community entered a state of *kitmān* soon after the fall of the Rustumid dynasty. They did not (even to the present day) establish another *imāma*, but evolved local councils (*ḥalqa*) of *'ulamā'* (also called *'azzāba*, sing. *'azzābī*) that ruled in the place of the Imām.[8] Although the state of *kitmān* and the suspension of the imāmate was a dispensation (*rukhṣa*) until such time as the community attained the ability to reestablish an Imām, the rule of the *ḥalqa* and the *'azzāba* effectively replaced the imāmate in North Africa.[9] In this manner, the North African Ibāḍī *'ulamā'* became the leaders of the community in the absence of the Imām, and ruled by virtue of their *'ilm*.

In Oman, the Ibāḍī community did not enter a state of *kitmān*, even after their second imāmate split over the controversy surrounding the deposition of the Imām al-Ṣalt b. Malik (d. 273/886). The modern Ibāḍī historian al-Sālimī, in a critique of Ibn Baṭūṭa's claim that the Omani "Khārijites" (meaning the Ibāḍīs) were not able to manifest their sect, stated: "we know of no time in Oman when the Ibāḍiyya have not been able to practice (*iẓhār*) their *madhhab* there, even though outside rulers (*malik min mulūk al-āfāq*) have established control over parts of the territory."[10] Nevertheless, medieval Ibāḍī jurisprudence recognized *kitmān* as a theoretical possibility, and recommended, in the absence of an Imām, that the *'ulamā'* assume control of the functions of the imāmate.[11] Thus, as in North Africa, the possession of *'ilm* qualified the *'ulamā'* in Oman to assume responsibility for the community in the event that the Omani Ibāḍiyya entered a state of *kitmān*.

Yet Ibāḍī historiography complicates the tenet that there could be no Imām during the state of *kitmān*. Both North African and Omani historical and legal tradition recognized certain prominent leaders of the early Basran quietist Khārijite movement—especially 'Abdullāh b. Ibāḍ, Jābir b. Zayd, and Abū 'Ubayda Muslim b. Abī Karīma—as Ibāḍī Imāms during an early period of *kitmān* in Basra.[12] In fact, these Imāms of *kitmān* remained a purely ideological aspect of the medieval Ibāḍī institution of the Imām: that is, the Ibāḍiyya retroactively claimed as Imāms certain early *'ulamā'* from their formative period in Basra in order to establish an unbroken line of Imāms (and a continuous line of *'ilm* transmission) reaching back to the Prophet.[13] Nevertheless, these early figures were certainly leaders (though not Imāms in the political sense) and *'ulamā'*; and furthermore, they existed during a time later regarded as *kitmān*. In the case of what would later become known as the *imām al-kitmān*, then, a retroactively imagined institution of authority, the fictive institution of the *imām al-kitmān* provides another example of the importance of *'ilm* to medieval Ibāḍī institutions of authority.

The concept of *'ilm* as an authoritative quality of leadership, and its subsequent institutionalization in the medieval Ibāḍī *imāma* as a recommended trait of the Imām, are features of the imāmate that the Ibāḍiyya share with their Sunni and Shi'a counterparts. However, the medieval Ibāḍī institutions of the *ḍa'īf* Imām, the imagined institution of the *imām al-kitmān*, and the (theoretical or actual) structures of authority that operated during the state of *kitmān* remain unique features of the Ibāḍī imāmate. In examining the concept of *'ilm* as a characteristic of legitimate authority, this chapter surveys its institutional manifestations in the pre-Islamic and early Islamic eras to show how preceding conceptions and institutions of *'ilm* as a type of legitimate authority functioned as the precedents for the Ibāḍī conception and subsequent institutionalization of *'ilm* in the medieval Ibāḍī *imāma* or, in the case of North African Ibāḍism, in the structures of authority that replaced the *imāma* during its abeyance.

'Ilm and Authority in the Pre-Islamic, Prophetic, and Early Caliphal Eras

During the pre-Islamic period, various authority figures possessed different types of knowledge that legitimated their leadership positions. Although no equivalent to *'ilm* as a specifically religious type of knowledge existed during the pre-Islamic period, the Arabs of this time believed that their soothsayers (*kāhin*) and poets (*shā'ir*) interacted with unseen spirits (*jinn*) and received inspiration for their work.[14] In fact, the term *shi'r* denotes both "knowledge" (in the sense of cognizance or knowledge of detail) and "poetry." Poetry was held to be "religious" in inspiration insofar as it came from the unseen world (*al-ghayb*), as well as being a type of knowledge.[15] In a tradition attributed to Ibn Sīrīn, 'Umar was reported to have said that the *'ilm* of the pre-Islamic Bedouin consisted of their poetry.[16] Likewise, Ibn Qutayba believed that pre-Islamic poetry was a treasure trove of the "knowledge of the Arabs (*'ilm al-'arab*), a book of their wisdom (*ḥikma*), a record of their history (*akhbār*), a treasury of their great days (*ayām*), and a rampart that protected their glorious deeds (*māthir*)."[17] Thus, poetry condensed military, cultural, social, and literary history, and the poets (or those who knew poetry) were prized as the protectors of and authorities on the tribal history and culture.

Although poets and soothsayers enjoyed a certain amount of authority in their tribe, the figure in authority of the tribe in pre-Islamic Arabia was the *sayyid*. As the spokesperson and orator for the tribe, many a *sayyid* knew and composed poetry. In fact, the roles of *kāhin*, poet, and *sayyid* were often blended.[18] For example, the famous poet of the pre-Islamic period, Imru' al-Qays of the Kinda, was also regarded as a *sayyid*.[19] Command of poetry, however, was not the only type of knowledge hoped for in a *sayyid*: the Arabs also desired that the *sayyid* have wisdom (*ḥikma*).[20] Additionally, some *sayyids*, such as Sa'd b. 'Ubāda, the *sayyid* of the Khazrāj in Yathrib (that is, Madīna), knew how to read and write.[21]

Moreover, if the *sayyid* could not resolve a disagreement, pre-Islamic Arabs could turn to another knowledgeable individual for arbitration. This person (known as the *ḥakam*) settled disputes between members of the same tribe and between tribes.[22] Like the *sayyids* and the poets, the *ḥakams* required a certain amount of knowledge—especially of genealogy and poetry—to fulfill their task.

Although persons possessing particular types of knowledge (*shi'r* or *ḥikma*) occupied positions of political authority in pre-Islamic Arabia, in the informal setting of the pre-Islamic Arabian tribe, where authority devolved upon those who demonstrated a propensity for exercising it, the possession of knowledge was not a formal requirement of leadership. In fact, if the *sayyid*s did not possess a sufficient command of poetry, the tribe's poets would advise them.[23] Thus those with authority tended to become those in authority, but the "office" of *sayyid* did not formally require knowledge (variously understood as *shi'r* or *ḥikma*), and other individuals such as the *ḥakam* periodically assumed certain responsibilities in the stead of the *sayyid*, or, alternately, other authorities such as the *shā'ir* functioned as advisors to the *sayyid*.

The advent of Islam introduced the concept of *'ilm* as a type of knowledge ultimately connected to divine revelation, and established the office of Prophet as an authority figure who possessed *'ilm*. The coming of Islam changed the concept of knowledge from *jinn*-inspired poetry to the knowledge given by God. According to the Qur'ān, knowledge is a trait of God. God is described as the most knowledgeable (*'alīm*): "And above every person of knowledge, there is [He who is most] knowledgeable."[24] He is also the "Knower of things unseen" (*'allām al-ghuyūb*).[25] As the ultimate source of knowledge, God teaches humankind and gives them *'ilm*. Verse 96:4–5 explains, for example, how God "taught by the pen; taught humankind what they knew not." The verb *'allama* in this verse is the verb "to teach," and is related both linguistically and conceptually to the word for knowledge—*'ilm*.[26] The Qur'ān speaks of God's action of teaching in connection with the gift of revelation: "the Compassionate, has made known (*'allama*) the Qur'ān";[27] "[He is] the Knower (*'ālim*) of the unseen, and He reveals to none his secret, except to every Messenger whom He has chosen."[28] The Qur'ān instructed Muhammad, in the context of recitation of the revelation, to say: "My Lord, increase me in knowledge."[29] Thus, the Qur'ān identifies authentic knowledge with revelation, and recognizes God as the ultimate source of all knowledge.

As recipients of the revelation, the Prophets possess divine knowledge, and have taught that knowledge to humankind. In 2:129, Abraham prays: "Our Lord! Raise up in their midst a Messenger from among them who will recite to them Your revelations, and will instruct them in the Scripture and in wisdom (*al-ḥikma*)." Moses asks the individual to whom God gave knowledge—who is identified in Islamic tradition as the Prophet Khiḍr—if he will "teach me right conduct from what you have been taught."[30] Likewise, 31:12 tells how God gave "wisdom" (*ḥikma*) to Luqmān; Ibn Kathīr clarifies the use of the term *ḥikma* in this verse by comparing it to knowledge (*'ilm*) and understanding of Islam (*al-fiqh fī al-islām*).[31] In these cases, those to whom God gave knowledge (usually identified as the Prophets) became authorities thereby.

In addition to being an authority by having the revelation, the Prophet was in authority over his followers, and like the pre-Islamic *sayyid*, the office of Prophet combined the possession of knowledge and the exercise of authority. However, unlike the *sayyid*, the Prophet alone delivered the revelation. There was no question of anyone advising the Prophet on the revelations (whereas the tribe's poets would advise the *sayyid* if he did not have sufficient command of poetry). Likewise, only the Prophet possessed final authority over his followers and he, and no one else, ultimately ruled the Islamic community.

After the Prophet's death, belief in the finality of prophethood—in Muhammad as the "seal of the Prophets"—insured that no Muslim would legitimately claim to possess revelation, or be an authority (or in authority) in quite the same manner as the Prophet.[32] Nevertheless, the possession of *'ilm* remained authoritative during the early Islamic period, and Muslims believed Abū Bakr and 'Umar to be knowledgeable. This conflation of *'ilm* and authority represents a continuation of the association between knowledge and leadership that operated throughout the pre-Islamic period, as well as during the Prophetic era.

During the early Islamic period, Muslims prized knowledge and believed it to be a characteristic that made an individual an authority. The Qur'ān stated: "God will exalt those who believe among you, and those who have knowledge (*utū al-'ilm*) to high ranks."[33] Likewise, al-Bukhārī, in the introduction to his tenth chapter in his book on *'ilm*, stated: "The *'ulamā'* are the heirs of the Prophets; who pass on *'ilm*, and whoso takes [knowledge], takes an abundant wealth (*ḥaẓẓ wāfir*); and whoso travels a road seeking [knowledge], God will ease his path to heaven."[34] To have *'ilm* meant to be an "heir" of the Prophet, and an authority on religion. Similarly, when 'Umar expressed surprise at his governor 'Usfān's choice to leave Ibn Ibzā, a client (*mawlā*) of the Quraysh, in charge of Makka during the governor's absence, 'Usfān justified his choice of deputy by saying: "Oh Commander of the Faithful! He is [versed in] the recitation of the Book (*qāri' lil-kitāb*), knowledgeable in the [Islamic] duties (*'ālim bi al-farā'iḍ*), and able to judge [according to Islamic law] (*qāḍin*)."[35] As the example of Ibn Ibzā shows, *'ilm* qualified in the eyes of 'Umar even a non-Arab (*mawlā*) to assume the duties of governance.

Of the individuals who were considered knowledgeable during the early period of Islam, Muhammad's close associates during his lifetime, the Companions of the Prophet (*ṣaḥāba*), came to be considered as particularly well versed in *'ilm* due to their proximity to the Prophet. Al-Bukhārī, for example, considers them to be authoritative sources of information on the deeds, words, and instructions of the Prophet.[36] In addition, al-Bukhārī holds the statements and actions of the *ṣaḥāba* to be worthy of imitation in their own right, especially with regards to the Islamic rituals (that is, prayer, fasting, *ḥajj*, and so on).[37] Likewise, the other main Sunni *ḥadīth* collectors—Muslim, Ibn Ḥanbal, al-Tirmidhī, Ibn Māja, Abū Dawūd, and al-Nisā'ī—consider the Companions to be reliable transmitters of the Prophetic *sunna*, as well as sources of it. Thus, in addition to being possessors of *'ilm* on the life and deeds of the Prophet, the Companions themselves became sources of *sunna*.

Of the Companions, Abū Bakr, 'Umar, 'Uthmān, and 'Alī became Caliphs and Imāms in their own right.[38] Although these early leaders owed their positions of authority to traits in addition to their knowledge of Islam—especially their membership in the Quyash tribe or, in the case of 'Alī, relation to the Prophet—they simultaneously possessed *'ilm*, and this possession became paradigmatic for later Sunni and Shi'ite theories of legitimate authority. Al-Māwardī, for example, names *'ilm* as one of the characteristics required of an Imām, so that the Imām may exercise *ijtihād*.[39] In the Shi'ite tradition, the possession of *'ilm* became one of the most important qualities of the Shi'ite Imām, and a proof of the Imām's authority.[40] As a result, Shi'ite sources preserve a wealth of reports regarding 'Alī's *'ilm*. Ibn 'Abbās reported, for example, that the Prophet said: "'Alī b. Abī Ṭālib is the most learned of my community and the most capable of giving legal decisions after me in [the matters in] which [people] differ."[41] In fact, one of the most prominent of early Shi'ite scholars, al-Mufīd, said of the *ḥadīth* that addressed 'Alī's knowledge: "examples of such reports are [so many] that a book would become [unduly] long in reporting them."[42] This incorporation of *'ilm* as a legitimating quality of leadership served as the precedent for the assimilation of the trait of knowledge into both the later Sunni and Shi'ite theories of legitimate authority.

During the medieval era, however, the Sunni world accepted a practical distinction between leadership and learning. The *'ulamā'* came to occupy an intermediate position between rulers and ruled, maintaining their authority over the *sharī'a* and legitimating the power of the Caliphs, wazīrs, amīrs, and sulṭāns. Al-Māwardī, for example, accepted the de facto rule of an amīr who seized power by force or usurpation.[43] Thus, although the Caliph, in theory, should be an *'ālim*, in practice the Sunnis accepted leaders who were not qualified scholars and, following al-Māwardī, classical Sunni legal theory posited no particular role for the *khalīfa* in formulating Islamic law. Similarly, the Prophetic *sunna* was generally limited to the actions of the Prophet and early Companions, some of whom happened to be early Caliphs (Abū Bakr, 'Umar, and 'Uthmān for example), with the exception of 'Umar II, who was included due to the belief in his exceptional piety.[44]

Nevertheless, the possession of *'ilm* by the first four Caliphs rendered meaningless the question, during the Madīnan phase of the caliphate, of an Imām or Caliph who did not possess *'ilm*, and, as a result, no data exists from the earliest period regarding the (then hypothetical) situation in which a leader did not have sufficient knowledge. Just as during the pre-Islamic era the poets or soothsayers of a tribe assisted the *sayyid* with their knowledge if the *sayyid* did not possess it, likewise, the learned members of the *umma* assisted the Caliphs in the early Islamic period, but such a situation was so widely accepted that the need to articulate a formal doctrine on it was not felt until much later.

To sum up, the idea that those in authority should possess knowledge as an aspect of their authority predated the emergence of Islam. The coming of Islam, however, redefined the concept of authoritative knowledge as *'ilm*, a knowledge that was based in and upon revelation, and associated that knowledge with the Prophets. After the death of Muhammad, the early Caliphs who assumed control of the Islamic state were simultaneously regarded as knowledgeable. This association between leadership and knowledge among the early Caliphs functioned as a potent precedent for all subsequent theories of legitimate leadership.

'Ilm and Authority in Early Islamic History: Umayyads, Shi'ites, and Khārijites

The pre-Islamic and early Islamic associations between knowledge and authority persisted into the Umayyad period, and were adapted by the Umayyads, the early Shi'ites, and the Khārijites. Although information remains rare regarding the various Khārijite views toward authority and its relationship to *'ilm*, the accounts that survive show an attitude toward leadership and knowledge similar to that of the pre-Islamic and Madīnan eras: leaders were also those who had knowledge, and if a leader did not possess knowledge, then those with *'ilm* should assist him with their *'ilm*. This Khārijite attitude existed alongside of the Umayyad and early Shi'ite approaches toward leadership and knowledge. In the Umayyad and Khārijite cases, the approach toward *'ilm* and leadership resembled the pre-Islamic (tribal) conception of knowledge and authority: that is, the Khārijites and Umayyads portrayed their leaders and possessors of knowledge, but seem to have simultaneously accepted the role of the *'ulamā'* as advisors to the Imām or Caliph.

The early Imāmite Shi'ite conception of the relationship between *'ilm* and authority, on the other hand, accorded authority to the Imām on the basis of his possession of esoteric *'ilm*. This knowledge was the sole possession of the Shi'ite Imāms as the result of their designation (*naṣṣ*) by the Prophet. Early Shi'ism, thus, leaned toward a Prophetic (and therefore exclusive) model of *'ilm* and authority.

The first hints of the Khārijite attitude toward *'ilm* and legitimate authority come from the Muḥakkima's association with the *qurrā'* at the battle of Ṣiffīn.[45]

The *qurrā'*, as those who recited (and therefore knew) the Qur'ān, undoubtedly enjoyed some authority thereby. As mentioned above, 'Umar's governor justified placing a *mawlā* in charge of Makka on the basis of his knowledge, using the phrase *qāri' lil-kitāb* (able to recite the Qur'ān) to indicate his proficiency in recitation. Additionally, the *qurrā'* at the Battle of Ṣiffīn reportedly forced 'Alī to accept arbitration against his better judgment, which is itself an indicator of a certain amount of authority.[46]

Although many sources preserve the Khārijite association with the *qurrā'*, few associate the possession of political authority with them.[47] Ibn Qutayba preserves a report that identifies 'Abdullāh b. Wahb al-Rāsibī, the Imām of the Muḥakkima at Nahrawān, as a *qāri'*.[48] While this association suggests an early affiliation with the *qurrā'*, it does not offer proof that the first Khārijite Imām, 'Abdullah b. Wahb al-Rāsibī, was chosen on the basis of his *'ilm*. Rather, it indicates that al-Rāsibī possessed the *'ilm* associated with being proficient in the recitation, and also became the leader of the Khārijites.

A report that is more suggestive of the association between *'ilm* and leadership among the Khārijites comes from Abū Mikhnaf, who recounts on the authority of Ja'far b. Huthayfa al-Ṭā'ī that in 42/662 (less than two years after the death of 'Alī) several Khārijites gathered in Kūfa and agreed to rebel against Mu'āwiya.[49] When they could not decide on whom to make their leader, Ma'āth b. Juwayn b. Ḥisn al-Ṭā'ī stated: "Not everyone is fit for leadership, so if all of [the candidates for leadership] are equal in merit (*fī al-faḍl*), then the Muslims should select the most experienced in war (*abṣarahum fī al-ḥarb*) and the most knowledgeable in religion (*afqahahum fī al-dīn*)." Thus, after "merit," Ma'āth believed military experience and the possession of knowledge to be the most important criterion for choosing a Khārijite leader.

Other reports on Khārijite leaders also indicate a correlation between leadership and the possession of *'ilm*. A report in al-Baghdādī mentions how a group of the followers of the first Imām of the Najdites, Najda b. 'Amr al-Ḥanafī, after forcing Najda to recant some of his beliefs, repented their action and stated: "you are the Imām, and it is for you [to perform] *ijtihād*, and it was not for us to make you recant."[50] Thus, among some of the Najdites, a belief in connection between *'ilm* as *ijtihād* and authority existed. Likewise, later Najdite doctrine, although it expressly rejects the *ijtihād* of the leader as any more valid than the *ijtihād* of each individual Najdite, nonetheless attributes the ability to perform *ijtihād* to the Imām.[51]

Likewise, al-Mubarrad, on the authority of Abū 'Ubayda Mu'ammar b. al-Muthannā, preserves an exchange between the leader of the Azāriqa, Nāfi' b. al-Azraq, and Ibn 'Abbās in which Nāfi' questions Ibn 'Abbās on the meanings and usages of Qur'ānic terms, as well as on the interpretation (*tafsīr*) of certain verses.[52] If this report is accurate, it indicates that Nāfi' pursued *'ilm*. Neither al-Mubarrad nor Ibn al-Muthannā indicates the date of the exchange, or if Nāfi' had yet assumed leadership (which he did in 65/684) of the Khārijite movement that subsequently adopted his name. Nonetheless, Nāfi' b. al-Azraq presents another possible example of a learned individual becoming (or being) a leader of the Khārijites.

Like Najda and Nāfi', the early Khārijite leader Ṣāliḥ b. Musarriḥ was known for his *'ilm*. In a report by Abū Mikhnaf, on the authority of a contemporary of Ṣāliḥ's, Qabīsa b. 'Abd al-Raḥmān, describes how Ṣāliḥ taught his followers the recitation of the Qur'ān and Islamic law.[53] Ṣāliḥ rebelled in 76/695 near Mosul in the Jazīra. He represents another example of an *'ālim* assuming the responsibilities of leadership. Moreover, al-Baghdādī reports that before Ṣāliḥ died, he appointed Shabīb b. Yazīd al-Shaybānī as his successor with the words: "I have made Shabīb my successor over you, even though I know there are more learned people among you; but he is a courageous man, and a scourge to your enemies, so, therefore let the knowledgeable (*al-faqīh*) among you assist him with their knowledge."[54] This report presents an example of a pre-Islamic attitude toward assisting a leader who is deficient in knowledge being utilized in a Khārijite context. Although it is not surprising that the Khārijites applied pre-Islamic/tribal structures of authority to their own organizations of authority, this sentence by Ṣāliḥ is the only evidence (before the Ibāḍiyya) of the persistence of such a practice among the Khārijites.

Finally, evidence from the early Ibāḍī epistle of Sālim b. Dhakwān supports the idea that the earliest Khārijites associated the possession of knowledge with the office of leadership. In a passage relating the Imām, Sālim recommends that the Ibāḍiyya appoint to the command of the Muslims the "most meritorious, and those with the greatest understanding [of religion] (*afāḍilahum wa fuqahā'ahum*)."[55] Thus, the early Ibāḍī Sālim equates the possession of knowledge (as "understanding"—*fiqh*) with leadership over the Ibāḍiyya.

These examples of the early Khārijite correlation between the possession of knowledge and the exercise of authority match the association between *'ilm* and authority that operated during the early Madīnan period, as well as during the pre-Islamic period. Moreover, Ṣāliḥ's suggestion that the knowledgeable among his community assist Shabīb with their understanding of religion (*fiqh*) is highly suggestive of the tribal system whereby those with knowledge helped those leaders without such knowledge. Although these pieces of evidence are fragmentary, and do not present a systematic exposition on the association between *'ilm* and authority in early Khārijite Islamic thought, they do indicate a continuation of the correlation between knowledge and authority that preceded the formation of the Khārijites.

Like the early Khārijites, the Umayyad Caliphs were viewed by their supporters as possessors of *'ilm*, and their knowledge was considered an essential aspect of their caliphate.[56] A report of Mūsā b. Ismā'īl in Ibn Sa'd explains how the Caliph Marwān b. al-Ḥakam narrated traditions on the authority of the Companions of the Prophet. This same report states that Marwān used to gather the Companions together in Madīna, and follow what they decided (by *ijmā'*) for him.[57] Likewise, Mu'āwiya described 'Abd al-Malik b. Marwān as a narrator of traditions;[58] another report explains how 'Abd al-Malik would sit with the *fuqahā'* and *'ulamā'* and memorize *ḥadīth* from them.[59] These reports portray the Umayyad Caliphs as acquiring knowledge from the *'ulamā'* and Companions of the Prophet, as being *'ulamā'* themselves, or as consulting with the *'ulamā'* of their time.

Other examples betray an implicit belief in the possession of *'ilm* by the Umayyad Caliphs by casting them as authoritative judges in Islamic law. Yazīd III, for example, in his letter to the people of Iraq, explains how the Umayyad Caliphs "followed one another as guardians of His religion, judging in it according to His decree."[60] This case illustrates how Yazīd III tacitly acknowledged the *'ilm* of the Umayyads by according them the right to judge (*qāḍā*) in God's religion. Likewise, Umayyad poetry flatters the Caliphs by comparing them to judges: "He is the Caliph, so accept what he judges for you in truth."[61] Likewise, the Umayyad Caliphs issued legal mandates, assuming the authority to do so: Mu'āwiya instructed his Madīnan governor on the rules regarding stolen property;[62] 'Umar II instructed his governor in Egypt on the treatment of non-Arab converts to Islam;[63] and the governor of Yemen wrote to 'Abd al-Malik questioning him on the procedures to be followed in a case of fornication.[64] These examples illustrate how the Umayyad Caliphs assumed their authority to adjudicate in questions of Islamic law, and implied their possession of the *'ilm* that was required to issue legal mandates. In such a fashion, the Umayyad Caliphs believed themselves to be (or were flattered by poets as) the possessors of knowledge; and at the same time they enjoyed the authority of being Caliphs. Although no early text systematized this relationship between knowledge and authority as a requirement of the Umayyad caliphate, the connection is suggestive of a necessary condition.

Among the supporters of 'Alī and his family, the correlation between *'ilm* and *imāma* became a cornerstone of Shi'ism at an early date. Among the Imāmite Shi'ites, the Imāms Muhammad al-Bāqir, Ja'far al-Ṣādiq, and their disciples first systematized the ideas of designation (*naṣṣ*) and esoteric knowledge (*'ilm*) into a coherent doctrine of the imāmate.[65] Al-Bāqir and al-Ṣādiq sought to exclude the extremist (*ghulāt*) Shi'ites, as well as those who advocated *jihād*-based activism as the only method of establishing the rights of the family of the Prophet.[66] One of al-Ṣādiq's prominent disciples, Hishām b. al-Ḥakam (who immediately recognized al-Ṣādiq's successor, Mūsā al-Kāẓim, after al-Ṣādiq's death), was a noted theologian, and elaborated a theory of the imāmate that remained the basis of Imāmī Shi'ite doctrine on the Imām.[67] According to the information preserved by al-Malaṭī, Hishām's theory rested on the principle that humankind required a divinely guided leader (an Imām) who would act as their authoritative teacher in all religious matters.[68] Hishām regarded belief in the (Shi'ite) *imāma* as a fundamental aspect of religion, and held that the Imām was the legatee (*waṣī*) of the Prophets. Muhammad had designated 'Alī and his progeny as his legatees, and successors (*khalīfa*) by explicit appointment (*naṣṣ*). Hishām held Muhammad's statement, "I am the city of knowledge, and 'Alī is its door," as evidence of Muhammad's designation of 'Alī as his successor. Accordingly, 'Alī, according to Hishām, was the most knowledgeable and meritorious person of the *umma*; he was "protected from error" (*ma'ṣūm*) and unable to be ignorant or senile.[69] With his designation, 'Alī became the possessor of exclusive and esoteric knowledge of religion (*'ilm*), a knowledge that would be passed by designation to his successors. Similarly, al-Kashshī, an early Imāmite biographer, states on the authority of al-Bāqir that authentic knowledge (knowledge of the Qur'ān and *ḥadīth*) could only be obtained from the Imāms.[70] In this way, early Imāmite thinkers argued that the Imām represented the sole legitimate authority of the age, and the only source of true guidance by his designation (*naṣṣ*) and knowledge (*'ilm*). Thus, in early Shi'ite (especially Imāmite) theories of legitimate leadership the *'ilm* of the Shi'ite Imām was fundamental to his authority. Although the Imāmite Imāms (after 'Alī) did not enjoy political power, they nevertheless remained in authority over their followers through their designation to the office of Imām, a designation that brought with it *'ilm*.

To summarize, the Shi'ite, Umayyad, and Khārijite correlation between the possession of knowledge and the possession of an office of authority (that is, being an authority and being in authority) represents, to a certain extent, the continuation of attitudes toward knowledge and authority that circulated during the pre-Islamic and early Islamic eras: namely, that a *sayyid*, Prophet, Imām, or Caliph should possess knowledge. Although the Imāmite Shi'ites made this connection explicit in their theory of the imāmate, among the Umayyads and early Khārijites the relationship between knowledge and political authority remained implicit until much later. Nevertheless, the informal Khārijite acknowledgement of the necessity of *'ilm* to political authority functioned as the precedent for the formal articulation of the necessity for the Ibāḍī Imām to possess knowledge in the medieval Ibāḍī theory of the imāmate. Moreover, Ṣāliḥ b. Musarriḥ's suggestion to his more knowledgeable followers to assist Shabīb al-Khārijī with their knowledge presents a continuation of the pre-Islamic, tribal attitude toward *'ilm*, and simultaneously suggests a precedent for the advisory role adopted by the medieval Ibāḍī *'ulamā'* in relation to a *ḍa'īf* Imām.

Quietist Khārijite *'Ulamā'*-leaders of Basra and the Emergence of the Ibāḍiyya

Although the correlation between *'ilm* and the Khārijite *imāma* remained a general feature of all Khārijite groups who boasted an Imām (that is, who existed in what the Ibāḍiyya would later call a state of *ẓuhūr*), certain Khārijites—who can be designated as the quietists—accepted a situation whereby the Khārijite community survived without an Imām, and entered a state of secrecy (*kitmān*). According to Islamic heresiographers and historians, the quietist Khārijites (those who would become the Ibāḍiyya, Ṣufriyya, and Bayhasiyya) split from the activist Khārijites (the Azāriqa and Najdāt) in Basra during the second *fitna* (61–65/680–684) over the question of secession (*khurūj*), the issue of separation from the wider Islamic community (which fell under the rubric of *hijra*), and the practice of *taqiyya*.[71] That is, the quietist Khārijites refused to secede from the Islamic community, preferring to remain among their fellow Muslims by practicing prudent concealment (*taqiyya*), hiding their beliefs and practices and/or denying them as a strategy for survival.[72] Although not stated explicitly in the texts, practicing *taqiyya* and remaining in a state of *kitmān* entailed living without an independent Khārijī Imām. However, in the state of *kitmān*, informal (and often secret) leadership of the quietist Khārijite community devolved onto the *'ulamā'*. Moreover, when the early Ibāḍī community emerged from the state of *kitmān*, the Ibāḍī *'ulamā'* retained their relationship to the *imāma* either by becoming Imāms or by advising them.

Due to the complexity of the early quietist Khārijite and early Ibāḍite period, as well as the sectarian nature of the sources involved in researching this era, several terms need to be clarified, and certain issues related to the sources of early Ibāḍite history need to be addressed. Although historical and heresiographical texts categorize the quietist Khārijites by their sectarian names—especially the Ibāḍiyya, Ṣufriyya, and Bayhasiyya—it is unlikely that sectarian distinctions such as Ibāḍī, Ṣufrī, or Bayhasī existed at the time of the activist-quietist Khārijite *tafrīq* (split) in 65/684. In fact, it is possible that they did not fully materialize until after 123/740, when the Ibāḍī sect emerged under the leadership of Abū 'Ubayda Muslim b. Abī Karīma. An Ibāḍī source, Abū Zakariyya, reports that Salama b. Sa'd, one of the first quietist Khārijite missionaries to Africa, and 'Ikrima, the *mawla* of Ibn 'Abbās, rode to Qayrawān in 105/723 on the same camel.[73] Abū Zakariyya labels Salama an Ibāḍī and 'Ikrima a Ṣufrī;[74] Ibn Ḥajar (a Sunni) also preserves a report in which 'Ikrima is described as a Ṣufrī.[75] Al-Ash'arī, on the other hand, labels 'Ikrima as one of the Ibāḍī predecessors (*salaf*).[76] This confusion over the sectarian affiliations of these figures may indicate a lack of fixed sectarian categories as late as 105/723. Wilkinson argues, convincingly, that the early quietists Khārijites of Basra should not be treated as separate sects, but rather as a loose confederation of like-minded Khārijites who adapted their lives so that they could blend with the wider Muslim population.[77] Therefore, the term "quietist Khārijites" will be used to refer to the diffuse and undefined Khārijite Muslim community that existed in Basra in a state of *kitmān* from the period of 65/684 to approximately 123/740. After 123/740, the term Ibāḍiyya is appropriate, as it is during the time of Abū 'Ubayda that the Ibāḍiyya most likely emerged as a distinct sect.

The main (though not the only) sources for the history of the Khārijite *'ulamā'*'s role in the emergence of the Ibāḍiyya from the quietist Khārijite movement in Basra are the medieval North African Ibāḍī biographical dictionaries (*kutub al-siyar*). These sources tend to portray the early history of the Ibāḍiyya according to the needs of the authors of such texts, whose own concerns did not necessarily reflect those of the early Ibāḍiyya about whom they wrote. Specifically, these authors wrote in accordance with the belief that the Ibāḍī sect was the unchanged and unchanging representative of authentic Islam. Consequently, Ibāḍī sources assume the existence of a fully developed Ibāḍī *madhhab* at the Khārijite split in 65/684, and a continuation of this *madhhab* in Basra up until the dissolution of the Basran Ibāḍī community in the late third/ninth century, by which time the North African and Omani Ibāḍiyya had assumed the mantle of Ibāḍī authority. As part of this narrative of origins, Ibāḍī sources retroactively claim certain members of the quietist Khārijite *'ulamā'* as their leaders, and even as Imāms. As Wilkinson argues, this "rationalization" of history by the Ibāḍiyya allowed them to claim an unbroken chain of *'ilm* transmission reaching back, through the early *'ulamā'* of Basra, to the Prophet.[78] In addition, the medieval Ibāḍī inclination to promote the early quietist Khārijite *'ulamā'* to full Imāms strengthened the story of a continuous line of "Ibāḍī" Imāms, even though the earliest leaders claimed the Ibāḍiyya cannot be properly called either Imāms or Ibāḍīs.

Despite the penchant in medieval Ibāḍī sources to create Ibāḍī Imāms out of early quietist Khārijite *'ulamā'*, the Ibāḍī biographical texts remain a valuable resource for the study of the *'ulamā'* during the quietist Khārijite period,[79] as well as the formative period of Ibāḍism. The medieval Ibāḍī transformation of the quietist Khārijite *'ulamā'* into full Ibāḍī Imāms was based upon the actual exercise of limited authority by the quietist Khārijite during the time of *kitmān*. Although these *'ulamā'* did not function as Imāms per se, the sources illustrate how they assumed partial political authority over the quietist Khārijite community.

In many ways, the maturity of the *'ulamā'* into a recognized category of religious specialists with an independent religious authority facilitated the assumption by the quietist Khārijite *'ulamā'* of limited positions of political authority over the quietist Khārijite community of Basra during the state of *kitmān*. In concert with the continued evolution of early Umayyad, Shi'ite, and Khārijite views toward authority and *'ilm*, the Umayyad era witnessed the development of the *'ulamā'* into a separate institution of religious authority. As Sachedina notes, the authority of the *'ulamā'* was based upon the *'ālim*'s comprehension of Islamic revelation, and remained "independent of any temporal investiture"; individuals became *'ulamā'* by demonstrating their knowledge, and having their authority accepted by other Muslims.[80] Moreover, this authority remained of a religious nature, which is to say that the authority of the *'ulamā'*, for the most part, involved the application of the Qur'ān and *sunna* to practical ethico-legal questions, and did not involve the direct enjoyment of political power (unlike the Umayyads, who, as shown above, held pretensions to scholarly authority in addition to the real power they wielded as Caliphs).[81]

Nevertheless, the exercise of religious authority by the *'ulamā* represented an institution of religious authority parallel to that of the Umayyad Caliphs. As an independent institution of authority, the *'ulamā'* remained potential rivals to the Caliphs in the realm of religious law and doctrine, and their opinions could have political ramifications. For example, al-Ḥasan al-Baṣrī endorsed of the doctrine of God's justice (whereby God, being just, demanded justice from His servants) and aroused the suspicions of the Umayyad Caliph 'Abd al-Malik. Although never openly stated by al-Ḥasan al-Baṣrī, the doctrine of God's justice could be taken to imply that it was the duty of Muslims to remove unjust rulers, a doctrine with subversive implications for the Umayyads. When the Caliph wrote to al-Ḥasan, expecting a disavowal of the doctrine, al-Ḥasan openly affirmed his belief in it, and 'Abd al-Malik could not retaliate lest he provoke a rebellion in al-Ḥasan's name. Clearly, in some cases, the institution of the *'ulamā'* presented an institution of religious authority with the capacity to challenge the authority of the Caliphs.

Among the Khārijites, this institution of religious authority became a de facto institution of semi-political authority. In the absence of the Imām, the quietist Khārijite *'ulamā'* assumed certain leadership roles in the community. Medieval North African Ibāḍī sources claim Jābir b. Zayd, also known by his patronymic name Abū Sha'thā', as the source (*aṣl*) of their movement, and its founder, viewing him as the individual who organized the movement during the state of *kitmān*.[82] Both medieval Ibāḍī biographers al-Darjīnī and al-Shammākhī use similar phrases when describing Jābir's role to the Ibāḍiyya, and both cite as a source for their information the biographical text of Abū Sufyān, which this early Basran scholar prepared for the Rustumid Imām Aflaḥ b. 'Abd al-Wahhāb (who ruled 209–259/824–872). As Wilkinson notes, Abū Sufyān probably used an earlier biographical or anecdotal source in the preparation of his work.[83] Thus, it is safe to conclude that al-Darjīnī and al-Shammākhī probably preserve early Ibāḍī views toward Jābir as the organizer of their sect. This supposition is supported by a passage in al-Ash'arī that notes how the Ibāḍiyya claimed Jābir as one of their predecessors (*salaf*).[84] Nevertheless, and in spite of the medieval (and probably the early) Ibāḍī claim that Jābir was the organizer of their sect, Wilkinson convincingly argues that he was probably only a leading figure of the quietist Khārijite movement in Basra.[85]

Sunni sources maintain a different view of Jābir. For example, Ibn Sa'd preserves numerous reports in which Jābir denied belonging to the Ibāḍiyya at all.[86] This denial may be understood with reference to Jābir's role in Sunni historical memory: Sunni sources also claim Jābir as a reliable source for *ḥadīth*, and so his name would have to be cleared of any sectarian affiliations deemed offensive.[87] Nevertheless, the sanitation of Jābir's image was not absolute: certain Sunni sources provide evidence of Jābir's affiliation with the Khārijites despite an overall effort to present him as a *jamā'ī*-Sunni. Ibn Ḥajar, for example, reports on the authority of Yaḥyā b. Ma'īn, that Jābir was, in fact, an Ibāḍī (that is, a quietist) Khārijite.[88]

Little reliable information exists on Jābir's birth and death dates, but it is clear that he lived during the quietist Khārijite period (that is, before the recognition of certain elements of the quietist movement as "Ibāḍī"). Ennami supposes that Jābir was born in Farq, near Nizwa in Oman, around 18/639.[89] Jābir's family would have migrated to Basra along with members of the Azd tribe during the Muslim conquests. He died, according to Ennami, in Basra between 91/709 and 104/722. Thus, although Jābir cannot be viewed as the founder and organizer of the Ibāḍiyya in the way that later Ibāḍī traditions presented him, it is clear that he was a prominent Basran personality, highly respected by Khārijites and non-Khārijites alike.

Both Ibāḍī and Sunni sources portray Jābir as an *'ālim* and *faqīh*; both al-Shammākhī and Ibn Ḥajar present Jābir as the student of Ibn Mas'ūd, 'Abdullāh b. 'Umar, Anas b. Mālik, and 'Abdullāh b. 'Abbās.[90] Jābir was especially close to Ibn 'Abbās, with whom he enjoyed a friendship.[91] Ibn 'Abbās is reported as saying, "Should the people of Basra turn to the knowledge (*'ilm*) of Abū Sha'thā', he would enrich them with understanding of the Book of God."[92] Ibn 'Abbās had such a high opinion of Jābir that he deferred his judgments to him. When a man from Basra asked Ibn 'Abbās for an opinion, he replied: "How can you ask me when you have Jābir b. Zayd among you?"[93]

To further strengthen Jābir's credentials as a scholar, Ibāḍī sources report that Jābir acquired his learning from seventy Companions of the Battle of Badr[94] and from his forty pilgrimages to Makka.[95] On one of his journeys to Madīna, Jābir is reported to have spoken with 'Ā'isha about the habits of the Prophet.[96] Likewise, it was said that his knowledge surpassed that of al-Ḥasan al-Baṣrī.[97]

Other reports on Jābir b. Zayd stress his simplicity and piety: both attributes that were expected of the *'ulamā'*. He is said to have desired only a good wife, a good riding camel, and bread to eat daily.[98] In addition, Ibn Sa'd reported that Jābir wore the same shoes for sixty years.[99] Similarly, Ibāḍī sources portray Jābir as refusing to compromise with the Umayyads; al-Darjīnī and al-Shammākhī report that when al-Ḥajjāj offered Jābir the position of *qāḍī* in Basra, he refused.[100] Thus, both Sunni and Ibāḍī sources laud Jābir's knowledge, simplicity, and piety in the highest terms, and associate Jābir with some of the most important figures of learning in early Islamic history. Clearly, he was a learned man, and respected as an authority on Islamic law by both Khārijites and non-Khārijites.

Moreover, Ibāḍī sources suggest that Jābir may have assumed some responsibilities as a leader of the early quietist Khārijite movement in Basra. Ibāḍī sources imply active missionary work by Jābir. Abū Sufyān reports that Jābir befriended a sister of the Muhallabid governor Yazīd, 'Ātika, who supported the quietist Khārijites (who, as the sources say, referred to themselves at this time as the *jamā'at al-muslimīn*).[101] In addition, he wrote letters to the members of the Muhallab family. Likewise, Jābir reportedly suggested the execution of an individual named Khardala who had given away the names of a group of Khārijites, ultimately getting them killed.[102] Likewise, Jābir hinted at giving bribes to Umayyad officials; when the persecution of Khārijites reaching its peak under 'Ubaydullāh b. Ziyād, Jābir was quoted as saying, "in that time, we found nothing more helpful to us than bribery."[103] Although these activities do not make Jābir an Imām of the early Khārijite community, they do indicate some level of leadership of the early Basran quietist Khārijites. This type of authority was not overtly political, and Jābir cannot be said to have been properly in authority. Nonetheless, among the early quietist Khārijites (as well as among non-Khārijites), Jābir commanded respect as a scholar, and was able to exert a certain amount of influence because of his status as an *'ālim*. Insofar as this authority could be considered political authority, it consisted of organizing missionary activity, offering bribes to protect the community, and suggesting the assassination of an informant. Although these activities do not make Jābir into a full-fledged Imām, they suggest an early correlation between the quietist Khārijite *'ulamā'* and the direction of the quietist Khārijī community during the absence of the Imām.

Other early Khārijite figures apparently fulfilled a similar role as scholars and leaders to the early quietist Khārijite community of Basra. Sunni tradition posits 'Abdullāh b. Ibāḍ al-Murra al-Tamīmī instead of Jābir b. Zayd as the source of the Ibāḍī sect.[104] However, significant evidence exists to doubt this supposition. First, the biographical information on Ibn Ibāḍ is vague and often contradictory. Al-Qalhātī suggests that he was born during the time of Mu'āwiya and died during the reign of 'Abd al-Malik (who ruled 66–86/685–705).[105]

Likewise, al-Baghdādī preserves a report that the Ibāḍī subsect, the Ḥārithīyya, claimed Ibn Ibāḍ as their Imām after Abū Bilāl Mirdās b. Udayya (d. 61/680).[106] Al-Shahrastānī, on the other hand, claims that he was a companion of ʻAbdullāh b. Yaḥyā (Ṭālib al-Ḥaqq) and was killed in the Battle of al-Tabāla (132/749).[107] Ibn Ḥazm implies that Ibāḍīs with whom he spoke in Andalusia were not even familiar with their supposed founder.[108] It has also been suggested that Ibn Ibāḍ did not exist at all, and that the name Ibāḍiyya derived from a color scheme designed to differentiate Khārijite sects by their degree of radicalism.[109] Thus, the Azāriqa (from *azraq*—blue) are the most radical, Ṣufriyya (*aṣfar*—yellow) are in the middle, and Ibāḍiyya (*abyaḍ*—white) are the moderates. In fact, the term "Ibāḍiyya" itself does not appear as a self-designation in Ibāḍī literature until the North African treatise of ʻAmrūs b. Fatḥ (d. 280/893), though the early Ibāḍī biographer Abu Sufyān places the term in the mouth of the Abbasid Caliph al-Manṣūr.[110]

Madelung has recently argued, primarily on the basis of a comment by the *adab* scholar Abū ʻUbaydullāh al-Marzubānī in his biography of the Shīʻī poet al-Sayyid al-Ḥimyarī, that Ibn Ibāḍ might have been a contemporary and rival of Abū ʻUbayda. This theory is perhaps the most convincing, as it enables Madelung to make sense of much of the heresiographical and historical comments on Ibn Ibāḍ. Madelung also argues that Ibn Ibāḍ's punishment at the hands of the Caliph al-Manṣūr may have caused al-Manṣūr to identify all of these particular quietist Khārijite branches—including the followers of Abū ʻUbayda—as "Ibāḍiyya." After the followers of Ibn Ibāḍ, led by al-Ḥārith al-Mazyad, disintegrated, the majority school of Abū ʻUbayda appropriated Ibn Ibāḍ as one of their own and eventually assumed the name "Ibāḍiyya" as well.[111]

Whatever the case, later Ibāḍī tradition embraced Ibn Ibāḍ and created a role for him in the early history of the movement as an advisor to the first Ibāḍī Imām, Jābir b. Zayd, from whom the later tradition tell us he received his orders.[112] As shown above, there is little historical evidence to prove Ibn Ibāḍ's connection to the mainstream Ibāḍī movement, and even his very existence is questionable. Nonetheless, medieval Ibāḍī heresiography states that he was a theologian who refuted the views of the Qadarites, Muʻtazilites, Murji'ites, Shiʻites, and extremist Khārijites.[113] Of the two letters attributed to him, one is addressed to the Caliph ʻAbd al-Malik b. Marwān with whom, the tradition claims, he had an extended correspondence.[114] The other epistle is devoted to debate with an anonymous supporter of ʻAlī. Thus, regardless of his historical existence, the Ibāḍiyya cast Ibn Ibāḍ primarily as an *ʻālim*, and such a portrayal reveals the importance of the *ʻulamā'* to the early (albeit imagined) history of Ibāḍism.

Later Ibāḍī tradition generally moves from Jābir straight to the next Ibāḍī "Imām," Abū ʻUbayda Muslim b. Abī Karīma. However, other *ʻulamā'* existed in the Basran quietist Khārijite circle through which we must trace the line of *'ulamā'* leaders of the Basran quietist Khārijite community before reaching Abū 'Ubayda. Ibāḍī biographical dictionaries mention Ja'far b. al-Sammāk and Ṣuḥār al-'Abdī as teachers of Abū 'Ubayda.[115] These men appear to be students of Jābir in Basra, and they excelled in their learning, asceticism, and piety. The sources also mention some contemporaries of Abū 'Ubayda, Ḍumām b. al-Sā'ib and Abū Nūḥ Ṣāliḥ al-Dihhān, as sources of Abū 'Ubayda's learning.[116] From the names of these early scholars, an idea of the social classes of some of the early Khārijites emerges. Ja'far, for example, was a fish seller (*sammāk*) and Abū Nūḥ a fat merchant (*dihhān*). None of the sources mention their tribe, so it is safe to assume that they were clients (*mawālī*) with no social status in Basra. Without standing or tribe, it would have been their knowledge alone that distinguished them from their contemporaries and earned them a place as leaders in the annals of Ibāḍī history.[117]

The association between *'ulamā'* and leadership of the community during a state of *kitmān* becomes more obvious during the direction of the quietist Khārijite community under Abū 'Ubayda Muslim b. Abī Karīma. Abū 'Ubayda presents an example of a quietist Khārijite *'ālim* who assumed significant political responsibilities: Abū 'Ubayda's systematization of quietist Khārijite doctrine, his organization of the economic resources of the Basran Khārijite community, and his creation of an active missionary institution (the *ḥamalāt al-'ilm*) permitted the Ibāḍiyya to emerge from the mass of quietist Khārijites as a recognizable sect. These actions also enabled the Ibāḍiyya to ultimately move from the state of *kitmān* to a state of *ẓuhūr*. Although historical circumstances favored the materialization of the Ibāḍiyya during Abū 'Ubayda's time, it was Abū 'Ubayda who lead the community toward that end.

Abū 'Ubayda himself came from humble origins; al-Shammākhī reports that Abū 'Ubadya was the client (*mawla*) of the Tamīm tribe, who studied under Jābir and (more likely) Jābir's students.[118] An anecdote about Abū 'Ubayda states that he spent forty years learning, and then forty years teaching.[119] Although anecdotal, it illustrates the esteem in which the scholarly activities of Abū 'Ubayda were held by Ibāḍī historians. Likewise al-Darjīnī describes Abū 'Ubayda as "the greatest of Jābir's students," and as "an *'ālim* with indifference to [things] worldly" (*'ālim ma' al- zuhd fī al-dunyā*).[120] Anecdotes such as these, while their historical accuracy may be disputed, portray Abū 'Ubayda as a typical *'ālim* and *faqīh*.

Stories from the biographical dictionaries regarding Abū 'Ubayda's organization of the early Ibāḍī *'ulamā'* illustrate the initial weakness of the Ibāḍī community during the state of *kitmān*. Ibāḍī sources mention the existence of all-night meetings (*majālis*) in the homes of prominent quietist *'ulamā'*; al-Darjīnī and al-Shammākhī mention *majālis* in the homes of Abū Mawdūd Ḥājib al-Ṭā'ī,

Abū Sufyān Qanbar, Abū al-Ḥurr 'Alī b. al-Ḥusayn, and 'Abd al-Malik al-Ṭawīl.[121] These *majālis* were kept secret from the Umayyad authorities, who sometimes raided them looking for Khārijites to arrest.[122] The quietists disguised themselves in order to attend the meetings: sometimes they dressed as women and went as far as carrying water on their heads to complete the disguise. Other meeting places included the caves around Basra. While the decentralized nature of the *majālis* lent itself to the loose-knit and secretive nature of quietist Khārijism in Basra during the state of *kitmān*, the need for secrecy and disguise demonstrates the powerlessness of the Ibāḍī community at this time.

Due to this weakness, Abū 'Ubayda at first counseled avoidance of the Umayyad rulers, and noninvolvement in politics. The situation of the quietists demanded tactful relationships with the Umayyads, who were eager to be rid of the Khārijites. Persecution under the Umayyads was a real and persistent concern: during the Umayyad governor 'Ubaydullāh Ibn Ziyād's general persecution of Khārijites, Abū 'Ubayda himself was jailed.[123] However, not all of the *'ulamā'* agreed with Abū 'Ubayda's quietist tactics. During the rebellion of Yazīd b. Muhallab in 102/720, Abū Nūḥ al-Dahhān, a prominent Shaykh and confidant of 'Ātika the Muhallabid, supported action against the Umayyads, whereas Abū 'Ubayda refused to allow direct involvement in the rebellion. Likewise, when Abū Muḥammad al-Nahdī (a famous preacher, *khātib*, in Basra) called for open rebellion against the Umayyad governor of Iraq, the Ibāḍiyya did not participate. Rather, it seems that the Ibāḍiyya under Abū 'Ubayda preferred to work from within the Umayyad system. Ibāḍī sources mention that the Caliph 'Umar b. 'Abd al-'Azīz, for example, appointed an Ibāḍī, Iyyās b. Mu'āwiya al-Madūnī, to the position of *qāḍī* of Basra.[124]

Despite Abū 'Ubayda's initial resistance to the idea of activism, and perhaps because of the more activist wing of the Ibāḍiyya, at some point between 105/723 and 123/740, Abū 'Ubayda began organizing the quietist Khārijites of Basra by establishing more formal missionary and economic institutions. Unfortunately, the texts do not mention when, exactly, these activities began. Ibāḍī sources reveal the existence of wealthy quietist Khārijite merchants whose funding supported the movement. For example, al-Darjīnī notes that one such merchant, Abū 'Ubayda 'Abdullāh b. al-Qāsim, engaged in trade as far as China.[125] Drawing on the considerable wealth available to the quietist Khārijite community, Abū 'Ubayda established a treasury (*bayt al-māl*) in Basra and appointed Ḥājib al-Ṭā'ī as its treasurer.[126] Al-Shammākhī mentions the existence of collectors, such as Abū Ṭāhir, who gathered funds from the wealthy members of the community.[127] In this fashion, Abū 'Ubayda amassed large sums of money for the movement; according to Ibāḍī sources he raised ten thousand *dirhams* in one day from among those of middle fortune (*al-awṣaṭ*).[128]

In addition to establishing and overseeing the economic institutions of the quietists Khārijites, Abū 'Ubayda established a missionary institution known as the "Bearers of Learning" (*ḥamalāt al-'ilm*). This process may have begun as early as 105/723, when Abū 'Ubayda sent Salama b. Sa'd to Qayrawān to promote quietist Khārijite ideals and scout out possible students.[129] Abū 'Ubayda personally trained the *ḥamalāt al-'ilm* in Basra for five years before sending them out to the distant provinces of the Islamic world.[130] A later Ibāḍī source, al-Sālimī, mentions Khurāsān, Oman, North Africa, Ḥaḍramawt, and the Yemen as places where the Bearers traveled.[131]

The figure of Abū 'Ubayda presents an example of a quietist Khārijite *'ālim* who assumed duties beyond those normally associated with the *'ulamā'*, duties that included managing the economic and missionary apparatus of the Ibāḍiyya. Abū 'Ubayda's actions represent the further development of the leadership of the Basran quietist Khārijites that began under Jābir b. Zayd, and they present a clear case of the assumption of the responsibilities of leadership by the prominent quietist Khārijite *'ulamā'* during the state of *kitmān*.

The further history of the correlation between *'ilm* and leadership among the early Ibāḍiyya presents a complicated picture: Abū 'Ubayda's missionary activities initially gave rise to several unsuccessful Ibāḍī rebellions in North Africa, the Ḥijāz, and Oman, but ultimately resulted in the establishment of Ibāḍī states in North Africa and Oman. In this way, the *ḥamalāt al-'ilm* were instrumental in bringing the Ibāḍī community out of the state of *kitmān* into *ẓuhūr* by proclaiming Ibāḍī states under the direction of Ibāḍī Imāms. With the transition into the state of *ẓuhūr*, several of the *ḥamalāt al-'ilm* assumed leadership of their movements as Imāms. The revolt of al-Julanda b. Mas'ūd in Oman represents one significant exception: al-Julanda was advised by the *ḥamalāt al-'ilm*, but was not an *'ālim* himself. However, this move from *kitmān* to *ẓuhūr* did not apply to Basra, where the Ibāḍiyya remained in a state of *kitmān* under the direction of the *'ulamā'*. The early Ibāḍī period (after 123/740) thus represents a time when certain Ibāḍī communities existed in *kitmān* under the direction of the *'ulamā'*, and others began to emerge into *ẓuhūr* under the leadership of Imāms. Nevertheless, despite the complexity of the early Ibāḍī political situation, an underlying theme pervaded each regional response to the question of *'ilm* and leadership; in all cases, *'ilm* remained associated in some capacity with the concept of legitimate political authority.

In Basra, the *'ulamā'* continued to function in a capacity of authority after the death of Abū 'Ubayda. According to Ibāḍī biographical sources, al-Rabī' b. Ḥabīb al-Azdī al-Farāhidī succeeded Abū 'Ubayda to the leadership of the Basran community.[132] Although the information surrounding the dates of al-Rabī''s assumption of the authority and his death are muddled, al-Rabī' fulfilled a vital role in the overall leadership of the Ibāḍī movement. Ibāḍī sources testify to al-Rabī''s status as an *'ālim*: he studied with Abū 'Ubayda, Ḍumām and Abū Nūḥ, and was considered a *muftī* during Abū 'Ubayda's lifetime.[133] Also, the collection of Ibāḍī *ḥadīth*, the *al-Jāmi' al-Ṣaḥīḥ*, is credited to al-Rabī'.[134] In addition to these scholarly activities, al-Rabī' used his position to influence the course of Ibāḍī politics: he endorsed the second Rustumid Imām, 'Abd al-Wahhāb, when the Nukkār schism challenged 'Abd al-Wahhāb's validity as Imām. Likewise, al-Rabī' maintained the institution of the *ḥamalāt al-'ilm* and trained missionaries for the Omani Ibāḍī community: he sent the famous *faqīh* al-Bashīr b. al-Mundhir to Oman after training him as an *ḥāmil al-'ilm*.[135]

After al-Rabī', the history of the Basran *'ulamā'* is one of the gradual eclipse of their authority by the Omani and North African Imāms. Abū Ayyūb Wā'il b. Ayyūb al-Ḥaḍramī (d. approx. 190/805) assumed leadership of the Basran Ibāḍīs after al-Rabī'. At this time, the Basran *'ulamā'* remained influential: Wā'il b. Ayyūb supported the actions of the Omani Ibāḍīs when they deposed their Imām, Muḥammad b. Abī 'Affān in 179/795, denouncing Ibn Abī 'Affān as a tyrant (*jabbār*).[136] Nonetheless, by the time of the last Basran *'ālim*-leader, Abū Sufyān Maḥbūb b. al-Raḥīl (d. 210/825), the influence of the Omani and North African Imāms began to eclipse that of the Basrans. The North African Ibāḍīs considered Abū Sufyān the most learned person in the east, and consulted with him when the followers of Khalaf b. Samḥ refused to recognize the Rustumid Imām 'Abd al-Wahhāb.[137] However, Abū Sufyān submitted to the authority of the Omani Imām in his dispute with Hārūn b. al-Yamān.[138] Abū Sufyān's delegation of authority to the Omani Imāms illustrates the declining influence of the Basran *'ulamā'* during the early part of the third/ninth century. By this time, the existence of Imāms in Oman and North African began to render the authority of the Basran Ibāḍī *'ulamā'* obsolete. Omani sources claim that Abū Sufyān migrated to Oman at the end of his life; one of his sons, Abū 'Abdullāh Muhammad b. Maḥbūb became *qāḍī* in Ṣuḥār.[139] With the departure of Abū Sufyān, no other prominent *'ulamā'* are recorded in Basra; the Ibāḍī community persisted, and presumably looked to Oman for their leadership, until the final destruction of the Basran Ibāḍī community in the Zanj uprising of 256/868–869.

The example of the Basran *'ulamā'* illustrates the assumption of limited authority by the quietist Khārijite *'ulamā'* during the absence of an Imām, a case that served as an obvious precedent for later medieval Ibāḍī institutions and theories about proper leadership during the state of *kitmān*. The quasi-political authority of the Basran *'ulamā'* came as consequence of the religious authority they wielded as religious scholars. That is, the possession of *'ilm*, which during the Umayyad era was already considered an informal institution of religious authority that functioned parallel and sometimes in competition with the assumed religious authority of the Umayyad Caliphs, easily justified, among those Khārijites who rejected the legitimacy of the Umayyad leaders but could not establish their own Imāmate, the assumption of an authority approaching that of an Imām by the *'ulamā'*.

Outside of Basra, the institution of the *ḥamalāt al-'ilm* gave way to full-fledged Imāmates as the Ibāḍī communities of North Africa, Ḥaḍramawt, and Oman openly revolted against the Umayyads and 'Abbasids. A revolt signaled the end of *kitmān* (at least as long as the revolt lasted) and the subsequent establishment of an Imām. With the move toward *ẓuhūr*, the Ibāḍiyya maintained the assumption that *'ilm* should be an essential aspect of leadership, and they selected knowledgeable people as Imāms to lead their revolts. Thus, the correlation between *'ilm* and *imāma* during the early Ibāḍī period mimicked that which was established during the Madīnan caliphate, and by the early, non-quietist Khārijites: namely, that the Imām should possess *'ilm* as an aspect of his legitimate authority.

Although little is recorded of the Bearers of Learning who initially arrived in North Africa after 123/740, their mission resulted in a small Ibāḍī-inspired uprising. Several Ibāḍī Berber tribal leaders took part in the revolt of 124/741; an Ibāḍī chief (*ra'īs*), 'Abdullāh b. Mas'ūd al-Tujībī, appears among the Hawwāra Berber tribe in the vicinity of Tripoli.[140] After his execution at the hands of the governor of Qayrawān, Ibn Ḥabīb, two other Ibāḍī chiefs appeared in Libya: 'Abd al-Jabbār b. Qays al-Murādī and al-Ḥārith b. Talīd al-Ḥaḍramī. Both were Berbers, and clients (*mawālī*), and they conquered all of Tripolitania. Unrecorded jealousies resulted in their deaths: they were reportedly found dead with their swords in each other. Another chief, Ismā'īl b. Ziyād of the Nafūsa tribe, is mentioned after 133/750, but he was killed shortly after becoming *ra'īs* and laying siege to Gabes.[141] It is safe to assume, despite the paucity of information available, that these leaders claimed authority on the basis of their tribal affiliations, a supposition supported by the use of the tribal title *ra'īs* to describe them. Nothing is recorded of their possession of *'ilm*, or of the *ḥamalāt al-'ilm* who inspired their rebellion.

In 140/757 Abū 'Ubayda sent additional *ḥamalāt al-'ilm* to North Africa, under the leadership of Abū al-Khattāb 'Abd al-A'lā b. al-Samaḥ al-Ma'ārifī, who was declared an Imām in that same year.[142] Although not able to hold Qayrawān, Abū al-Khattāb raised a revolt in Libya and shortly seized all of Tunis and eastern Algeria.[143] After holding Qayrawān for a brief time, he was killed in 144/761. His successor, the Imām Abū Ḥātim al-Malzūzī, maintained political control over much of Tripolitania until his death in 157/772.[144] When the imāmate of Abū Ḥātim collapsed, 'Abd al-Raḥmān Ibn Rustum, another *ḥāmil al-'ilm*, was declared Imām in Tahert.[145] The basis of Ibn Rustum's claim to the imāmate rested partially on his credentials as an *ḥāmil al-'ilm*, his Persian ancestry, and his service as a judge under Abū al-Khattāb. When considering 'Abd al-Raḥmān b.

Rustum for the imāmate, the heads of the Berber tribes declared: "the Imām Abū al-Khattāb appointed 'Abd al-Raḥmān as a judge (*qāḍī*) and overseer (*nāẓir*) for you, and you entrusted your affairs to him."[146] Thus, both Abū al-Khattāb and Ibn Rustum owed their authority, in some capacity, to their possession of *'ilm*.

In the Ḥaḍramawt in Arabia, initial Ibāḍī revolts involved an Imām who was simultaneously an *'ālim*: the first large-scale Ibāḍī revolt in the east took place during end of the Umayyad dynasty, under the direction of the *'ālim* 'Abdullāh b. Yaḥya al-Kindī, known as Ṭālib al-Ḥaqq. 'Abdullāh b. Yaḥya was the *qāḍī* of Ḥaḍramawt on behalf of the Umayyad governor.[147] He was described as a diligent scholar (*mujtahid*) and pious (*'ābid*).[148] During the pilgrimage of 129/746, he met with the Basran Ibāḍī scholars Abū Ḥamza al-Mukhtār b. 'Awf al-Azdī and Balj b. 'Ukba al-Azdī. They persuaded 'Abdullāh b. Yaḥya to revolt against the Umayyads and extended him the oath of allegiance (*bay'a*). In this fashion, 'Abdullāh b. Yaḥya became the Imām with the support of the Basran Ibāḍī scholars. However, the revolt of Ṭālib al-Ḥaqq did not last long. After taking the Ḥaḍramawt, Ṣan'ā', Makka, and Madīna, the Ibāḍīs were beaten back by the advancing Umayyad army. Both 'Abdullāh b. Yaḥya and Abū Ḥamza were killed. Nonetheless, 'Abdullāh b. Yaḥya presents another case of an early Ibāḍī Imām who came from the ranks of the *'ulamā'*.

The figure of al-Julanda b. Mas'ūd, who revolted in Oman in 136/752, presents an exception to the rule of *'ālim*-Imāms in early Ibāḍī history. Al-Julanda was not an *'ālim*; rather, he was chosen on the basis of his membership in the traditional ruling tribe of Oman, the Julanda.[149] The Ibāḍīs needed to utilize the legitimacy of the Julanda tribe's reputation for leadership without accepting its current leaders, who were loyal to the 'Abbasids (al-Julanda b. Mas'ūd's acceptance of the Ibāḍī imāmate immediately caused a feud among his kinsmen).[150] Nevertheless, Abū 'Ubayda sent Bearers of Learning to Oman to assist with the revolt of al-Julanda b. Mas'ūd, and al-Julanda consulted with these Omani *'ulamā'* during his brief reign.[151] Al-Julanda b. Mas'ūd ruled for two years as Imām before falling to 'Abbasid troops in 137/754.[152] While exceptional in that al-Julanda b. Mas'ūd was not himself an *'ālim*, his rebellion prefigured later developments in Omani and North African Ibāḍī imāmate history when Imāms consulted with the *'ulamā'* more often than hailing from their ranks. Such a development is not especially surprising in a movement that was in the process of developing into a full-fledged polity.

The early Basran quietist Khārijite period, and the emergence of the Ibāḍiyya from the quietist Khārijites during the early Ibāḍī period, presented a wealth of precedents for the later medieval Ibāḍī imāmate. On the one hand, the assumption of limited leadership by the *'ulamā'* during the period of *kitmān* in Basra functioned as a paradigm for the (theoretical or actual) rule of the *'ulamā'* during the medieval period. Moreover, the examples of Abū al-Khattāb, Ibn Rustum, and ʻAbdullāh b. Yaḥya illustrate the reemergence after the period of *kitmān* of the paradigm of the Ibāḍī Imām who possessed *ʻilm*. This model of *ʻālim*-Imāms did not differ significantly from the idealized paradigms of knowledgeable leadership that developed under the Madīnan Caliphs or the pre-Islamic period—nor did it deviate from the dominant notion of *ʻilm* and legitimate authority that operated during the Umayyad caliphate. In fact, the reappearance of *ʻālim*-Imāms represented a logical continuity with earlier Islamic ideals. This continuity resulted in the medieval Ibāḍī association between *ʻilm* and the imāmate.

Al-Julanda b. Mas'ūd, on the other hand, became the model for the medieval Omani Ibāḍī institution of the *ḍa'īf* Imām—the Imām who ruled without the possession of *ʻilm* and with the assistance of the *ʻulamā'*. Nevertheless, the correlation between *ʻilm* and *imāma* that has been sketched throughout this chapter continued to function in the case of al-Julanda b. Mas'ūd, and the quality of *ʻilm* continued to be an essential aspect of the Ibāḍī *imāma* even when, as in the case of the *ḍa'īf* Imām, the *'ulamā'* exercised it on behalf of the Imām. This condition of "weakness" in the Imām represented an intermediate position between the correlation of *ʻilm* and authority that ideally resided in the Imām during a state of *ẓuhūr*, and the connection between *ʻilm* and leadership that devolved on the *ʻulamā'* during a state of *kitmān*. The role of the *ʻulamā'* in relation to the *ḍa'īf* Imām thus presents a logical development, given the underlying Ibāḍī concern with *ʻilm* and the *imāma*. Moreover, the assistance rendered to al-Julanda b. Mas'ūd by the *ʻulamā'* suggests continuity with pre-Islamic models of authority wherein the knowledgeable members of the tribe aided a *sayyid* who did not possess knowledge. Unsurprisingly, this pre-Islamic paradigm of assistance to a non-*ʻālim* Imām also became an aspect of the medieval Omani imāmate theory.

ʻIlm and the Medieval Ibāḍī Imāmate

The intricate relationship between the possession of *ʻilm* and the enjoyment of leadership that originated in the pre-Islamic period, and developed into a complex institutional apparatus during the early quietist Khārijite and early Ibāḍite eras in Basra, reached its culmination in medieval Ibāḍī theories of the imāmate. The medieval Ibāḍī conception of *ʻilm* agreed with the general Islamic understanding of knowledge as based in and upon the religious: *ʻilm*, the tenth-century Omani jurist al-Kudamī argues, is entirely based upon the Qur'ān. That is to say that *ʻilm*, as a form of knowledge that is specifically religious knowledge, comes from God primarily in the form of His book. Al-Kudamī also accepts as valid sources of knowledge the Prophetic *sunna*, the actions of previous Ibāḍī Imāms, and the agreement (*ijmāʿ*) of the scholarly Ibāḍī community. He argues that rational proof (*ḥujjat al-ʿaql*) and qualified opinions (*al-raʾy*) also constitute a valid form of religious knowledge as long as they are based upon the Qurʾān. Thus, all knowledge that qualifies as *ʿilm* comes ultimately from God.[153]

In fact, the pursuit of *ʿilm* was not limited to the Imāms and remained a general obligation in Ibāḍī Islamic thought; al-Kudamī argued that each Muslim should acquire *ʿilm* as part of the duties of religion (*ʿibāda*).[154] The Imām, however, was expected to be exemplary in his attainment of *ʿilm*. In his legal digest, the fifth/eleventh-century Ḥaḍramawtī scholar Abū Isḥāq states that the Imām must be chosen from among the "people of knowledge and piety" (*ahl al-ʿilm wa al-warʿ*) and that the Imām must be among those most knowledgeable.[155] Similarly, Omani jurists require *ʿilm* of the Imām: Abū Muʾthir stipulates that the Imām be chosen from among the "most learned" (*afqāh*);[156] al-Bisyānī obliges the Imām to "accumulate knowledge in his mind."[157] Additionally, in North African historical texts, where the Imām ideal was preserved in narrative form, the first Rustumid Imām ʿAbd al-Raḥmān b. Rustum was recognized as an *ʿālim* from his apprenticeship with Abū ʿUbayda.[158] Likewise, Abū Zakariyya praises the entire Rustumid family as knowledgeable—particularly as experts in the fundamentals of religion (*al-usūl*), law (*al-fiqh*), Qurʾānic interpretation (*tafsīr*), the diversity of peoples (*ʿilm ikhtilāf al-nās*), grammar, poetry, prose and astronomy.[159] Although Abū Zakariyya's praise is undoubtedly exaggerated, it nevertheless expresses the ideal of the Imām as a possessor of knowledge. This correlation in the medieval Ibāḍī imāmate theory between the possession of *ʿilm* and legitimate authority is the obvious continuance of the association between knowledge and leadership that stretches back through the early Khārijite and early Islamic eras to the pre-Islamic period.

Ideals, of course, do not always match realities, and a telling anecdote about the second Rustumid Imām, ʿAbd al-Wahhāb, illustrates the practical issues that the Ibāḍiyya faced even as they held to the ideal of an Imām-*ʿālim*. ʿAbd al-Wahhāb held the position of Imām after the death of his father ʿAbd al-Raḥmān for nearly forty years until his own death in 208/823. The reign of ʿAbd al-Wahhāb was marked by the development of extensive political and economic power, combined with ʿAbd al-Wahhāb's absolute authority. Ibāḍī sources rarely mention ʿAbd al-Wahhāb in his capacity as a religious leader, and they make it clear that ʿAbd al-Wahhāb was not, in fact, an *ʿālim*. Abū Zakariyya, for example, preserves a story about the Imām in which ʿAbd al-Wahhāb was unable to follow the thread of a debate between five Ibāḍī *ʿulamāʾ* from Jabal Nafūsa and some Muʿtazilites.[160] Assuming that the anecdote is historically accurate (and such candid criticism should hardly be otherwise), it serves as testimony to how far the ideal of the Imām as *'ālim* eclipsed the actual possession of *'ilm* during the reign of the Rustumid Imāms.

Likewise, the medieval Omani *'ulamā'* eventually institutionalized exceptions to the general rule that the Imām be an *'ālim*. The sixth/twelfth-century Omani *qāḍī* Ibn 'Īsā permitted the imāmate of a non-*'ālim* Imām in the case where no learned Imām could be found, and the Ibāḍī community was threatened from without with destruction.[161] Similarly, al-Kindī allows the rule of a non-*'ālim* Imām in cases of "necessity" (*ḍarūra*).[162] As mentioned above, Omani Ibāḍī jurists identified such Imāms as "weak" (*ḍa'īf*) Imāms, and considered them inferior to full Imāms.[163] Legal scholars stipulated as a condition (*sharṭ*) of their imāmate that the *ḍa'īf* Imām consult with the *'ulamā'* on any major decision, though it seems that the issue was not unanimously agreed upon. Ibn 'Īsā also wrote a tract arguing against "some scholars of our time who accept the contract of the imāmate and the entrusting of the affairs of the *umma* to an Imām whether he be knowledgeable or not (*'ālim aw ghayr 'ālim*)."[164] Clearly some scholars saw no need for special conditions for a non-*'ālim* Imām. Nevertheless, these exceptional cases became part of the medieval Omani Ibāḍī imāmate tradition, so that the institution of the *ḍa'īf* Imām was widely accepted by the late medieval period.

Like their North African Ibāḍī counterparts, the Omani institution of the *ḍa'īf* Imām possesses significant precedents in the pre-Islamic era insofar as the tribal conception of knowledge and authority permitted those who had knowledge to assist a leader who did not possess it. As shown above, certain early Khārijite groups likewise encouraged their *'ulamā'* to help a non-*'ālim* Imām. The institution of the *ḍa'īf* Imām, therefore, represents a systematization of a "tribal" understanding of authority and knowledge that became part of the medieval Ibāḍī institution of the Imām via the early Khārijites and Caliphs.

In addition to the exceptional status of the *ḍa'īf* Imām, the Ibāḍiyya recognized the possibility of a situation in which there was no Imām. North African and Omani texts refer to this state of affairs as *kitmān*; the North African Ibāḍī historian al-Darjīnī states: "*kitmān* is the pursuit of affairs in secret (*mulāzamat al-amr sirran*) without an Imām."[165] Likewise, the Omani jurist al-Kindī states: "there is no *imāma* except in *ẓuhūr*."[166] In Oman, where the state of *kitmān* remained a theoretical possibility but not a reality, Ibāḍī jurists recommended that the *'ulamā'* assume responsibility for the direction of the community during the absence of the Imām. Al-Kindī states: "the Muslims have agreed that in the absence of the covenant of the Imām, it is permitted to empower (*wallā*) one of the *'ulamā'* of the Muslims to administer what it is permitted for the Imām to administer."[167] These duties included rendering judgments, protecting orphans and women, performing marriages, and "commanding the good and forbidding evil." Al-Kindī mentions a difference of opinions among jurists regarding the application of the

Qur'ānic penalties (*ḥudūd*): some jurist claim that only the just Imām may apply the *ḥudūd*, while others allow the community (*al-jamā'a*—meaning, in this case, the *'ulamā'*) to apply them.

In North Africa, where the institution of the Imām ended with the destruction of the Rustumid dynasty in the 297/909, councils (*ḥalqa*) of Ibāḍī *'ulamā'* rapidly assumed leadership of the North African Ibāḍī community.[168] Abū Zakariyya mentions the *ḥalqa* of Abū al-Qāsim Yazīd b. al-Makhlaf (d. late fourth/tenth century) and Abū Khazr Yaghlā b. Zultāf (d. late fifth/tenth century) that these scholars established in order to teach those who sought *'ilm*, good behavior (*al-adab*), and information on the traditions of the righteous (*siyar al-ṣāliḥīn*).[169] This *ḥalqa* operated during the mid-fourth/tenth century. Although Abū Zakariyya does not describe the political authority of this *ḥalqa* (if, in fact, it possessed any at this time), it is suggestive that an institution consisting of *'ulamā'* called a *ḥalqa* existed during the fifth/tenth century, and that shortly thereafter (probably by the sixth/twelfth century), the institution of the *ḥalqa* effectively ran the various Ibāḍī communities in North Africa.[170] The authority of these *ḥalqa* clearly rested on the *'ilm* of its members. Theoretically, the state of *kitmān* in North Africa represented an exceptional situation, in which the Ibāḍī community possessed a dispensation (*rukhṣa*) to forego their Imāmate until such time as they accumulated the strength of numbers to reinstitute it.[171] In North Africa, however, the *ḥalqa* councils became permanent, and effectively replaced the imāmate. Thus, the actual practice of *kitmān* in North Africa, and the hypothetical condition of *kitmān* in Omani jurisprudence, led jurists in both areas to stipulate that the Ibāḍī *'ulamā'* should take control of the affairs of the Ibāḍī *umma* during the absence of the Imām. In many ways, the North African councils of *'ulamā'* and the postulated rule of the *'ulamā'* in Omani jurisprudence recall the original situation of quietist Khārijism in Basra during the state of *kitmān*. In such a way, the Basran period of quietist Khārijism provided a valuable precedent for the rule of the *'ulamā'*, just as the early Islamic period and the rule of the Madīnan Caliphs (especially Abū Bakr and 'Umar) provided a precedent for the rule of a knowledgeable Imām during the state of *ẓuhūr*.

Medieval Ibāḍī historical texts, however, complicate the conception of *kitmān* as a state in which there is no Imām by casting the early leaders of the Basran quietist Khārijite community, who ruled during a time of *kitmān*, as Ibāḍī Imāms. The North African jurist and theologian al-Warjlānī, for example, portrays Jābir b. Zayd as an Imām (*huwwa imām fī maqām al-jamā'a*).[172] Likewise, other North African texts imply that Jābir and Abū 'Ubayda functioned as leaders during the time of *kitmān* (although these texts do not use the word "Imām" to describe them).[173] Similarly, Omani texts depict the early Basran quietist Khārijite *'ulamā'* as Ibāḍī Imāms: al-Kindī mentions the "Imām of the Muslims,"

'Abdullāh b. Ibāḍ;[174] Abū Mu'thir includes 'Abdullāh b. Ibāḍ, Jābir b. Zayd, Ṣuḥār al-'Abdī, Ja'far b. al-Sammāk (who he calls al-Sammān), Abū Nūḥ al-Dihhān, and Abū 'Ubayda Muslim b. Abī Karīma in his list of "Imāms of the Muslims" (*ā'immat al-muslimīn*).[175] Al-Qalhātī unambiguously identifies 'Abdullāh b. Ibāḍ as the Imām of the Ibāḍiyya.[176] In this manner, medieval Ibāḍī texts elevate the early Basran *'ulamā'* to the rank of full Imāms and create for them a position of Imām during the time of *kitmān*.

In order to make sense of the promotion of the early Basran *'ulamā'* to Imāms, reference must be made to the type of text—and the kind of discourse—in which this discussion occurs. Abū Mu'thir and al-Kindī speak of the early Basran *'ulamā'* as Imāms in the context of tracing the line of true Islam back to the Prophet. Similarly, al-Qalhātī's identification of Ibn Ibāḍ as an Imām occurs in his heresiography, that is, in a polemical text aimed at showing Ibāḍism as the true version of Islam. Likewise, al-Warjlānī (the only North African author to identify Jābir b. Zayd as an Imām) upheld the notion of an unbroken chain of *'ilm* transmitters reaching back directly to the Prophet: in fact, al-Warjlānī compiled the first collection of Ibāḍī *ḥadīth* and probably used the narrative of the early Basran Imāms to make his *isnād*s appear more plausible.[177] Thus, the institution of the Imām of *kitmān* represents an institution that was imagined for the ideological purposes of tracing the line of true Islam (and a chain of continuous *'ilm*) back to the Prophet Muhammad. This fictive institution existed alongside of the legal descriptions of *kitmān* as a state without an Imām. Apparently, the ideological value of claiming the early Basran quietist *'ulamā'* as Ibāḍī Imāms was more important than the contradiction that arose from simultaneously portraying *kitmān* as a condition with no Imām.

The theme underlying all of the aforementioned medieval Ibāḍī institutions of authority is a concern for keeping *'ilm*, in some capacity, associated with the leadership of the community. In the ideal situation, the Ibāḍī Imām, ruling the community in a condition of *ẓuhūr*, possessed knowledge. However, if necessity required the community to select an Imām without knowledge, they would be able to do so as long as the *'ulamā'* assisted him. Finally, in the unfortunate circumstance of the Ibāḍī community entering a state of *kitmān* and subsisting without an Imām, the *'ulamā'* assumed leadership of the community. Likewise, in the primarily imagined institution of the Imām of *kitmān*, the supposed Imāms of this phase of Ibāḍī history were all primarily *'ulamā'*, and their knowledge justified their elevation to the rank of Imām. This correlation between leadership and knowledge that lies behind the medieval Ibāḍī imāmate theory was based upon earlier conceptions of *'ilm* as appropriate to leadership positions. The early role of knowledge and leadership in pre-Islamic Arabia, as well as the relationship between *'ilm* and the office of Prophet, and knowledge and the office of the early caliphate, all set the precedent for the Ibāḍī requirement for *'ilm* in their Imām. In addition, the assumption of limited (and secret) political authority by the early Basran quietist Khārijite *'ulamā'*—from whom the Ibāḍiyya emerged as a distinct sect—provided a powerful precedent for the rule of the *'ulamā'* during the state of *kitmān*.

According to the medieval Ibāḍī imāmate ideal, the traits of knowledge remained an essential characteristic for all Ibāḍī leaders, be they Imāms or *'ulamā'* (*'ilm* is, after all, the defining characteristic of the *'ulamā'*). In fact, though medieval Omani Ibāḍī jurisprudence does not explicitly mention piety as a necessary trait for those who assume control of the community during the state of *kitmān*, the characteristic of piety also figured prominently in the portrayals of the *'ulamā'* who led the community during *kitmān*.[178] These two traits comprised the essential characteristics of an Ibāḍī leader—be he an Imām or *'ālim*.

3

The Shārī Imām

The type of Imām known in North Africa and Oman as the *imām al-shārī* (the Imām dedicated to the practice of *shirā'*) presents a unique case in Islamic political theory. No other sectarian group possesses this peculiar institution, or the concept—*shirā'*—that is associated with it. *Shirā'* and the *imām al-shārī*, it seems, are an inheritance of the Ibāḍiyya exclusively from their early Khārijite predecessors, though important foundations for the Khārijite notion of *shirā'* may be found in the Qur'ān and in the accounts of martyrdom from the early Islamic community. Tracing the lineage of *shirā'* from its conceptual roots, through its use by the early Khārijites, to its final articulation as an aspect of the Ibāḍī imāmate institution will be the focus of this chapter.

The concept of *shirā'*, and its subsequent use in early Khārijite and Ibāḍī thought, possesses a particularly complex history. The term *shirā'* encompasses a range of overlapping concepts; it literally means "to give for a price," "to sell" or "to exchange"; and the person who performs the action of *shirā'* is known as *shārī* (plural—*shurāt*).[1] The term occurs in the Qur'ān in the context of the believer who "sells/exchanges" (*sharā*) his soul to God by fighting and dying for His cause: "Let those fight in the way of God who sell (*yashrūn*) the life of this world for the other"; "And there is a type of person who sells (*yashrī*) his life to earn the pleasure of God, and God is full of kindness to His devotees."[2] The Khārijites applied the Qur'ānic metaphor of *shirā'* to the action of fighting and dying for Khārijism, a cause they identified with establishing a just and moral social order on earth. Simultaneously, they regarded *shirā'* as the quality of pious bravado that made an individual a *shārī* person, willing to sell his life to further God's purposes. Moreover, the Khārijites employed the term *shurāt* to describe themselves as well as their movement.[3] In the Ibāḍī context, Ibāḍīs spoke of the *imām al-shārī* as possessing the characteristic of *shirā'*—a certain reckless bravery, a desire to "sell" his life on behalf of Islam—that inspired him to pursue *shirā'* as the military expansion of Ibāḍī territory. These various usages indicate that for both Khārijites and Ibāḍites, the concept of *shirā'* came to denote a characteristic of an individual, as well as the actions associated with that characteristic.

Ibāḍī imāmate theory later associated *shirā'* with the qualities of bravery and heroism, and the *imām al-shārī* personified these characteristics in a leader. Both North African and Omani conceptions of the *imām al-shārī* shared this underlying correlation between *shirā'* and authority. Due to different historical situations of the North African and Omani communities, however, the regional institutions of the *imām al-shārī* differed slightly. In North Africa, the *imām al-shārī* remained a largely theoretical institution; the North African Ibāḍī community recognized the early Khārijite (that is, pre-Ibāḍite) heroes Qarīb b. Murra, Zuḥḥāf b. Zuḥar al-Ṭā'ī, and Abū Bilāl Mirdās b. Udaya as members of the first Ibāḍī "generation" (*ṭabaqa*) and examples of leaders who performed *shirā'*, but they did not designate any of the subsequent Rustumid Imāms as *shārī* Imāms.[4] In Oman, on the other hand, the ideal of the *imām al-shārī* remained a living tradition: Omani historians considered many of the early Omani Imāms to be *shārī* Imāms,[5] but unlike the North African Ibāḍīs, the Omani Ibāḍīs did not so label Qarīb, Zuḥḥāf, and Abū Bilāl. Rather, these individuals (among others) functioned as forerunners to the *imām al-shārī* insofar as they were portrayed as martyrs, heroes, and pious predecessors.[6]

Additionally, differences in the conception of *shirā'* as a supplementary or separate institution of authority existed between the North African and Omani Ibāḍī communities. Omani Ibāḍī jurists conceived of *shirā'* as a supererogatory practice that could be voluntarily adopted by a group of qualified individuals, or by an existing Imām. An Imām opted to take the contract (*'aqd*) of *shirā'*, and thereby became an *imām al-shārī* in addition to his being an Imām.[7] In North Africa, jurists conceived of the state of *shirā'* as separate from the states of *ẓuhūr*, *kitmān*, and *difā'*, implying that the *imām al-shārī* was a distinct institution from the *imām al-ẓuhūr*, *imām al-difā'*, and the *imām al-kitmān*.[8]

Although the differences between the medieval North African and Omani institutions remain significant, the underlying conception of the *imām al-shārī* as an institution of authority associated with the quality of *shirā'* as a particular kind of authority associated with bravery and self-sacrifice link the medieval North

African and Omani institutions of the *imām al-shārī*, and set off the office of the *shārī* Imām from other types of Imāms. Omani jurists viewed the *shārī* Imām as the highest degree of Imām—an Imām who possessed *all* of the desirable qualities of an Imām. That is, in addition to the moral probity and knowledge expected of the *ẓuhūr* Imām, the *imām al-shārī* possessed the desire to perform *shirā'*.

Like the Omanis, North African jurists distinguished the *imām al-shārī* from other Imāms by the practice of *shirā'*.[9] After the dissolution of the Rustumid dynasty, however, the *imām al-shārī* remained a theoretical (and therefore unelaborated) institution in North African Ibāḍism. Finally, both North African and Omani Ibāḍiyya recognized certain historical individuals (Qarīb, Zuḥḥāf, and Abū Bilāl) as leaders in connection with the concept of *shirā'*: in North Africa as *shārī* Imāms proper, and in Oman as heroes and martyrs. These commonalities between the North African and Omani notions of *shirā'* and the *imām al-shārī* constitute the distinctive features of both North African and Omani conceptions of the *imām al-shārī*, and illustrate its centrality to the medieval Ibāḍī *imāma*. Despite the overall complexity of the institution of the *imām al-shārī* in its distinctive North African and Omani articulations, its underlying connection to the concept of *shirā'* anchors the process of institutional development in earlier conceptualizations of legitimate violence and martyrdom.

Two points must be borne in mind when investigating how the medieval Ibāḍī institution of the *imām al-shārī* assimilated the early Khārijite phenomenon of *shirā'*, appropriated the Khārijite figures associated with the phenomenon of *shirā'*, and adapted the concept of *shirā'* to a political institution of authority. First, prior to the medieval Ibāḍī *imāma*, the concept of *shirā'* was not necessarily associated with political authority, but rather with popular notions of heroism and martyrdom. The heroic deeds of the early Khārijite *shurāt* constituted an "authority" of sorts that was opposed to dominant political authorities of the time. The practice of *shirā'* created, foremost, a heroic image that was captured by the popular imagination in the form of poetry and legend.

Second, as a consequence of their formation in Basra, the Ibāḍiyya inherited and assimilated Iraqi Khārijite *shurāt* stories. Later, the Ibāḍiyya manipulated the stories of *shurāt* so that the *shurāt* individuals appeared as examples of *shārī* Imāms (in the North African case), or as heroes and martyrs associated with the concept of *shirā'* (as in Oman), and thereby as forerunners to the *imām al-shārī*. In such a way, the Ibāḍiyya appropriated the "authority" of the *shurāt*'s heroic image, but transformed it into a type of political authority (that is, the *shurāt* became Imāms or models for Imāms).

In tracing the process of assimilation, appropriation, and adaptation that produced the medieval Ibāḍī office of the *shārī* Imām, it is helpful to examine the precedents for the Ibāḍī conception of *shirā'* in the Qur'ānic concepts of *jihād* and *shahāda* (martyrdom). We shall look at examples of martyrdom from the Prophetic and early Islamic eras, including those of some early Khārijite *shurāt*. The popular appeal of *shurāt* and the existence of the informal institution of Khārijite martyrs and heroes served as precedents for the individuals in Ibāḍī texts who functioned in North Africa as the examples of the *imām al-shārī*, and in Oman as the forerunners to the *shārī* Imām. Finally, the medieval North African and Omani institutions of the *imām al-shārī* illustrate the transformation of *shirā'* into a political institution (that is, an Imām).

The adaptation of the concept of *shirā'* into a political office included limiting the potentially destabilizing power of the *shurāt*. As inheritors of the Iraqi Khārijite *shurāt* cycle, the Ibāḍiyya appropriated the image of the early Khārijī rebels to bolster their claims to power, but defused the destabilizing potential of *shirā'* by creating the office of the *imām al-shārī*. In such a way, the concept of *shirā'* developed from an indigenous Khārijite expression of pious bravado into a cult of the martyrs and heroes, and finally into the medieval Ibāḍī institution of the *shārī* Imām.

Militancy and Martyrdom in Early Islamic History

The Qur'ān presents the notion of fighting (the Qur'ān uses the terms *jihād* and *qitāl* in association with martial actions) as a one of many types of activities that are potentially associated with piety. Although the militant aspect of the concept of *jihād* was not the only way in which the Qur'ān speaks about *jihād*, it does provide a precedent for the Khārijite notion of *shirā'*.[10] Likewise, the concentration on *shahāda* as martyrdom that bestowed divine reward and enhanced the physical presence of the martyr's body with extraordinary properties does not exhaust the topic of martyrdom in the Qur'ān or in early Islamic history, but these aspects of the notion of martyrdom are of prime importance to the Khārijite notion of *shirā'*.

As an indigenous Khārijite concept of militancy and martyrdom, the idea of *shirā'* came from a Qur'ānic metaphor (later used in Khārijite poetry) of those who "sell" (*sharā*) their soul to God, who "buys" (*ashtarā*) the souls in exchange for paradise. Verse 9:111 reads:

> Lo! God has bought from the believers (*ashtarā min al-mu'minīn*) their persons and their wealth because the Garden will be theirs: they shall fight in the way of God (*yuqātilūn fī sabīl Allāh*) and shall slay and be slain. It is a promise, which is binding on Him in the Torah and the Gospel and the Qur'ān. Who fulfills his covenant better than God?

> Rejoice then in your bargain that you have made, for that is the supreme triumph.

In 2:207, the believers "sell themselves" for the pleasure of God, while 4:74 commands: "Let those fight in the way of God who sell (*yashrūn*) the life of this world for the other." These verses explicitly connect the Qur'ānic metaphor of "selling" one's life to God (*shirā'*) in exchange for reward to the idea of militancy.

Fighting, so long as it was conducted "in God's way," presented a means by which Muslims could further the cause of Islam and, as such, became a method associated with Islamic piety (*taqwā*). The Qur'ān states: "Have you not seen those unto whom it was said: Withhold your hands, observe prayer and pay the alms tax, but when fighting (*qitāl*) was prescribed for them, a group of them fear people as much as they fear of God."[11] This verse associates fighting with the other cornerstones of Islamic behavior (prayer and *zakāt*). In addition, it makes reference to fighting as an aspect of Islamic piety, insofar as piety stems from a "fear" of God.

The Qur'ān connects warfare with establishing a just social order on earth, and thereby further cements the association between piety and fighting "in God's way." In 4:75, the Qur'ān rhetorically asks: "What is wrong with you that you do not fight in the way of God when weak men, women, and children are crying: Our Lord! Bring us out of this town of evil people and give us from Your presence a protector! Oh, give us a defender." Similarly, 2:193 commands Muslims to fight until "there is no more persecution (*fitna*) and the religion becomes God's (*wayakūn al-dīn lil-lāh*)."[12] In conjunction with Qur'ānic verses commanding the Islamic community to establish justice, the prosecution of warfare can primarily be interpreted as a means to further the creation of a just social order on earth. The qualifying phrase "in God's way" (*fī sabīl Allāh*) specifically distinguishes warfare as advancing the cause of God's justice.

Ḥadīth from the Prophet Muhammad further strengthen the link between piety and warfare. The Prophet was recorded as saying: "I have been commanded to fight people until they say, 'There is no God but God,' establish [regular] prayers, and pay the alms tax."[13] This *ḥadīth* establishes warfare as a means to institute Islamic practices aimed at the betterment of humanity. Likewise, the range of meaning covered by the concept of *jihād* testifies to an array of pious activities associated with *jihād*, one of which is warfare proper. These activities, according to *ḥadīth*, distinguished the true believers:

> Every Prophet sent by God to a people (*umma*) before me has had disciples and followers who followed his ways (*sunna*) and obeyed his commands. But after them came successors who preached what they did not practice and practiced what they were not commanded. Whoever strives

> (*jāhada*) against them with one's hand is a believer, whoever strives against them with one's tongue is a believer, whoever strives against them with one's heart is a believer.[14]

In addition, the Prophet Muhammad was credited with saying: "The best *jihād* is [speaking] a word of justice to a tyrannical ruler."[15] These associations between pious activity—of which combat is included—and *jihād* establish warfare as a form of pious action (that is, so long as it is conducted in the proper manner and with righteous cause).

As the logical extension of the concept of *jihād fī sabīl Allāh*, the Qur'ān established the notion of martyrdom (*shahāda*) for those who died fighting in the way of God. The Muslim martyr—the *shahīd*—is one for whom death becomes a defining moment. However, the *shahīd* is also a witness, one who sees and who is seen, and one who will testify to what has been seen.[16] The Qur'ān uses the same terms for martyr and witness: "thus We have appointed you a middle nation, that you may be witnesses (*shuhadā'*) against humankind, and the messenger may be a witness (*shahīd*) against you";[17] "And the witnesses/martyrs (*shuhadā'*) are with their Lord."[18] Verse 3:140 clearly presents the term *shahīd/shuhadā'* in the sense of martyr:

> If you have received a blow, the [disbelieving] people have received a blow the like thereof. These are [only] the vicissitudes which We cause to follow one another for humankind, to the end that God may know those who believe and may choose *shuhadā'* from among you; and God does not love the unjust.

As a testament, the martyr's death offered an authentication (*shahāda*) of the truth of the Islamic path.

As an act of supreme witness to the validity of Muhammad's message, Muslim martyrs were promised great reward in heaven. The Qur'ān, in 3:170, refers to a grand recompense for those slain fighting in God's way: "Jubilant [are they] because of that which God has bestowed upon them of His bounty, rejoicing for the sake of those who have not joined them but are left behind: that no fear shall come upon them neither shall they grieve." In 3:169 the Qur'ān states, "think not of those who are slain in the way of God as dead. No—they are living! They have provision with their Lord." Similarly, Islamic tradition describes the rewards awaiting the martyr: all his sins will be forgiven, he will be protected from torment in the grave; he will wear a crown of glory on his head; he will marry seventy-two *ḥūri*s (heavenly consorts); his intercession will be accepted for his relatives.[19]

So powerful was the belief in the efficacy of martyrdom in early Islamic history that it became a desirable end in itself. As a corollary to the soteriological aspects of martyrdom in Islam, the fervor and faith of the new religion saw individuals "longing for *shahādat*," that is, desiring martyrdom. The early history of Islam presents numerous examples of this phenomenon. A man named 'Amr b. Jamuh was lame, but had seven sons who went to fight at the Battle of 'Uhud. 'Amr himself wanted to fight, but his sons protested on the grounds that he was not obligated due to his infirmity. 'Amr approached the Prophet Muhammad and asked for permission to fight, which the Prophet granted. 'Amr was then killed in the battle, along with one of his sons.[20]

Just as the martyrs were believed to be exalted in heaven, their bodies and tombs were treated with special respect on earth. The bodies of the *shuhadā'* were thought to be especially purified and sanctified by their act of martyrdom. This special status is reflected in the later codification of law regarding the burial of certain martyrs. Later Sunni law made a distinction between those killed fighting for the defense or propagation of Islam, and those who died for their faith in other ways: the former were known as "battlefield martyrs" (*shuhadā' al-ma'raka*) while the latter were subsumed under the general heading of martyr.[21] The main difference between battlefield and other martyrs lie in the burial rites of the battlefield martyr; under normal circumstances, a dead body was washed and wrapped in a white shroud after death. This process cleansed the body in preparation for its final meeting with God. In the case of the battlefield martyr, the body was not washed, nor was it covered in the traditional white shroud.[22] The blood of the martyr and the force of his act was enough to cleanse the body, and the garments that the martyr wore at the time of his act were believed to have been sanctified in the process.[23] Thus, just as the sincere utterance of the profession of faith (*shahāda*) wiped away the former sins of the individual, the act of martyrdom (also *shahāda*) purified the martyr's body.

Similarly, Islamic martyrs are set apart from Muslims who die a normal death by the fact that mourning is encouraged at their graves. This practice dates to the death of Ḥamza b. 'Abd al-Muttalib during the Prophet Muhammad's lifetime. Ḥamza lived alone, and at his death there was no one to lament his passing. The Prophet commented on this fact, and the women who had been lamenting their sons and husbands went immediately to his house and began mourning. It became a tradition that before anyone wept for their fallen relatives they first went to the house of Ḥamza and cried there. Although the Prophet discouraged weeping after a death, lamenting the deaths of the martyrs was encouraged.[24]

In addition, the graves of the martyrs (which are sometimes identical with the site of their martyrdom) were believed to emanate the same sanctity that infused the body of the martyr. Muṭahharī relates that Fātima gathered materials for her prayer beads at the grave of her uncle, the martyr Ḥamza b. 'Abd al-Muttalib.[25] Likewise, the earth of Karbalā', because of its inherent sanctity from the martyrdom of al-Ḥusayn, is still utilized today for the prayer stones of the Shiʿa. The physical presence of sanctity at the grave of the martyrs is a reflection on the consecrated status of the martyrs.

Practices such as veneration of the grave sites of the martyrs, lamentation at their tombs, and belief in the efficacy of their bodies, in addition to the Qur'ānic and Prophetic paradigms for martyrdom created a powerful precedent during the first centuries of Islam. Such examples form the backdrop against which indigenous Khārijite notions of militant activism undoubtedly formed. Although the dating and reliability of much, if not most, of the materials relating to the concept of martyrdom and *jihād* during the early period can be called into question, there is no doubt that such ideas circulated in some form in the earliest periods. It was these early notions of martyrdom and militancy that coalesced into the Khārijite concept of *shirā'*.

Shirā': The Concept of Militant Activism in Early Khārijite Religious Thought

The frequency of violent Khārijite rebellions in early Islamic history testifies to the importance of the concepts of militancy among the early Khārijites; Islamic heresiographers and historians mention some ten Khārijite military campaigns against ʿAlī and Muʿāwiya following the Battle of Nahrawān.[26] In addition, the recorded early Basran uprisings of Sahm b. Ghālib, Qarīb b. Murra, Zuḥḥāf b. Zuḥar al-Ṭā'ī, Ṭawwāf b. ʿAlāq, and Abū Bilāl Mirdās b. Udaya occurred over a mere twenty-three year period. Later rebellions, such as those of Shabīb al-Khārijī in the Jazīra (northern Mesopotamia), Ḥamza b. Ādhrak al-Khārijī in Sīstān (southeastern Iran), Ṭālib al-Ḥaqq in the Ḥijāz, and al-Julanda b. Masʿūd in Oman confirm the continued magnitude of Khārijite military activities. In part, these large numbers of Khārijite rebellions in the early Islamic period can be understood with reference to the theme of militant activism—the Khārijī rebel's zeal to "sell his soul" to God in exchange for heaven (*shirā'*)—that runs through them. The early Khārijite rebels viewed themselves as fighting injustice as a righteous remnant of true believers, and buying Paradise with their lives.

Accounts of the early Khārijite rebellions, however, remain problematic. The inevitable biases of the Sunni authors toward treating the Khārijites as deviant rebels, combined with the virtual extinction of the Khārijites as a sectarian block in Islam, resulted in the preservation of very few unedited Khārijite texts from which an accurate picture of the Khārijī interpretation of *shirā'* may be developed. Fortunately, a small but significant amount of early Khārijite poetry survived in various historical and literary sources from which a picture of the Khārijite attitude toward acts of violence can be drawn. This early Khārijite poetry illuminates how the Khārijites adopted the Qur'ānic metaphor of *shirā'* to describe indigenous Khārijite conceptions of *jihād* and *shahāda*. The notion of "selling" one's soul to God in exchange for paradise was taken from the Qur'ān and applied to Khārijite concepts of militancy. For example, an early militant Khārijite, Ma'dān b. Mālik al-Iyādī, employed the metaphor of *shirā'* in connection with warfare: "Greetings to the one who God has bought as a *shārī*; and not to those who are a party of quietists (*ḥizb al-muqīm*)";[27] an anonymous Khārijite begged God to grant him piety (*taqwā*), sincerity (*ṣidq*), and provision in the world until he could "sell that which is fleeting (*al-ladhī yafnā*) for the hereafter."[28] In addition, the Khārijites employed other related metaphors, such as *bī'* ("buying" as a corollary to "selling"). These terms collectively share what Wittgenstein would call a "family resemblance" in their references to the concept of militancy. In this manner, *shirā'* functioned as the general term for the concept of Khārijite militancy and martyrdom, even though it did not formally become a theological or legal term among the Khārijites.

Similar to the Qur'ānic and Prophetic notion of militancy as a way of fulfilling one's religious duties, the Khārijites conceived of *shirā'* as a method of being religious. Early references to *shirā'* in Khārijite poetry testify to a commitment to pious militancy from the beginning of the Khārijite movement. 'Abdullāh b. Wahb al-Rāsibī, the Imām of the Muḥakkima, is credited on the day of Nahrawān with the verses:

> I am Ibn Wahb al-Rāsibī the *shārī*,
> I strike among the enemy to take vengeance,
> Until the state of the evil ones (*dawlat al-ashrār*) may vanish,
> And truth may return to the virtuous.[29]

Al-Rāsibī's usage of *shirā'* connects militancy with the removal of "evil" rulers and the return of righteous government to power. Similarly, the early Khārijite al-'Ayzār b. al-Akhnas al-Ṭā'ī recited: "Do not spare any effort for piety (*taqwā*) and do not follow whims; for God will not forsake those who are *shārī*."[30] Like al-Rāsibī, al-'Ayzār associates piety with *shirā'*. Other verses, without explicitly employing the notion of *shirā'*, illustrate the nature of the Khārijite commitment to pious militancy. Abū Bilāl stated: "Fear (*taqwā*) of God and fear (*khawf*) of the Fire sent me out (*akhrajanī*); to sell my self (*bī' nafsī*) for that which has no price."[31] In this way, the Khārijites conceived of *shirā'* as part of the realm of religion: in particular, they considered *shirā'* a means to combat injustice, and an essential aspect of pious service to God (*taqwā*). This particular understanding of *shirā'* enabled the Khārijites to ascribe an elevated status to those who engaged in it: the *shurāt* came to be regarded as exemplary because they were willing to struggle in God's way.

In addition, Khārijite poetry clearly shows that the Khārijites hoped for divine reward as a result of *shirā'*. For example, the mother of 'Imrān b. al-Ḥārith al-Rāṣibī, in a lament to her son killed with Nāfi' b. al-Azraq at the Battle of Dūlāb, speaks of him as "purified" by God through death.[32] Ka'b b. 'Amīra eulogized Abū Bilāl stating: "God has bought (*sharā*) Ibn Ḥudayr's soul and he has embraced Paradise with its many blessings."[33] Al-Rahīn b. Sahm al-Murādī eulogized several early rebels, who he portrays as residents of Paradise (*firdaws*).[34] The attainment of heaven came as the direct result of *shirā'* for, indeed, the very metaphor of *shirā'* implied purchasing heaven with one's life. Thus, beyond its efficacy as an aspect of general Islamic piety, the act of *shirā'* was believed to have potent soteriological power, and the Khārijites clearly viewed their acts of *shirā'* as synonymous with martyrdom (*shahāda*).

Similar to early Islamic conceptualizations of martyrdom whereby the martyrs displayed a characteristic disregard for their own lives, the Khārijites actively sought death through *shirā'*. For example, Thābit b. Wa'la al-Rāsibī pledged: "I will follow my brethren [that is, I will die like them] and drink of their cup with a cleaving, two edged, Indian sword in hand."[35] As death came to everyone at some time, the Khārijites believed they should seek it through fighting for God's cause: "Death is a thing inevitable and true; whoever it does not greet by day, it comes to by night."[36] Abū Bilāl asked:

> What do we care if our souls go out [of our bodies];
> What good to you were bodies and limbs anyway?
> We look forward to the Gardens [of paradise],
> When our skulls lie [here] in the dust like rotten melons.[37]

This disregard for death in favor of the attainment of paradise illuminates how the Khārijite concept of *shirā'* was believed to possess the same soteriological effect as *shahāda*, and can thereby be treated as synonymous with it.

Along with belief in the divine reward for the practice of *shirā'*, the Khārijites considered the bodies and gravesites of the *shurāt* to be infused with a kind of blessing. Evidence exists of the belief in the purification of the bodies of the slain *shurāt*, and of the gravesites of early Khārijite *shurāt* being regarded as places of special power. 'Imrān b. al-Ḥārith al-Rāsibī, for example, was believed to have been "purified" by God through his death.[38] The gravesite of the Khārijite rebel Sāliḥ b. Muṣarriḥ became a pilgrimage place for Khārijites before they made their rebellions (*khurūj*).[39] It is also reported that the people of Basra feared that the graves of slain Khārijites would become pilgrimage sites.[40] From these examples, it becomes clear that the Khārijites subscribed to the belief in the purity of the bodies of the *shurāt*, as well as their ability to transmit this sanctity through the place of their burial.

From these examples of the conflation of *shirā'* with the concepts of *jihād* and *shahāda*, it has been shown that the early Khārijite notion of *shirā'* combined the concepts of militancy and martyrdom as a pious pursuit for which God would reward the practitioner. Much like the concepts of *jihād* and *shahāda*, *shirā'* represented a heroic and pious action insofar as it involved a suspension of the "normal" rules of human behavior in favor of divinely sanctioned action (that is, the *shārī* sought death in the service of God, whereas human beings usually sought life). As such, the practice of *shirā'* insured the practitioner's place among the heavenly elect, and conferred a certain ineffable power to the bodies and gravesites of the slain Khārijite *shurāt*.

The practice of *shirā'*, however, did more than simply insure the salvation of the *shurāt*. For those who witnessed or heard of the martyr's sacrifice, the power of the act resonated with the truth for which the *shārī* had died, and endowed martyrs with an authority that they did not possess before their death. This authority was not necessarily political in nature, though the *shurāt* were often regarded as politioreligious and military leaders during their lives. Rather, the stories and legends of the Khārijite *shurāt* transformed them into popular heroes and established their heroic image, so that they became potent ideological symbols. As symbols, the image of the Khārijite *shurāt* would be used to justify and bolster sectarian claims to political and religious authority.

The Heroic Image: Early Khārijite *Shurāt* Narratives

As much of the latent power of the *shurāt* derives from their heroic image, it is imperative to investigate the metamorphosis of the Khārijite *shurāt* into mythic figures, heroes, and legends. Four Khārijite heroes from early Islamic history—Abū Bilāl Mirdās b. Udaya, Ṣāliḥ b. Muṣarriḥ, Shabīb al-Khārijī and Ḥamza b. Ādhrak al-Khārijī—exemplify this transformation. A relatively large amount of material exists for these four figures, which will establish the nature of their legends, allow for a comparison of their heroic images, and illustrate how the heroic image of the Khārijī *shurāt* became an informal and popular "institution" in early Islamic history. Moreover, they illustrate how the anti-authoritarian characteristics of the early Khārijī *shurāt* myths are vital to understanding the subsequent use and institutionalization of the *shurāt* figures.

It should be stressed that it is the stories, rather than actual historical events, so far as they could be reconstructed from the sources, that will concern us here. As such, the early Khārijite *shurāt* appear in their accounts as semi-mythic, semi-real characters. Certainly, the stories of Abū Bilāl, Ṣāliḥ, Shabīb, and Ḥamza were based upon some actual events in their lives. Nevertheless, it is their legends that survive them, just as it is their legends that inspired those who looked to them as heroes. And as legendary heroes, Hobsbawm's comment on the social bandit's status vis-à-vis those who preserve and revered their stories remains important to the discussion. Hobsbawm states: "The point about social bandits is that they are peasant outlaws whom the lord and state regard as criminals, but who remain within peasant society, and are considered by their people as heroes, as champions, avengers, fighters for justice, perhaps even leaders of liberation, and in any case men to be admired, helped and supported."[41] True to Hobsbawm's maxim, the Khārijites enjoyed a duality of status in relation to the dominant authorities and rural populations: the Umayyads and 'Abbasids regarded them as rebels while the local populations frequently rallied to their cause, regarding them as heroes. They did not have a conscious revolutionary program; rather, they restored things to the way they "should be," righted wrongs, and avenged injustices without constituting an organized movement.[42] Their appeal came from their connection to the peasantry and to its values. As primitive rebels, the Khārijite *shurāt* captured the rebellious zeitgeist of their eras and gave form to undercurrents of resistance. In their own minds, the Khārijites undoubtedly viewed themselves as reestablishing the original and authentic Islam while fighting against the injustices of the dominant regimes. It was this connection to the non-Arab majority, in conjunction with their resistance to the Umayyads and 'Abbasids, which gave their movement a broad base of popularity.

Mention should also be made of the socioeconomic conditions that set the stage for the early Khārijite heroes. Hobsbawm points out certain economic conditions in which social banditry thrives: specifically, among societies in transition from tribal and kinship-based social organizations to capitalist and industrially based societies, including "the phases of disintegrating kinship society and transition to agrarian capitalism."[43] In each case, class conflict exists between the social bandits, who fight for the peasantry, and the dominant classes. In a somewhat similar vein, Khārijism developed under economic conditions that approximate Hobsbawm's criteria for social banditry. The Umayyad era witnessed the development of an Arab ruling elite, consisting primarily of old Makkan families, who administered lands populated by large, non-Arab peoples. The old tribal system of social organization that had existed in the Arabian Peninsula slowly became absorbed in the agrarian societies outside Arabia. At the same time, economies founded upon *jihād* gave way to agrarian-based economies dependent on taxing the peasantry.[44] These social and economic conditions paved the way for popular support of the Khārijites insofar as they represented an attempted to reinstitute a kinship-like form of social organization (replacing kinship with membership in the Khārijite sect), incorporated non-Arabs into their movement, and frequently released the peasants from their tax obligations to the Islamic state. Hobsbawm's observations may be borne in mind when considering the context of the early Khārijite heroes.

Another preliminary consideration involves the variety of sources in which the narratives of Abū Bilāl, Ḥamza, Ṣāliḥ, and Shabīb are preserved. Due to the widespread appeal of Abū Bilāl, his cycle is preserved in both Sunni and Ibāḍī sources—but especially in the Ibāḍī biographical dictionaries of al-Shammākhī and al-Darjīnī—and in the histories of al-Ṭabarī, al-Mubarrad, and al-Balādhurī. Likewise, the story of Ṣāliḥ and Shabīb is preserved in al-Ṭabarī and Ibn Qutayba. Ḥamza's narrative, on the other hand, comes exclusively from the *Tārīkh-e Sistān*. While the similarities in the narratives of Abū Bilāl, and to a certain extent, Ṣāliḥ and Shabīb's, across a variety of sources points toward a possible common source (or sources) for their stories, nothing indicates how the narratives came to have their specific, semi-legendary form.[45] Nevertheless, the preponderance of eulogies devoted to Abū Bilāl in Khārijite poetry suggests that his story was well known among the Khārijites and their sympathizers.[46] Likewise, eulogies to Ṣāliḥ and Shabīb exist in Khārijite poetry, suggesting a similar popular familiarity with their narratives.[47] It is entirely possible, even probable, that the semi-legendary form of these narratives resulted from repeated tellings, which were eventually written down and used by the authors and editors of various historical works.

The narrative of Abū Bilāl presents a Khārijite version of a semi-legendary hero. Sunni and Ibāḍī sources report that Mirdās b. Udaya, also known by his patronymic Abū Bilāl, witnessed the battles of Ṣiffīn and Nahrawān.[48] His brother 'Urwa was among the first, if not the first, person to utter the famous Khārijite slogan *lā ḥukm illā lil-lāh*.[49] Such credentials established Abū Bilāl as a solid Khārijite and linked him to the very font of Khārijism, the Battle of Ṣiffīn. However, Abū Bilāl rejected the extremist tactics of some fellow Khārijite rebels, and his public disavowal of extremism vindicated the harsh tactics employed by the Basran governor Ziyād b. Abīhi (governed 40–56/660–675) against the extremist Khārijites in Basra.[50] Nonetheless, under Ziyād's son, 'Ubayd Allāh (governed 56–76/675–695), Abū Bilāl and other Khārijites were imprisoned in Basra for their views.

Ibāḍī sources preserve an anecdote about Abū Bilāl's prison stay that captures the legendary side of his moral qualities. According to the myth, Abū Bilāl was on good terms with his jailer, who allowed him to visit his home at night, so long as he returned to his cell by the morning. On one of his visits, Abū Bilāl learned of the impending execution of all Khārijite prisoners, to include himself. Nonetheless, he returned to his cell to honor his word to his jailer. The jailer was impressed by Abū Bilāl's action, and mentioned the incident to the governor, who then freed Abū Bilāl.[51] Although this is not the only occasion for which Ibāḍī authors laud Abū Bilāl's moral traits, it is an example of the type of piety that was esteemed by Muslims.[52] Although this story was undoubtedly exaggerated, the attribution of moral heroism to Abū Bilāl strengthened his appeal as a hero to the average Muslim.

Abū Bilāl's most celebrated act was his revolt against the 'Ubayd Allāh in the year 61/679. The governor's cruelty in the execution of a Khārijī woman named al-Baljā' roused Abū Bilāl's anger and, gathering forty of his companions, he led his followers away from Basra in open rebellion against the governor.[53] The story presents Abū Bilāl as a champion who brings justice and rights wrongs, as the execution of the Khārijī woman is presented, even in Sunni sources, as excessive: 'Ubayd Allāh cut off her hands and feet and then displayed her dead body in the marketplace.[54] Abū Bilāl, disgusted by this injustice, voiced his desire to escape from "the rule of... tyrants."[55] In such a manner, Abū Bilāl's rebellion became a stance against the injustice of 'Ubayd Allāh, and Abū Bilāl became a champion of the weak and a righter of wrongs. His mythical persona encapsulated the Islamic hope for justice against injustice, and became a symbol of resistance against the hated Umayyads.

By all accounts, Abū Bilāl exercised moderation during his rebellion. Both Sunni and Ibāḍī sources preserve Abū Bilāl's speeches in which he pledged to defend himself only against those who attacked his band.[56] In addition, after capturing the man carrying the Umayyad taxes and allotments (*'atā'*), Abū Bilāl took only his and his men's fixed share and then returned the rest to the Umayyad carrier.[57] This moderation earned him the lasting respect of the Ibāḍiyya, who eulogized Abū Bilāl's rebellion as a paradigm for all just uprisings.

Like other heroes, Abū Bilāl is presented as invincible in the face of impossible odds, and his military prowess became legendary.[58] According to the sources, he and his forty men defeated an Umayyad force of two thousand sent against them.[59] This victory, though probably exaggerated, highlighted Abū Bilāl's role as champion of the Basrans and Khārijites. As the champion of justice in the face of injustice, his myth showed that a small force of determined men could defeat the corrupt Umayyads. So humiliating was this defeat for the Umayyad commander Aslama b. Zur'a that 'Ubayd Allāh officially banned heckling Aslama in the market.[60] Abū Bilāl also earned the love of the populace through canceling their taxes, an action that undoubtedly strengthened his connection with the general public.

As is common in stories of noble heroes, their deaths occur not through weakness or hubris (which they are not shown to possess), but through betrayal.[61] Accordingly, Abū Bilāl and his men died through the deceitfulness of the Umayyad general, 'Abbād b. Akhḍar al-Māzinī.[62] Faced with an army of four thousand, Abū Bilāl and his men fought until the time of prayer. They then agreed with 'Abbād to cease fighting, put down their weapons and pray. Abū Bilāl's men put down their weapons and began to pray, but in between prostrations the Umayyad army fell upon them and slaughtered them where they sat.[63] This kind of duplicity by the heroes' enemies served to highlight the righteous nature of Abū Bilāl in contrast to his opponents: Abū Bilāl's piety is exaggerated by his murder during the prayer, in a state of ritual consecration, while his enemy's treachery is all the more perfidious thereby.

Although the historical and mythical elements of Abū Bilāl's story are hopelessly intertwined, it is the image of Abū Bilāl that survived and established his popularity. This image even transcended sectarian boundaries; he was the hero of the Basran people, who cherished and preserved his memory and later made it part of their sectarian narratives. Both Ibāḍites and Ṣufrites looked to him as one of their founding leaders.[64] In addition, Mu'tazilites and Shi'ites claimed him as one of their own.[65] This widespread popularity across sectarian lines indicates the level of Abū Bilāl's appeal as hero and martyr among the general Islamic population.

Like that of Abū Bilāl, Ḥamza al-Khārijī's story contains obviously mythologized elements that reflect Ḥamza's status as a popular hero. Ḥamza b. Ādhrak al-Khārijī began his career as a *shārī* in 181/797 as the result of an altercation with a local administrator (*amel*) in his village of Raven-va-Jul. Although the *Tārīkh-e Sistān* only states that Ḥamza left his village to begin a pilgrimage because "the administrator wanted to destroy him," it is clear that the author links Ḥamza's career as a Khārijite rebel with the injustice of the administrator.[66] Ḥamza returned from his pilgrimage with a group of supporters of Qaṭarī b. al-Fujā'a al-Azraqī, and became the leader of the Sistānī Khārijites who seceded from the Khalafiyya Khārijites in Khurāsān.[67] During his tenure as Khārijī military leader, Ḥamza reportedly defeated all armies sent against him. At the same time, Ḥamza was described as merciful in his dealings with the populace: upon arriving at the gates of Sistān and preparing to lay siege to the city, Ḥamza heard the "numerous prayer chants and calls to prayer emanating from the city."[68] Ḥamza, realizing that "the sword cannot prevail against a city that so esteems and praises God," refused to wage war against the people of the city, but invited the 'Abbasid army to fight outside of the city gates. Likewise, in a show of mercy to the population of Sistān, Ḥamza abolished 'Abbasid taxation, ordering the populace not to "give another *dirham* in taxes and goods to the governor." As the Islamic equivalent of taking from the rich and giving to the poor, the actions of Ḥamza portray him as an excellent example of the heroic robber.

Just as Abū Bilāl's heroic narrative revolves around his role as champion of justice, so Ḥamza is also presented as a champion of justice. The *Tārīkh-e Sistān* preserved a letter from Ḥamza, a response to the missive of the 'Abbasid Caliph Harūn al-Rashīd, in which Ḥamza explained his reason for fighting as combating injustice on the part of the local officials:

> As for what has been related to you regarding my wars against your governors, these wars did not take place because I disputed your

> authority, nor because of my desire for worldly gain, or prestige, or fame; nor did I begin hostilities with any of the governors, although their bad conduct is known to all. They have taken lives, confiscated property, and committed debauchery, and other acts which God prohibited man from doing.[69]

Ḥamza's self-proclaimed motive for rebellion remained the establishment of justice and the righting of wrongs. In addition, the *Tārīkh-e Sistān* reports that before Ḥamza left Sistān to fight in India, he instructed his followers not to permit tyrants to oppress the weak.[70] Thus, Ḥamza's dedication to the principle of justice made him a prime example of the hero in early Islamic history.

In contrast to Abū Bilāl and Ḥamza, the figures of Ṣāliḥ b. Musarriḥ and Shabīb b. Yazīd present a different type of hero: what Hobsbawm calls the bandit avenger.[71] As Robinson notes, Muslim historians have taken liberties with the historical text in an effort to present the rebellions of Ṣāliḥ and Shabīb as contiguous.[72] What in fact were two consecutive and apparently nonrelated rebellions in the Jazīra have been transformed into a seamless uprising. However, what is of interest is not the historical separateness of Ṣāliḥ and Shabīb's uprising, but their contrived connectedness.

In the story as it is preserved, Shabīb derives his legitimacy from his connection to Ṣāliḥ b. Musarriḥ, who presented himself (in his speeches) as someone who fought against the impiety and tyranny of the Umayyads. In these renderings, Ṣāliḥ has something of the champion about him. However, his extreme views, if we accept as authentic the accounts of his speeches preserved by Qabīṣa b. 'Abd al-Raḥmān in the reports of Abū Mikhnaf, resembled those of the Azāriqa and would not have endeared him to the majority of Muslims (unlike Abū Bilāl, who clearly enjoyed mass popularity even across sectarian lines).[73] Nor were Ṣāliḥ's military exploits spectacular: he took riding animals from the Umayyad authorities in 76/695, and raided the villages in the area of Nisibis, Dārā, and Sinjār. Shortly thereafter he was defeated and killed by an Umayyad army.

Ṣāliḥ's appeal lay, rather, in his piety and his ability to inspire his followers, even after his death. Al-Ṭabarī reports, via Abū Mikhnaf, that he was an ascetic whose face became yellow (*muṣaffar al-wajh*) from excessive prayers.[74] His speeches called on the Muslim tribesmen of the Jazīra to follow the example of the tribesmen of the Prophet's day and rise up against the unbelievers (by whom Ṣāliḥ meant the Umayyads). Equally important to the story is the fact that Ṣāliḥ endorsed Shabīb as his successor: "I have chosen Shabīb even though he is not the most learned among you; he is, however, a courageous man (*shujā'*) and a scourge (*muhīb*) to your enemy."[75] Ṣāliḥ's power reached its height after his death; Ibn Qutayba mentions that no Jazīran Kharijite would rebel without first shaving his head at the tomb of Ṣāliḥ in Mosul.[76] This is precisely, according to the same source, what Shabīb did before launching his rebellion.

Shabīb's rebellion, it seems, was more successful than Ṣāliḥ's, and the stories preserved about him contain the elements of myth that transformed him into a hero. Shabīb led his group of Kharijites south through Nahrawān, al-Madā'in, and Kūfa and then north to Khūzistān. Facing ever-greater numbers of Umayyad forces, Shabīb, rather than attempting to defeat his opponents, engaged in military activities to humiliate them. His exploits, none of which were particularly noble, portray Shabīb as avenging the poor on their oppressors. As such, Shabīb's image rested on his ability to inspire terror and on his bravado. Shabīb's myth is replete with examples of this type of behavior. Among the more colorful exploits was his taking of the mosque in Kūfa. Shabīb beat on the door of al-Ḥajjāj's palace in Kūfa, and then stormed the mosque to lead his group in prayers.[77] Such bravado earned Shabīb the title of "illustrious horseman and mighty champion" in an early Syriac Christian source.[78] Likewise, al-Ṭabarī preserves a dialogue with Shabīb and the Christians of al-Batt in which the Christians hail Shabīb as their hero. Shabīb's justice is contrasted to the injustice of the Umayyads, whom the townspeople describe as "tyrants; they will not be spoken to and will not accept a plea (*'udhr*)."[79]

Rather than specific acts of nobility or restraint, Shabīb's heroism and bravery in the face of superior Umayyad forces earned him the respect of the Jazīran townspeople. Because Shabīb defied the Umayyads, the local population loved him. His role was that of symbolizing a collective discontent with the rulers from Damascus. More than any specific act of nobility or restraint, it was Shabīb's lack of restraint and violent rebellion that earned him a place in the mythology of the early Khārijite *shurāt*.

This examination of the early Khārijite narratives about the *shurāt* illuminates certain aspects of the Khārijite myth cycles: they were popular, and expressed a primitive form of rebellion through their longing for justice. As myth cycles, the *shurāt* narratives perpetuated a heroic image associated with the pious bravado and martyrdom (that is, the quality of *shirā'*) of these early Khārijite figures. Although the institution of *shirā'* in early Khārijite history remained one of charismatic individuals rather than political authorities, the value of the Khārijī *shurāt* legends as propaganda endowed them with a narrative authority; the heroic image of the Khārijite *shurāt* could inspire further acts of *shirā'* or sway the sympathies of those who heard the narrative of the *shurāt*. It was precisely this popularity that made such narratives ripe for appropriation by emerging sectarian groups.

The Iraqi Khārijite *Shurāt* Cycle and Its Appropriation

A collection of *shurāt* narratives, similar to those outlined above, circulated in Iraqi during the second/eighth century. This collection formed an indigenous Iraqi Khārijite myth cycle that functioned as a precedent for the Ibāḍī notion of *shirā'* and the *imām al-shārī*. Although the early Ibāḍiyya undoubtedly inherited this Iraqi *shurāt* cycle as the natural consequence of their formation in Basra, no record of it exists in early ("formative") Ibāḍī sources. Nevertheless, numerous other sources attest to its existence, including early Khārijite poetry, Sunni texts, and medieval Ibāḍī sources. Moreover, the recurrence of the same individuals across various textual traditions proves that the Iraqi cycle concerned a relatively fixed set of individuals and their narratives; the Iraqi *shurāt* cycle consisted, for the most part, of stories of individuals who were considered Khārijī *shurāt*. However, one figure, 'Ammār b. Yāsir, was claimed by the mainstream (both Sunni and Shi'ite) traditions as well by the Khārijites. In addition, the Ibāḍiyya later added two indigenous (and non-Iraqi) Ibāḍī rebels, 'Abdullāh b. Yaḥya and al-Julanda b. Mas'ūd, to the cycle.

It should be noted that the charismatic appeal and propaganda value of the *shurāt* narratives made them a battleground for competing sectarian groups. That is, different sectarian groups appropriated the authority of the early Khārijite figures and put them to different uses. In the case of 'Ammār b. Yāsir, even his status as a Khārijite or Shi'ite was contested. The divergence between Khārijī, Shi'ite, and mainstream Muslim appropriations of the early Muslim heroes must be borne in mind for two reasons. First, the dichotomy of interpretation remains important for an understanding of the sources. Sunni texts portray the early Khārijite *shurāt* according to their perception of them as rebels (*bughāt*), while the Khārijites and Ibāḍites wished to portray the *shurāt* as heroes and martyrs who engaged in the pious practice of *shirā'*. Second, this difference in interpretation of the role of the Khārijite rebels/*shurāt* represents a conscious judgment with ideological ramifications. By treating the early Khārijites as rebels (*bughāt*), Sunni authors wished to dissociate the Khārijites from the laudable actions of *jihād* and *shahāda*.[80] Conversely, the Khārijites and Ibāḍites portrayed the *shurāt* as *mujāhidūn* and *shuhadā'* precisely because they wanted to associate them with the piety associated with these actions, and to appropriate these figures for their own ends.

The stories of the *shurāt*, as they are preserved in Sunni, Ibāḍī, and early Khārijite sources, exist in the form of "fictive truths." That is, the narratives of the heroic figures and martyrs have been appropriated and manipulated toward sectarian ends by the various groups who preserved their stories. "Fictive truths" are narratives that depict a significant occurrence without being burdened by strict application of historical or factual accuracy. What is essential to the fictive truth is not the actual happening of an event or the authentic existence of a character, but rather the necessity of conceiving, developing, and representing the important incident. As such, its style of language remains normative: it directs its audience to see the truths it is trying to glorify.[81] The different sectarian appropriations of the individuals who make up the early Iraqi *shurāt* cycle must be acknowledged so that the different sectarian interpretations of their narratives may be examined.

The existence of an Iraqi *shurāt* cycle will first be established by a comparison of Sunni texts, early Khārijite poetry, and medieval Ibāḍī sources. Attention will be paid to the different ways in which these traditions adapted the image of the *shurāt*, because the method of appropriation will show how non-Khārijite sources (that is, the Sunni and pro-ʿAlid traditions) either claimed certain figures for their own (as in the case of ʿAmmār b. Yāsir or Abū Bilāl) or denigrated the *shurāt* as rebels. The early Khārijite method of adopting the *shurāt* will be the most difficult to establish due to a general lack of sources from the early Khārijites. Nevertheless, references to the early Iraqi *shurāt* survive in early Khārijite poetry. In addition, the medieval Ibāḍī appropriation of the Iraqi *shurāt* cycle as a fictive truth offers clues as to how the Ibāḍiyya transformed the essentially heroic image of the *shurāt* into a precedent for a political institution; the Ibāḍiyya portrayed the early Iraqi *shurāt* as Imāms, or as the models for Imāms. Although this claim was surely ideological, it created a potent precedent for the institution of the *imām al-shārī*.

It is important to remember that the medieval Ibāḍī lists of *shurāt* include several individuals who, historically speaking, existed long before the emergence of the Ibāḍiyya in Basra and, in the case of ʿAmmār b. Yāsir, before the formation of the Muḥakkima at the Battle of Ṣiffīn. The stories surrounding the martyrdom of ʿAmmār b. Yāsir illustrate the way in which a hero can be claimed by Khārijites, Shiʿites, and Sunnis alike, and used to serve whatever sectarian interest the editor of their narrative might require. ʿAmmār's example works particularly well in this respect. Due to his early association with the Prophet, and his death at the Battle of Ṣiffīn, each sect group wanted to claim ʿAmmār as their partisan, and fashioned their narratives accordingly.[82] The pro-ʿAlid author Abū Mikhnaf portrays ʿAmmār as an early Companion of the Prophet Muhammad, and uses his story to highlight the illegitimacy of the Umayyad regime. The story, as given in al-Ṭabarī on the authority of Abū Mikhnaf, begins with anecdotes about ʿAmmār and the Prophet, specifically the Prophet's praise for ʿAmmār and his promise that he would see paradise. This narration tells how the Prophet foretold that ʿAmmār would be killed by a "rebellious party" (*al-fiʾa al-bāghiya*).[83] This narrative provides the background necessary to cast Muʿāwiya (and by association the Umayyads) as the enemy of Islam.

Abu Mikhnaf's narrative portrays 'Ammār fighting on the side of 'Alī's army at the Battle of Ṣiffīn; his death in the struggle against Mu'āwiya identifies Mu'āwiya's supporters as the "rebellious party" mentioned by the Prophet. The "martyrdom" of 'Ammār as it appears in this context is directly related to making the Umayyads appear to have been condemned by the Prophet, an enterprise in keeping with the pro-'Alid concerns of the 'Abbasid era. The death of 'Ammār thus directly challenges the legitimacy of the Umayyads while portraying 'Ammār as solidly within the pro-'Alid tradition.

The story of 'Ammār as it appears in Ibāḍī sources is, not surprisingly, different. The text contains the same stories that establish 'Ammār as a pious individual to whom the Prophet promised paradise.[84] However, 'Ammār espouses the Khārijite line that the enemies should be fought until they "return to the command of God" or are totally defeated.[85] 'Ammār's speech at Ṣiffīn is a paraphrase of 49:9, which is simultaneously the verse cited by the Ibāḍiyya as proof against the arbitration.[86] Moreover, 'Ammār, before his martyrdom, explicitly warns 'Alī against arbitration with Mu'āwiya.[87] These acts cast 'Ammār as sympathetic to the Khārijite interpretation of the events at Ṣiffīn, and thereby portray him as a proto-Khārijite. His martyrdom challenges the foundation of Umayyad authority, while his association with the Khārijite interpretation of the events of Ṣiffīn lends legitimacy to the Khārijite cause.

Although the dual interpretations of 'Ammār's affiliation ('Ammār the pro-'Alid and 'Ammār the proto-Khārijite) cannot both be historically accurate, they share a core narrative that portrays 'Ammār's death as a discredit to the Umayyads. It is this core narrative of martyrdom that gives 'Ammār's story its power. Once 'Ammār became a symbol of legitimacy against the Umayyads, various protest groups rushed to assert solidarity with him. In claiming 'Ammār as their own, they fashioned his story to fulfill their specific sectarian requirements. In addition to using 'Ammār's story to bolster their own sectarian image, Omani Ibāḍī jurists present 'Ammār as one of their early predecessors; al-Kindī includes 'Ammār among those he lists as one of the preservers of the true (that is, the Ibāḍī) religion;[88] Abū Mu'thir portrays 'Ammār as one of the early "Imāms" of the Muslims (*ā'immat al-muslimīn*);[89] Munīr b. Nayyar al-Ja'lānī presents 'Ammār as one of the "good examples" (*uswa ḥasana*) for the Muslims and their leaders.[90] In this manner, the medieval Ibāḍiyya appropriated the image of 'Ammār by including him among the early supporters and Imāms of the sect.

The Iraqi *shurāt* cycle also incorporated the Khārijites who were killed fighting Mu'āwiya at Nukhayla, a small plain outside of Kūfa. Al-Mubarrad, using an account from Abū al-'Abbās, reports that the People of Nukhayla were those who rejected the leadership of 'Abdullāh b. Wahb al-Rāsibī at Nahrawān by refusing to fight against 'Alī and abandoning the battlefield.[91] Al-Ṭabarī, on the authority of

'Awāna, mentions their number as five hundred, under the leadership of Farwa b. Nawfal al-Ashja'ī.[92] After the defeat of the Khārijites at Nahrawān, the remaining Khārijites at Nukhayla prepared to fight Mu'awiya as he camped in Kūfa.[93]

According to 'Awāna's report in al-Ṭabarī, the remaining Khārijites decided to attack Mu'āwiya when he approached Kūfa. Although Mu'āwiya sent a contingent of Syrian cavalry to meet them, his cavalry was defeated. Exasperated, Mu'āwiya threatened the Kūfans, goading them to fight the Khārijites. The Khārijites attempted to dissuade the Kūfans from attacking them, claiming that Mu'āwiya was their mutual enemy, but the Kūfans insisted on fighting. In a final dramatic flair, the narrative tells of how the Khārijites repented of leaving their fallen brethren at Nahrawān: "They knew you better, Oh people of Kūfa!"[94] In the end of this narrative, the Kūfans slaughtered the Khārijites of Nukhayla, implying that Mu'āwiya and nameless "Kufans" were to blame for the destruction of the Nukhaylites. Their deaths simply underlined the ability of Mu'āwiya to bully others into fighting for him. Al-Ṭabarī achieves with this narrative the denigration of Mu'āwiya as representative of the Umayyad regime. That is, al-Ṭabarī's portrayal of the Umayyads must be understood in the context of the 'Abbasid era in which he wrote: 'Abbasid historians sought to devalue the formative figures of the Umayyads (such as Mu'āwiya) in order to make themselves appear justified in overthrowing them. Although writing about Khārijites, al-Ṭabarī's manipulation of the story achieves this objective of maligning the Umayyads.

From the early Khārijite and Ibāḍite perspective, the Basran Khārijite poet 'Irmān b. Hiṭṭān (d. 84/703) preserved a line of poetry in which he names the *ahl Nukhayla* as *shurāt*, and declares his approval of them: "I profess that which the *shurāt* professed on the day of Nukhayla."[95] Little else survives from the early Khārijites regarding the *ahl Nukhayla*. Nevertheless, the story of the martyrs of Nukhayla, as it appears in medieval Ibāḍī sources, is presented in a slightly different manner from 'Awāna's report in al-Ṭabarī. In al-Qalhātī's version, as in Ibn Qaḥṭān's, the Kūfans were specified as followers of 'Alī's son al-Ḥasan—in other words, they are specifically identified as partisans (*shī'a*) of 'Alī.[96] In the Ibāḍī version, al-Ḥasan surrendered his right to rule to Mu'āwiya, and then rode to fight the people of Nukhayla in solidarity with Mu'āwiya. Al-Ḥasan reminded his followers that they pledged allegiance to him on the condition that they fight whom al-Ḥasan fought, and make peace with those who made peace with al-Ḥasan. To underscore al-Ḥasan's unity with Mu'āwiya, al-Ḥasan declared to his followers, "I have made peace with Mu'āwiya."[97] In the Ibāḍī version, it is al-Ḥasan's army that slaughtered the Nukhaylites.[98] This version of the martyrdom of the Nukhaylites leaves no doubt that Ibāḍī authors wish the martyrdom to be understood as the fault of 'Alī's supporters acting in collusion with the wishes of Mu'āwiya. 'Alī's supporters and Mu'āwiya are cast as equally responsible for the martyrdom of the Nukhaylites.

This openly anti-Shi'ite line reflects the later concerns of the Ibāḍī scholars Ibn Qaḥṭān and al-Qalhātī.[99] The scholar Abū Qaḥṭān Khālid b. Qaḥṭān lived in Oman in the third/ninth century during the reign of the Omani Imām al-Muhannā b. Jayfar (reigned 227–237/841–851).[100] At this time, the North African Ibāḍī imāmate was facing increased Ismā'īlī activity in Tūnis, as well as the Shi'ite Idrīsids on their western border. The Omani and Ḥaḍramawtī Ibāḍiyya had contact with Zaydī Shi'ism through the Yemen. Although the Ibāḍiyya in Tahert were known for their tolerance of different sects, anti-Shi'ite propaganda was not below them when it served their interests.[101]

Similarly, Abū Sa'īd Muhammad b. Sa'īd al-Qalhātī was an Ibāḍī scholar who lived in Oman in the sixth/twelfth century. By al-Qalhātī's time, the Fātimids had destroyed the Ibāḍīs of Tahert, and anti-Shi'ite polemics had become a well-entrenched discipline among Ibāḍīs. Al-Qalhātī himself devotes several pages of his heresiographical *al-Kashf wa al-Bayān* to anti-Shi'ite argumentation.[102]

Among the other uses to which the medieval Ibāḍiyya put the story of the *ahl Nukhayla*, Ibāḍī jurists unabashedly claim them as Ibāḍī martyrs, Imāms, and affiliates (*awliyā'*) in religion. Abū Mu'thir describes Farwa b. Nawfal al-Ashja'ī and Wadā' b. Ḥawthara al-Asadī, along with those who were killed on the "day of Nukhayla" as martyrs.[103] Similarly, Munīr b. Nayyar al-Ja'lānī includes them among the predecessors of the Ibāḍiyya, and lists them along with the other "good models" of conduct for the Ibāḍīs.[104]

Like 'Ammār and the *ahl Nukhayla*, other figures in early Khārijite history became part of the Iraqi Khārijite myth cycle. Al-Ṭabarī, on the authority of Abū Zayd, names the first Khārijites to rebel in Basra after the Battle of Nahrawān as Sahm b. Ghālib al-Tamīmī and Yazīd b. Mālik al-Bāhilī, known as al-Khaṭīm.[105] With seventy men, they raised their rebellion in 44/664, killing in the process a man that they found near a bridge outside Basra. The governor, Ibn 'Āmir, pardoned them after they surrendered, but they rebelled again during the reign of the governor Ziyād b. Abīhi. Fleeing to the Ahwāz (southwestern Iran), Sahm and al-Khaṭīm killed those who refused to profess Khārijism.[106] Nothing came of this rebellion, and Sahm returned to Basra abandoned by his companions. He surrendered to the governor, expecting clemency, but was crucified at the door of the governor's palace. Al-Khaṭīm was banished to Bahrain, but returned to Basra and was placed under house arrest. The leader of his tribe executed him when he broke the conditions of his arrest.[107] As is clear, the story of Sahm and al-Khaṭīm in Sunni sources presents them as simple rebels.

Early Khārijī poetry, on the other hand, suggests that the Khārijites revered Sahm to a certain extent. A line of anonymous Khārijī poetry exists that praises

Sahm: "If the parties will admit to crucifying him, God will not abandon Sahm b. Ghālib."[108] Evidence for the admiration of Sahm and al-Khaṭīm in medieval Ibāḍī sources is likewise scant. Nevertheless, Munīr b. Nayyar al-Ja'lānī lists the Companions of al-Khaṭīm (*aṣḥāb al-Khaṭm*) as predecessors in religion.[109] This acknowledgment of obscure Khārijī rebels in a medieval Ibāḍī text lends credence to the suggestion that the early Ibāḍiyya inherited an Iraqi *shurāt* cycle and put it to their own uses.

Among the more well-attested Basran Khārijite *shurāt* were Qarīb b. Murra and Zuḥḥāf b. Zuḥar al-Ṭā'ī. According to Wahb b. Jarīr's account in al-Ṭabarī, they were the first to rebel in Basra after Nahrawān (apparently al-Ṭabarī forgot that this honor was also bestowed on Sahm and al-Khaṭīm).[110] Their rebellion was short lived, and they were both killed fighting around Basra in 50/670. The sources mention that they killed a Shaykh who they mistook for the leader of Ziyād b. Abīhi's police force. Al-Baghdādī and al-Balādhūrī corroborate this accusation with reports that Qarīb and Zuḥḥāf engaged in random killing (*isti'rāḍ*),[111] which earned them the condemnation of Abū Bilāl.[112] Thus, the image of Qarīb and Zuḥḥāf in the Sunni sources is that of two rebels who slaughtered those who did not profess Khārijism; so horrible was their rebellion that a fellow Khārijī, Abū Bilāl, condemned them.

Only one poem from the early Khārijites preserves the memory of Qarīb and Zuḥḥāf: an anonymous Khārijī poem that eulogizes Zuḥḥāf as "the humble Zuḥḥāf."[113] Medieval Ibāḍī sources, however, revere Qarīb and Zuḥḥāf as predecessors, martyrs, and leaders of the *shurāt*: al-Jā'lānī lists Qarīb and Zuḥḥāf among those who function as models for Ibāḍī behavior;[114] Abū Mu'thir describes them as martyrs;[115] and al-Darjīnī lists them among the first generation (*ṭabaqa*) of Ibāḍīs.[116] Importantly, a North African Ibāḍī source describes them as leaders of *shurāt*: al-Talātī, in his commentary on al-Shammākhī's *Muqaddimat al-Tawḥīd*, includes Qarīb and Zuḥḥāf among those leaders who engaged in the practice of *shirā'* with no fewer than forty persons.[117] From these examples, it is obvious that Ibāḍī sources unambiguously identify Qarīb and Zuḥḥāf with the *shurāt*, and appropriate their images so that they appear as models for Ibāḍī behavior, or as members of the first Ibāḍī generation. These same traditions remember Qarīb and Zuḥḥāf as martyrs and heroes, despite Abū Bilāl's disapproval of them, and the fact that their rebellion only served as an excuse for Ziyād to persecute the Basran Khārijites. While it is possible that the medieval Ibāḍī sources for information on Qarīb and Zuḥḥāf contained no information on the details of their uprising, it is more plausible to believe that the heroic image of Qarīb and Zuḥḥāf was more useful to the Ibāḍiyya as a means of consolidating opposition against the Umayyads than the brutality of Qarīb and Zuḥḥāf's actions. If the Ibāḍīs coopted an already extant Khārijī tradition of hero narratives in order to bolster their own sense of legitimacy and authenticity, it would be difficult to selectively renounce certain individuals. Thus, the heroic image of Qarīb and Zuḥḥāf as martyrs, purged of its potentially embarrassing details, persisted among the Ibāḍiyya.

The figure of Abū Bilāl Mirdās b. Udaya, his myth cycle, and popularity among the early Khārijite poets have already been discussed above. What needs to be mentioned here is that many of the stories about Abū Bilāl in medieval Ibāḍī texts match those found in the Sunni materials, suggesting a common source for Abū Bilāl's narrative. For example, both Sunni and Ibāḍī sources preserve the stories about Abū Bilāl returning to his jail cell after being informed about the impending execution of the Khārijite prisoners; about the execution of al-Baljā' that prompted Abū Bilāl's rebellion; and about the treachery of 'Abbād b. Akhḍar al-Māzinī that resulted in the slaughter of Abū Bilāl and his followers while they prayed.[118] Although the common source of the Abū Bilāl cycle remains unnamed and therefore unknown, its existence illustrates Abū Bilāl's widespread popularity, and accounts for his place in the Iraqi *shurāt* cycle.

In addition, medieval Ibāḍī jurisprudence mentions Abū Bilāl as a martyr, predecessor, and leader of *shurāt*: Abū Mu'thir includes Abū Bilāl in his list of martyrs and Imāms;[119] al-Ja'lānī presents him as one of the pious predecessors to the Ibāḍiyya;[120] al-Darjīnī includes him in the first *ṭabaqa* (generation) of Ibāḍīs;[121] and al-Talātī describes him as a leader of the *shurāt*.[122] Likewise, the North African jurist Abū Zakariyya names Abū Bilāl as an example of a leader during the stage of *shirā'*, thus explicitly connecting Abū Bilāl with the concept of the *imām al-shārī*.[123]

The diffusion of a similar set of individuals across a wide and varied group of texts suggests the existence of a fixed tradition of Iraqi heroes and martyrs. Although no single source contains all of their names, comparisons of Sunni texts, early Khārijite poetry, and Ibāḍī sources yields a compelling correspondence among the identities of these Iraqi Khārijite individuals. Moreover, Khārijite poetry and medieval Ibāḍī jurisprudence identifies these same individuals as martyrs, heroes, and persons who engaged in *shirā'*, implying the existence of an Iraqi *shurāt* cycle.

In addition to the individuals who made up the Khārijite Iraqi *shurāt* cycle, medieval Ibāḍī authors add two other figures to their list of martyrs and heroes. In their attempts to establish Ibāḍī political entities in North Africa, the Yemen, and Oman, the Ibāḍīs engaged in military exploits aimed at establishing an Ibāḍī state. Many of these attempts failed, but later came to be regarded as acts of *shirā'*. For example, Abū Mu'thir mentions among the Imāms and martyrs of the early Ibāḍiyya the Imām 'Abdullāh b. Yaḥya (Ṭālib al-Ḥaqq) and his companion, Abū Ḥamza al-Mukhtār b. 'Awf, as well as the Omani Imām al-Julanda b. Mas'ūd.[124] Like their earlier Basran counterparts, these Ibāḍī *shurāt* narratives possessed a semi-legendary quality, and were used for the purpose of focusing attention on the righteousness of the Ibāḍī cause while simultaneously rallying and support for it. As the addition of the title Imām suggests, the heroic images of Ṭālib al-Ḥaqq and al-Julanda b. Mas'ūd for Ibāḍīs centered on their attempts to establish political entities, more so than on their roles as popular champions of justice. Their heroic exploits, to a certain extent, remained incidental to their function as founders of political centers in Ḥaḍramawt and Oman. This shift away from the ideological role of the *shurāt* (as champions of justice or avengers) toward a political role (as Imāms) represents an important shift in the development of the concept of *shirā'* under the Ibāḍīs. *Shirā'* became the attempt to establish an Ibāḍī polity, and the leaders of the *shurāt* thereby came to be regarded as political leaders (Imāms).

Another critical difference between the early Iraqi *shurāt* and later Ibāḍī *shurāt* lies in the fact that the later Ibāḍī rebels had a greater chance of success. Early Iraqi rebels were often outnumbered, and faced an organized and determined Umayyad army. They knew their cause was hopeless, and their heroic image incorporated their reckless pursuit of death in the name of fighting injustice. The later Ibāḍī rebels, on the other hand, operated with moderate chances of success. This gave their rebellions a political edge that the early Iraqi Khārijites only sporadically enjoyed. Undoubtedly, it also contributed to their image as Imāms.

The example of 'Abdullāh b. Yaḥya, who assumed the title of Ṭālib al-Ḥaqq, illustrates the shift toward treating the Ibāḍī *shurāt* as political and administrative figures. Ṭālib al-Ḥaqq began his revolt in Ḥaḍramawt in 130/747 amid the degeneration of the Umayyad caliphate. Seizing Ṣan'ā', the seat of the Umayyad governor, Ibn Yaḥya sent Abū Ḥamza al-Mukhtār b. 'Awf north to capture Makka.[125] Abū Ḥamza's lieutenant, Balj b. 'Ukba al-Azdī, also took Madīna in 131/748. An Umayyad army sent by Marwān II, however, halted the Ibāḍī advance in the Ḥijāz and recaptured Makka and Madīna. Abū Ḥamza was hung, while 'Abdullāh b. Yaḥya died in the battle with Umayyad forces north of Ṣan'ā'.[126]

The application of the title "martyr" and *shārī* to 'Abdullāh b. Yaḥya appears somewhat formal in comparison to the commemoration of the exploits of heroes like Abū Bilāl. Ṭālib al-Ḥaqq was primarily an administrator whose main accomplishments were the establishment of a short-lived Ibāḍī polity in Ṣan'ā'. Ibāḍī sources praise him for equitably distributing the wealth of Ṣan'ā' among its *'ulamā'* and insisting on the application of *sharī'a* punishments for crimes such as theft and adultery. Although undoubtedly pious and brave, Ṭālib al-Ḥaqq's exploits lack the popular heroics of earlier Iraqi heroes. Nonetheless, al-Darjīnī describes 'Abdullāh b. Yaḥya, Abū Ḥamza, and their companions as *shurāt*.[127]

Similarly, the heroic narrative of al-Julanda b. Mas'ūd focuses attention on the deeds of al-Julanda as an Imām, rather than as a champion of justice or avenger of wrongs. One year after the destruction of the Ibāḍī polity in the Yemen, Ibāḍī *'ulamā'* in Oman appointed al-Julanda b. Mas'ūd to lead an Ibāḍī uprising against the newly established 'Abbasid regime.[128] After successfully defeating other members of the Julanda tribe who sought to limit his power, al-Julanda b. Mas'ūd sent his lieutenants Hilāl b. 'Aṭīyya al-Khurasānī and Yaḥya b. Najīḥ to meet a Khārijite army—Ibāḍī sources call them Ṣufrites—led by Shaybān al-Khārijī.[129] Slaughtering their Khārijite brethren, al-Julanda claimed the sword and seal of Shaybān as his prize. Upon the request of the 'Abbasid governor to Oman, Khāzim b. Khuzayma al-Khurasānī, al-Julanda surrendered these items to the 'Abbasids. However, despite this accommodating gesture to the 'Abbasids, they soon set out to destroy the Ibāḍī rebels with an army under Ibn Khuzayma. The Ibāḍī forces, led by al-Julanda, were defeated by the 'Abbasids in 133/750. In an anecdotal story related by al-Sālimī, the 'Abbasids killed all but al-Julanda b. Mas'ūd and Hilāl b. 'Aṭīyya. Al-Julanda then invited Hilāl to be the first to die, but Hilāl replied, "You are my Imām, so be ahead of me" (*inta imāmī fa-kun amāmī*). Al-Julanda then achieved his martyrdom, followed by Hilāl.[130] Like Ṭālib al-Ḥaqq, al-Julanda's martyrdom is a formality bestowed on a figure that is primarily remembered as an Imām. Although al-Julanda's martyrdom narrative retains the heroic quality of earlier martyrs, his importance lies in his role as founder of the political Ibāḍī entity in Oman. Nevertheless, the figures of 'Abdullāh b. Yaḥya and al-Julanda b. Mas'ūd became appended to the Ibāḍī *shurāt* cycle. Ibāḍī use of the title Imām in connection with their exploits suggests a move toward affiliation of *shirā'* with temporal authority.

Despite the implications of the association between the notion of *shirā'* and the imāmate of 'Abdullāh b. Yaḥya and al-Julanda b. Mas'ūd, a general a lack of Khārijite and Ibāḍite sources from the early period makes it difficult to determine how, if at all, the notion of *shirā'* (that is, martyrdom and heroism) was connected to the idea of religiopolitical authority during the early Khārijite era. Evidence from the epistle of Sālim b. Dhakwān suggests that the early Ibāḍiyya actively encouraged (during their formative period) the practice of *shirā'* under the direction of an Imām. Sālim's epistle describes the position of leadership in the Ibāḍī community in terms reminiscent of the *imām al-shārī*, but Sālim does not use the terms *shirā'* or *imām al-shārī*: "We hold that a band of Muslims should pay allegiance to the Imām only on [the condition that he will wage] *jihād* in the path of God and that they will obey him in what is approved (*ma'rūf*), until they perish in that pursuit or prevail over the enemy."[131] As one of the earliest extant Ibāḍī texts, the epistle illustrates the early Ibāḍī encouragement of a practice that is the very definition of *shirā'*: *jihād* under an Imām who will lead the Ibāḍiyya to success, or perish in its pursuit. Nevertheless, although Ibn Dhakwān's epistle is suggestive of a link between the notion of *shirā'* and the enjoyment of temporal authority by an

Imām, undisputed evidence for the existence of the temporal office of the *imām al-shārī* comes only from the later medieval era.

One possible early Ibāḍī source for the medieval Ibāḍī interpretation of the Basran *shurāt* cycle is the now lost work of the last Basran Imām, Abū Sufyān Muḥbūb Ibn al-Raḥīl (d. mid-third/ninth century). Abū Sufyān's work, which was probably commissioned by the Rustumid Imām Aflaḥ Ibn 'Abd al-Wahhāb (ruled 250–255/864–868), was biographical in nature, and concerned with creating a line of development from the Khārijites who seceded at Nahrawān to the Ibāḍiyya of Abū Sufyān's day.[132] Large portions of the *Kitāb Abī Sufyān* survive in the biographical works of the North African historians al-Darjīnī, al-Shammākhī, Abu Zakariyya, and al-Barrādī. As Wilkinson observes, Abū Sufyān probably used an earlier source (also lost), an anecdotal and biographical treatment of the early Khārijites by Abū Yazīd al-Khwārzimī (d. mid-second/eighth century), who was a contemporary of the Basran Imām Abū 'Ubayda.[133] While Abū Sufyān's work survived primarily in North African texts, the scattered references to early Khārijite martyrs and heroes in Omani texts may ultimately be the influence of Abū Yazīd. Thus, the appropriation of the early Iraqi *shurāt* cycle by the North African and Omani Ibāḍiyya most likely commenced at a very early date, despite the lack of early Khārijite texts to prove this assertion.

The appropriation of the Iraqi *shurāt* cycle by the early Ibāḍiyya provided a precedent for the concept of *shirā'* and the creation, in the medieval Ibāḍī imāmate theory, of the office of the *shārī* Imām. By assimilating the popular myth cycle of heroes and martyrs, the Ibāḍiyya bolstered their own image by establishing an association between their sect and the early *shurāt*. In so doing, the Ibāḍiyya incorporated the concept of *shirā'* into their religious discourse, and cast the early Iraqi martyrs and heroes as predecessors and models for behavior. The perpetuation and association of the *shurāt*'s heroic image with the Ibāḍī sect continued into the early Ibāḍī period with early Ibāḍī martyr-Imāms Ṭālib al-Ḥaqq and al-Julanda b. Mas'ūd. In such a way, the notion of *shirā'* began to be connected to the notion of political authority.

The Medieval Ibāḍī Shārī Imām

The practical application of *shirā'* in the medieval Ibāḍī era, as well as the concentration of the leadership of the *shurāt* in the *imām al-shārī* represented a significant break with the practice of *shirā'* in the early Khārijite era. Medieval Ibāḍī jurists adapted the practice of *shirā'* to fit the needs of their political situations. That is, they created rules to contain and govern what had originally been a spontaneous and informal institution of martyrs and heroes. While preserving the concept of *shirā'* as a type of pious militancy, the medieval Ibāḍī adaptation of *shirā'* to the office of the *imām al-shārī* transformed it into an aspect of political authority.

Just as it does in the early Khārijite sources, the medieval Ibāḍī concept of *shirā'* denotes a type of pious militancy associated with martyrdom and heroism. Al-Talātī, a North African jurist, defines the concept of *shirā'* as "earning a reward by sacrificing one's self and one's money in the way of God."[134] Likewise, al-Kindī glosses the meaning of *shirā'* as selling something (in this case, the self) for a price.[135] Ibāḍī texts make it clear that *shirā'* involved militant actions to establish the rule of the Ibāḍiyya. These actions were to be prosecuted until the *shurāt* achieved success or died in the process.[136] This notion of *shirā'* matched the early Khārijite conception of *shirā'* as violent action for the purposes of establishing justice, an action that usually resulted in the deaths of the Khārijite *shurāt*.

Although the medieval Ibāḍī conception of *shirā'* was substantially the same as the early Khārijite notion of *shirā'*, the medieval Ibāḍiyya adapted the practice of *shirā'* to the needs of the Ibāḍī state. With the establishment of the Rustumid dynasty in Tahert and the first Ibāḍī dynasty in Oman, the practice of *shirā'* was recognized to have potentially dangerous implications for the Ibāḍī state; the inherent danger of *shirā'* lay in its latent ability to inspire rebellion in the name of Islamic justice. In an effort to diffuse the potentially destabilizing effect of *shirā'*, the Ibāḍī *'ulamā'* developed the office of *al-imām al-shārī* as the leader of the *shurāt*. Likewise, the term *shurāt*, which had once referred to the early Khārijite heroes, became divorced from its original heroic connotations and came to specify the volunteer Ibāḍī soldiers who defended the Ibāḍī state against its enemies.[137] In such a way, the practice of *shirā'* was kept under the control of the Ibāḍī state. As a result, the practice of *shirā'* changed from being a spontaneous practice to being a formal institution governed by social and legal regulations.

The practice of *shirā'* as such could not be imposed, as it was conceived as a voluntary action that was incumbent upon those who took it upon themselves. As the medieval North African jurist Abū 'Ammār put it: "our *'ulamā'* have not made the condition of *shirā'* a matter of obligation (*wujūb*) and duty (*farḍ*), as they have made the condition of *ẓuhūr* and the state (*dawla*): whoever wishes, let them sell their self for the pleasure of God, and whoever wishes, let them remain hidden (*muktatim*) among their people."[138] However, once Muslims accepted the duties of *shirā'*, they became obliged to follow certain tenets. For example, the Omani Ibāḍī jurist al-Kindī explains that a group of persons who wish to perform *shirā'* should pledge their allegiance to an Imām who would agree to lead them in the practice of *shirā'*.[139] The *shurāt* were required to follow him in his capacity as *imām al-shārī*. This Imām, according to the Omani jurist al-Bisyānī, should possess all the characteristics of a qualified Imām, in addition to his willingness to perform *shirā'*.[140]

Other regulations that were imposed on those who wished to practice *shirā'* involved giving up their obligations to the world; the *shurāt* were ideally required to forego marriage, pay their debts, and renounce their homes in order to prepare themselves for death in the way of God. This vision of the *shurāt* is preserved in a mytho-historical narrative attributed to Abū Bilāl, who addressed potential *shurāt* with the following advice:

> You go out to fight in the way of God desiring His pleasure, not wanting anything of the goods of the present world, nor have you any desire for it, nor will you return to it. You are the ascetic and the hater of this life, desirous of the world to come, trying with all in your power to obtain it: going out to be killed and for nothing else. So know that you are [already] killed and have no return to this life; you are going forward and will not turn away from righteousness till you come to God. If such is your concern, go back and finish up your needs and wishes for this life, pay your debts, purchase yourself, take leave of your family and tell them that you will never return to them. When you have done so I will accept your pledge.[141]

Here, the practice of *shirā'* became associated with ascetic conditions in addition to the requirement to perform *jihād* under the direction of an Imām. In a similar vein, the North African commentator al-Talātī explains that the *shurāt* should abandon fixed residences.[142]

Finally, Ibāḍī jurists sought to control the practice of *shirā'* by setting conditions on how many persons were required for its instigation. Abū Isḥāq, the fifth/eleventh-century Ḥaḍramawtī scholar, set the minimum number of followers required to support a *shārī* Imām at forty (following the model of Abū Bilāl, who rebelled with forty of his followers).[143] Likewise, al-Talātī states that the minimum number of individuals required to prosecute *shirā'* at forty, adding that they should fight until there are three of them remaining.[144] By imposing certain conditions of the practice of *shirā'*—especially the condition that it be headed by an Imām who would be recognized by the *'ulamā'*—the Ibāḍī *'ulamā'* effectively brought the potentially destabilizing effects of *shirā'* under their control.

Despite the similarities between the North African and Omani conception of *shirā'*, these communities conceptualized the *shārī* Imāms in different ways. These differences are the result of the divergent histories of the North African and Omani Ibāḍī communities. In North Africa, the institution of *al-imām al-shārī* remained a purely theoretical aspect of the North African Ibāḍī *imāma*, a reflection of the Ibāḍī inheritance of the early Iraqi Khārijite *shurāt* tradition, but no longer a living tradition. Certain historical figures in early Ibāḍī history, such as Abū Bilāl, Qarīb, and Zuḥḥāf, were retroactively cast as *shārī* Imāms, but no new leaders were acknowledged as such.[145] By appropriating the early Iraqi *shurāt*, the North African Ibāḍiyya maintained the important narrative of an unbroken chain of Imāms stretching back to the era of the Prophet. In this manner, the North African *'ulamā'* reinforced the legitimacy of the North African imāmate by presenting a continuous line of authoritative rule.

As a result of the theoretical nature of the *shārī* Imām in North Africa, the state of *shirā'* was conceived as a separate condition between that of *ẓuhūr* and *kitmān*. Al-Tanwātī explains:

> If the Muslims do not have the capacity for the *imāma*... it is better for them to act as they do in the state of *kitmān*, for that is permitted to them; except for those who bring on [themselves] the condition of *shirā'*: *shirā'* is one of the most beloved affairs of God and the Muslims. If they are not able to [bring about] *ẓuhūr* and a state (*dawla*), then [*shirā'*] is the closest stage (*masālik*) to *ẓuhūr*.[146]

This conception of the stage of *shirā'* separates it from the stage of *ẓuhūr* and *kitmān*, and implies that the *shārī* Imām was distinct from the Imāms who ruled during the stages of *ẓuhūr* and *kitmān*. Unfortunately, North African jurists did not develop the notion of the *shārī* Imām, and therefore it remains a somewhat vague institution: the state of *kitmān* in North African Ibāḍism, and the rule of the North African Ibāḍī community by their *'ulamā'*, precluded the need for the development of the institution of the *shārī* Imām except as a theoretical counterpart to the notions of *ẓuhūr*, *kitmān*, and *difā'*.

In Oman, on the other hand, the institution of the *shārī* Imām developed into a practical office. Medieval Omani Ibāḍī jurisprudence explicitly recognized the Omani Imām al-Muhannā b. Jayfar as a *shārī* Imām, and implied that the other Omani Imāms functioned as *shārī* Imāms. For example, the *'ālim* Abū 'Abdullāh Muhammad b. Maḥbūb (d. 260/873) censured the Ḥaḍramawtī Ibāḍīs for not having *shārī* Imāms like the Omanis: "It is our opinion that your path should be like the path of the people of Oman, who have elected for *shirā'* (*'aqd al-shirā'*) and this is the higher level."[147] The *shārī* Imām thus represented the Imām who possessed all the desirable traits of an Imām, and symbolized the highest level of leadership in the Omani Ibāḍī community.[148]

Like the North African Ibāḍiyya, the Omani Ibāḍīs appropriated the early Khārijite *shurāt* (especially Abū Bilāl) and requisitioned their images toward their own ends. In Oman, Ibāḍī historians employed the heroic image of the early Khārijite *shurāt* as a model for the volunteer Omani soldiers who defended Ibāḍī territory; and their leaders became models for the *shārī* Imāms. In addition, Ibāḍī historians portrayed the early Iraqi *shurāt* as martyrs, heroes, and predecessors to the Ibāḍiyya. In such a way, the early Iraqi *shurāt* added an aura of legitimacy to the later Ibāḍiyya who presumed to inherit the mantle of their authority.

The later history of *shirā'* is dominated by the Ibāḍī sect, who remained the only Khārijite sect to survive and develop the notion of *shirā'*. As inheritors of the Iraqi Khārijite traditions, the Ibāḍiyya incorporated the narratives of the *shurāt* into their own sectarian identity, and embraced the notion of *shirā'* as a valid method of fighting injustice. During their formative period, the Ibāḍīs labeled several ultimately unsuccessful rebellions acts of *shirā'*, and remembered their leaders as *shurāt*. With the establishment of Ibāḍī states in North Africa and Oman, the destabilizing potential of *shirā'* was contained by institutionalizing *shirā'* in the figure of *al-imām al-shārī*. The institution of the *shārī* Imām persisted in North Africa as a theoretical construct, and in Oman as a practical institution of authority.

The *shārī* Imām represents the third aspect of the medieval Ibāḍī imāmate that the Ibāḍiyya inherited from their predecessors in earlier eras. Like the qualities of piety and knowledge, *shirā'* became embedded in the Ibāḍī imāmate ideal. These three characteristics describe the traits that an Imām may or may not possess; they are three potential facets of the Imām's legitimate authority. There remains, however, another aspect of the Ibāḍī imāmate institution that corresponds to a different type of authority. This authority does not pertain to the Imām exclusively, but also concerns the role of the Ibāḍī community in relation to the Imām.

4

Imām al-Difā‘, Imām al-Ḍa‘īf, and Community

This chapter tells the story of the *imām al-difā‘* (the Imām of defense) and, as sometimes appears in Omani works of jurisprudence, the *imām al-ḍa‘īf* (weak Imām). More precisely, it addresses the equilibrium of powers and responsibilities that are negotiated between these types of Imāms and the symbolic Ibāḍī "community" (*umma*) as concretely represented by the *‘ulamā’*. Whereas the second chapter dealt with knowledge and its role in legitimizing the rule of the *‘ulamā’*, especially during the state of *kitmān*, this chapter examines the careful balancing of authority between Imām and community.

As is apparent from the role of the Ibāḍī *‘ulamā’* in relation to the various types of Imāms examined thus far, the Ibāḍī community, represented by their *‘ulamā’*, carried out a vital responsibility in the medieval Ibāḍī institution of the Imām. In North Africa, the *‘ulamā’* administered the community in the absence of the Imām after the dissolution of the Rustumid dynasty. Under the dispensation (*rukhṣa*) granted to them by the state of *kitmān*, the *‘ulamā’* assumed the duties of the Imām, even while maintaining the formal principle of the necessity of the Imām.[1] For this reason, in North Africa the *imām al-difā‘* was, like the *shārī* Imām and the *imām al-kitmān*, a purely theoretical institution.[2]

In Oman, where the imāmate ideal remained a live tradition, the *‘ulamā’* assumed an active role in the maintenance of the Ibāḍī community. By the medieval period, medieval Omani jurisprudential texts granted the *‘ulamā’* (on behalf of the Ibāḍī community) the responsibility to choose, monitor, and depose the Imāms, and to impose consultation on the *imām al-difā'* and on weak (*ḍa'īf*) Imāms. In this manner, the Omani Ibāḍī "community" (that is, the *'ulamā'*) touched every aspect of the *imāma*, and became thereby a facet of the general Ibāḍī institution of authority.

Ultimately, what underlies the balance of powers and responsibilities between Imām and community is a belief in the collective responsibility of the Ibāḍiyya to insure their success in both the world and the hereafter. Such success, it is believed, requires in part the insurance of proper leadership. Ideally, Imām and community exist in a state of equilibrium, whereby the Imām retains certain privileges while the *'ulamā'* holds others. In such an ideal situation, both agents work for the collective good of the Ibāḍī community. In medieval Ibāḍī imāmate theory, this equilibrium manifests itself in the expressions of the necessity and integrity of the imāmate, balanced by the role granted to the *'ulamā'* in monitoring and deposing the Imāms.

However, when the Ibāḍiyya find the well-being and success of the community threatened from either within or without—a situation that became all too common in medieval Oman—such circumstances might require the acceptance of provisional leaders, such as an *imām al-difā'* or *imām al-ḍa'īf* who would not be acceptable under optimal conditions. In such a situation, the balance of power tipped toward the Ibāḍī *'ulamā'*, who assumed the responsibility to regulate the Imām in the interest of the overall success of the community. Such a formally regulated and situation-based approach to the question of the imāmate is, to my knowledge, unique to the Ibāḍiyya.

The Ibāḍī balance of powers between Imām and community as it is presented in the medieval Ibāḍī *imāma* reflects the conceptual and historical legacy of the Ibāḍiyya from their forerunners. In keeping with the historically grounded methodology explored in previous chapters, this examination of the precedents for the balance of authority between Imām and community will first illuminate how the unique relationship between the Ibāḍī *'ulamā'* and Imām developed from earlier pre-Islamic, and Islamic (including early Khārijite) norms of authority. Comparisons between the early Umayyad attitude toward their Caliphs as religious guides and the early Khārijite (especially early Ibāḍī) interpretation of the Imām will reveal a shared acceptance of the notion of the Imām as religious guide for the community. However, different understandings of the efficacy of the Imām's guidance led to divergent interpretations of the role of the community in relation to the Imām; early Ibāḍī sources show a continuity with tribal and early Islamic models of leadership that encouraged as necessary communal structures of power in relation to the leader. The Umayyads, on the other hand, discouraged communal interference with their powers, tending more toward authoritarian models of rule (this tendency actually broke with the practices of the first

Caliphs). A further comparison between early Khārijite and late Najdite notions of the need for an Imām will reveal that the necessity of the Imām was implied for the early Khārijites as well. It will show how the rejection of the necessity of the Imām by some late Najdite Khārijites remained an anomaly, unique in the history of Khārijism. Finally, all of these precedents will serve to illuminate how medieval Ibāḍī imāmate theories preserved the stipulation of the necessity and integrity of the Imām, but balanced the authority of the Imām by granting the Ibāḍī *'ulamā'* the authority to select, monitor, and depose the Imāms, and to further assume added duties in relation to *ḍa'īf* and *difā'ī* Imāms.

Tribal Models of Authority in the Pre-Islamic and Early Islamic Eras

The belief in the necessity and integrity of the medieval Ibāḍite Imām, and the subsequent balance of powers between the Ibāḍī community and Imām point to unacknowledged precedents in the pre-Islamic *sayyid*'s significance to the continued existence of his tribe, as well as in the diffusion of authority to other figures and institutions of leadership in pre-Islamic Arabia. As Watt notes, the survival of the pre-Islamic Arabian tribe often depended on the effectiveness of its leadership.[3] Disputes between tribes, and stability within the tribe, required institutions of authority that could negotiate the customs that made up tribal law. Such complex requirements on pre-Islamic institutions of authority insured that those institutions evolved elaborate methods for insuring their own success.

The office of the *sayyid* or *shaykh* partially fulfilled the need for effective leadership in pre-Islamic Arabia. The *sayyid* directed the actions of the tribe, and so long as he fulfilled the duties incumbent upon him, his decisions remained binding upon the tribe's members. These duties included representing the interests of the tribe in relation to other groups, as well as settling disputes within the tribe on the basis of custom or tradition. However, pre-Islamic tribes informally limited the powers of their *shaykh* by reserving the right to disregard his advice should he prove incapable of successfully completing his duties as leader. As Watt notes: "If the *sayyid*'s wisdom were respected, disputes between parties within his tribe would be brought to him. In other cases, however, and where he was not sufficiently respected, recourse could be had to those men of wisdom and integrity who were widely accepted as arbiters (sing. *ḥakam*)."[4] Thus, while the *sayyid* was respected as an indispensable institution in pre-Islamic Arabia, the actual authority of the *sayyid* depended on his effectiveness. The tribe held a modicum of power in relation to their *sayyid* insofar as they ultimately judged the efficacy of their leader, and could consult other sources of authority if the *sayyid* proved ineffective.

Moreover, Arabian tribes retained a degree of authority over their *sayyid* insofar as the selection and recognition of a *shaykh* was usually conducted in consultation (*shūrā*) with the leading personalities of the tribe. The tribe expressed their acceptance of a *sayyid* through a symbolic handshake known as the *bay'a*. The *bay'a*, therefore, was both an acknowledgement of the authority of the *sayyid* and a tacit recognition of the source of the *sayyid*'s authority, the tribe's members. Additionally, the distribution of authority over multiple pre-Islamic institutions of authority effectively restricted the powers of the pre-Islamic *sayyid*:

> Leadership in war was usually given by a special decision, and might be for a fixed period only. Mostly, it would seem, it was not the *sayyid* who was appointed as a war leader. In some tribes, again, before adopting some new plan the soothsayer (*kahin*) would be consulted, and this would give some power to the soothsayer at the expense of the *sayyid*.[5]

Thus, the power of the *sayyid*s in pre-Islamic Arabia was limited by the structure of pre-Islamic authority, which diffused the power of leadership into various persons, insuring that a *sayyid* never possessed total control.

In addition to the *kāhin*, *ḥakam*, and military leader, still other intuitions of authority existed in pre-Islamic Arabia. In pre-Islamic Makka, for example, a grouping of chiefs and clan leaders formed a council (*malā'*).[6] Although each clan functioned independently, the *malā'* was able to make semi-unanimous decisions affecting the tribe as a whole; for example, the boycott of the Hāshimites during the lifetime of the Prophet was one of the Makkan *malā'*'s decisions.

The need for survival in pre-Islamic Arabia thus ensured that a balance and distribution of powers existed between the numerous figures and institutions of political authority. This balance of power would later be tacitly incorporated into the Islamic, and later the Khārijite and then Ibāḍite, conceptions and institutions of legitimate authority.

The Prophetic era provided another, different, precedent for medieval Ibāḍī communal structures of authority insofar as the advent of Islam adapted the pre-Islamic connections between communal structures of authority and leadership to an Islamic worldview. While Qur'ānic notions of salvation, as well as the means of achieving salvation, differed in form from their pre-Islamic precursors, an underlying belief in the need for efficacious leadership, and in the role of the Islamic community in realizing their success or salvation, provided underlying themes running throughout the Prophetic era. These themes provided a basis upon which an interpretation of an active role for the community in relation to their leader—justified in Islamic terms—could be established.

Although the pre-Islamic Arabs were undoubtedly aware of Christian, Jewish, and Zoroastrian notions of salvation or damnation in an afterlife, it was the acceptance of Islam that truly incorporated the idea of the hereafter into the Arab consciousness.[7] In many ways, the Qur'ānic ideas about an afterlife build upon pre-Islamic conceptions of survival: the notion of persisting in heaven was, in some sense, the idea of survival beyond the grave. Salvation was envisioned in terms of success (*falāḥ*) in the world and in the afterlife (that is, success in the afterlife meant going to heaven). Likewise, damnation was presented in terms of loss (*khusrān*).[8] The attainment of salvation was based on the adherence of the individual as well as the community to which that individual belonged to a divinely revealed standard of behavior and belief: to *islām*. Salvation, therefore, required proper guidance, which came in the form of prescriptive commands (the Book—*al-kitāb*), and also in the individuals who embodied the divine message, the Prophets.

The Qur'ān thereby equated salvation (to a certain extent) with the acceptance of properly guided leaders. In 25:74, the term *imām* denotes a model for behavior, or an example that can be followed: "And those who say: Our Lord! Vouchsafe us comfort of our wives and of our offspring, and make us patterns (*imāman*) for those who ward off evil." In other verses, these "models" have been given the ability to guide other human beings, and thus are identified as Prophets. A verse referring to the Prophets Isḥāq (Isaac) and Yaʿqūb (Jacob) states: "And we made them models (*ā'imma*) who guide by Our command."[9] Likewise, certain interpretations of 17:71 associate proper leadership of the community with the final judgment on the Day of Judgment: "On the day when We shall summon all people with their leader (*bi-imāmihim*), whoever is given his book in his right hand—such will read their book and will not be wronged a shred."

Ibn Kathīr reports a variety of interpretations of the term *imām* in this verse; on the one hand, certain commentators equate the term *imām* with the Prophets (*bi-nabīhim*).[10] Others, such as Ibn ʿAbbās, interpret the phrase to refer to the record of a person's actions (*kitāb ʿamālihim*). For those who interpreted the phrase to indicate an individual—especially a Prophet—the verse seems to indicate that salvation is associated with the Prophets in their capacities as guides for humanity.

Other Qur'ānic verses imply that the efficacy of a leader is not guaranteed simply by his being an *imām*. The acceptance of human leadership can negatively affect the salvation of a community, in fact, insofar as an Imām can also lead a community to misguidance and damnation: "And We made them examples (*ā'imma*) that invite unto the Fire, and on the day of Resurrection they will not be helped."[11] Elsewhere, the Qur'ān provides the Pharaoh as an example of the negative soteriological implications of leadership:

> And We sent Moses with Our revelations and a clear warrant; Unto Pharaoh and his chiefs (*malā'ihi*), but they did follow the command of

> Pharaoh, and the command of Pharaoh was no right guide; he will go before his people on the Day of Resurrection and will lead them into the Fire, and woeful will be the place where they are led.[12]

The verse indicates that Pharaoh's people will end up at a place of damnation by following him—their choice of leader will lead them to destruction. Insofar as individuals choose whom they will accept as a guide, they have a certain amount of control over their destiny. This choice was synonymous with the fundamental choice of accepting the strictures of Islam, becoming a Muslim, and accepting Muhammad as a Prophet, and thus as an efficacious guide.

This Qur'ānic notion of efficacious leadership—of the Prophet who guided his *umma* to earthly and heavenly success—shares an affinity with the pre-Islamic conception of effective tribal headship, of the pre-Islamic *sayyid* who worked for the survival and success of his tribe. Moreover, in both cases, success was not guaranteed, but depended in part on the choice of leader; just as tribal survival depended on a competent *sayyid*, so proper guidance hinged on the acceptance of a proper guide, that is, a Prophet.

Beyond this identification of the Prophets as divinely inspired guides for humanity, and the consequent implications of the acceptance of their message for the conduct of human affairs, the Qur'ān does not advocate an authoritative role for the Islamic community in relation to the Prophets. There is no need to monitor the behavior of the Prophets, as their divine sanction precluded any such necessity. However, certain verses of the Qur'ān, taken in conjunction with the concept of efficacious leadership, imply a more active role for the community in insuring their own salvation by insuring proper leadership of the community.

First, while the Qur'ān reserves agency for establishing and restricting the authority of the Prophets to God, it does not comment on the possible responsibility of the Muslim community in monitoring non-Prophetic institutions of authority. The Qur'ānic requirements of piety constrain the authority of the Prophets in their roles as Imāms and Caliphs. For example, God makes Abraham an *imām*, but promises authority only to those of his progeny who refrain from tyranny.[13] Similarly, the Prophets Isḥāq and Ya'qūb are described as *imām*s who "guide by Our command,"[14] and the Children of Israel are described as becoming *imām*s after they believed in the signs of God.[15] Likewise, the Qur'ān commands the Prophet Dawūd (David), as Caliph (*khalīfa*): "O Dawūd! Lo! We have set you as a viceroy (*khalīfa fī al-arḍ*) in the earth; therefore judge aright between mankind."[16] In these verses, God limits valid leadership of the Prophets to those who believe in God and follow His commands, especially the command to establish justice on earth. Thus, God sets and enforces standards by which human beings become Prophets. While God alone directs the Prophets, the Qur'ān, by avoiding comment on temporal institutions of authority, leaves open the possibility for communal supervision of the worldly offices of the Caliphs and Imāms.

Although the Qur'ān limits the authority of the Prophets to the practice of justice, it actively encourages communal participation in realization of its religio-political goals, and thereby allocates to the *umma* an interest in the community's success. Just as the Prophets, in their roles as Imāms and *khalīfas*, are instructed to establish justice, so the community of believers was to serve God by establishing His plan for humanity: "This nation is one nation (*umma*), and I am your Lord, so keep your duty to Me";[17] "And of those whom We created there is a nation who guides with the truth and establishes justice therewith";[18] "Oh you who believe, be staunch in justice."[19] Responsibility for the *umma*'s success rested equally on every Muslim, and even on the Prophet: "Thus We have appointed you a middle nation, that you may be witnesses against mankind, and the messenger is a witness against you."[20] This equal accountability of leader and community toward the completion of God's will on earth connotes an equal effort in creating a just society. In other words, the Qur'ān, by its insistence on the establishment of a just society, insured the Muslim community an active role in the moral-political scheme for humanity.

Insofar as the community is responsible for its own destiny, the Qur'ān can be interpreted as empowering the community to check the authority of their leaders if the actions of the leader threatened the central mission of establishing justice. Although the Qur'ān speaks of the *umma* as the "best community that was raised up for mankind," this does not insure the Muslim community paradise on the Day of Judgment.[21] God repeatedly warns the believers that they will be tested: "Had God willed He would have made you one community—but that He might try you by that which He gave you";[22] "Do men imagine that they will be left [at ease] because they say, We believe, and will not be tested with affliction? Lo! We tested those who were before you—thus, God knows who is sincere, and knows who is feigning."[23] Ultimate responsibility for the success of the community thus resided with the community itself. Just as God does not "change the condition of a people until they [first] change what is in their hearts,"[24] the *umma* must assume the duty of insuring its own destiny.

Thus, the verses constraining the authority of the Prophets, taken in conjunction with the Muslim community's responsibility for its own salvation, seem to imply the duty of the community to monitor the conduct of leaders and, possibly, to remove them if they do not conform to the standards of justice. Of course, this must be inferred from an interpretation of the Qur'ān that accepts the association of communal success with human leadership, and posits a positive role for the community in insuring its own triumph through insuring proper leadership. This situation did not apply to the Qur'ānic era: the Qur'ān unambiguously instructs the Muslims in 4:59 to follow the Prophet and "those in authority over you." As a Prophet, the efficacy of Muhammad's leadership was assumed, and his authority unambiguously commanded by the Qur'ān. Questions of communal responsibility to insure proper leadership were rendered meaningless by the divine sanction of the Prophet Muhammad. Thus, the import of these Qur'ānic verses, and of the particular interpretation of them that the Khārijite community assume responsibility for insuring its own success through insuring the legitimacy of its own leadership, did not become apparent until many years after the death of the Prophet. However, the essential elements of the particular Khārijite interpretation of communal authority in relation to their leaders existed implicitly in the Qur'ān; communal responsibility for its own destiny and the relation between such destiny and communal leadership pointed toward an active role of the Khārijite community vis-à-vis their Imām.

Moreover, during the lifetime of the Prophet, Muhammad incorporated the Islamic community into the process of governance, despite the absolute authority granted him as Prophet of God. For example, the principle of consultation (*shūrā*) was adopted, practiced, and encouraged by the Prophet Muhammad as a legitimate form of sharing authority with the community. The Qur'ān advised Muhammad to consult with the people of Makka after its conquest: "So pardon them and ask forgiveness for them and consult with them upon the conduct of affairs."[25] In another verse, the Qur'ān generalized Muhammad's specific command to practice *shūrā*, encouraging all Muslims to employ consultation.[26] A Prophetic *ḥadīth* stated: "Consultation (*mushāwara*) is a fortress against regret and a safeguard against blame."[27] Although the use of consultation during the Prophetic era cannot be described as equilibrium of powers between the Prophet and the community, it nonetheless granted some authority to the community. In this way, the Qur'ānic and Prophetic sanctions of consultation made it an important aspect of early Islamic governance.

In addition, the Prophet's demeanor implied a certain self-restraint in the exercise of his powers. That is, the nature of Muhammad was such that authoritarianism did not seem to suit him. By all available accounts, the Prophet was merciful in both his personal and political personas. For example, it is reported that Muhammad forgave his former enemies in Makka and acted leniently toward the Bedouin tribes who converted to Islam. He favored consultation and persuasion over autocratic fiat. If such accounts can be believed, then, in many ways, Muhammad earned the love of his followers by not exercising his absolute authority, and encouraging people to do good by his own example. Thus, while it is inaccurate to say that Muhammad's authority was constrained or dependent upon his followers, it is also inaccurate to claim that he relied on the absolute authority that was granted him by divine appointment in the implementation of his power.

In other words, the nature of Muhammad's authority was not legitimated or monitored by the tribal norms that applied to a pre-Islamic *sayyid*, but it was also not exercised in an authoritarian manner.

With the death of Muhammad, the comprehensive leadership of the Prophet gave way, under the first two Caliphs, to a structure of authority that was deeply rooted in the pre-Islamic pattern of leadership. Although the Islamic era introduced novel institutions of leadership such as the Prophet to the Arabs, the nature of authority and conduct of the Caliphs borrowed from institutions that operated in the pre-Islamic period, such as the tribal *sayyid*. As such, the authority of the first two Caliphs, Abū Bakr and ʿUmar, was characterized by the adaptation of the tribal model of leadership along Islamic lines, and the consequent acceptance of a restrictive influence of the community on their authority that was much like the influence the community had exercised during the pre-Islamic era.

The lack of systematic treatises on the nature of political authority from the era immediately succeeding the Prophetic era translates into a general lack of materials on the underlying conceptions of authority that animated the early caliphate. Nonetheless, the historical accounts of the early caliphate illuminate its nature as a revision in Islamic terms of tribal structures of leadership. That the community required an efficacious leader after the death of the Prophet, one who would lead them in accordance with the strictures of Islam, and thus lead them to success in this world and in the next, was almost self-evident. The Qur'ān had ordered the believers to follow God, the Prophet, and "those in authority over you."[28] Thus, the necessity of leadership after the death of the Prophet was assumed.

Due to the lack of specific direction from Muhammad and the Qur'ān regarding the issue of succession, however, the exact qualities of an efficacious Islamic leader remained unclear. In what became the majority response to the question of effective leadership, Muhammad's successor (*khalīfa*) was envisioned (much like Muhammad himself) as a supra-*shaykh* presiding over a supra-tribe, the Islamic *umma*. As became apparent from the proceedings on the porch of the Banū Saʿīda, as well as from the *ridda* wars, Abū Bakr explicitly rejected the call for separate leadership for the various tribes who had submitted to Islam, and insisted on a single leader for the Islamic community. As mentioned in previous chapters, Abū Bakr's candidacy rested on a combination of Islamic and pre-Islamic qualifications: his Companionship with the Prophet, his early conversion to Islam, his ability to deal with the tribal chiefs, and to be accepted by them—a trait directly related to his membership in the Quraysh.[29] Similarly, and in addition to the explicit designation of Abū Bakr, ʿUmar possessed the necessary Islamic and pre-Islamic credentials for leadership of the community. Although far from universally accepted (among the Shiʿa, all but the Zaydī Shiʿite traditions, for example, view Abū Bakr and ʿUmar as usurpers of ʿAlī's rights to leadership of the Islamic community), later Islamic tradition recognized Abū Bakr and 'Umar as successful rulers—"rightly guided" Caliphs—and as sources of salvation for the Islamic community insofar as Abū Bakr and 'Umar came to be regarded as sources of right practice (*sunna*). Thus, their "efficacy" as rulers depended on a combination of the Islamic characteristics (Companionship, early conversion, piety) and pre-Islamic traits (knowledge of genealogy, ability to influence other tribal leaders) that were prized by the early Muslim Arabs.

In addition, Abū Bakr and 'Umar's style of rule resembled that of a tribal *sayyid*. That is, the size of the *umma*, and the face-to-face setting of Madīna, allowed Abū Bakr and 'Umar to personally address themselves to the duties of the caliphate. During their reigns, the caliphate functioned less as an office and more as direct relationship with those they ruled. Like the Arab *sayyid* whose powers rested on his abilities and rapport with his tribe, Abū Bakr and 'Umar felt themselves personally beholden to the Islamic *umma* for the conduct of their rule. 'Umar, for example, despite being the leader of the Muslim army and Caliph of an expanding empire, understood his powers to be limited by his responsibilities to God and the Muslim community, and viewed himself as accountable before the *umma* for his actions as leader. An anecdote about the life of 'Umar from al-Ṭabarī relates that 'Umar once compensated a man named Salama six hundred *dirham*s for having struck him with his cane in the marketplace of Madīna a year earlier. When Salama remarked that he did not remember the incident, 'Umar replied that he had not been able to forget it.[30] Another anecdote recounts how 'Abdullāh b. 'Umayr came to 'Umar and demanded a stipend on behalf of his father, who was killed at the Battle of Ḥunayn. When 'Umar ignored him, 'Abdullāh jabbed him with his walking stick to get his attention. 'Umar then ordered that the man be given a stipend.[31] These two anecdotes illustrate how, according to the chroniclers, 'Umar felt both directly responsible for his actions as leader and ultimately beholden to the Islamic community for his position.

Concurrent with the personal character of the authority of the early Caliphs, and as a natural side effect of the adaptation of tribal models of leadership along Islamic lines, members of the Islamic community reassumed their role in insuring effective leadership. Although an actual demonstration of communal authority in relation to the Caliph would not materialize until the resistance to 'Uthmān, evidence of the Islamic community as an accepted check on the powers of the Caliph comes from the era of Abū Bakr and 'Umar. For example, Abū Bakr's speech, delivered in the mosque at Madīna during the public pledge of allegiance (*bay'a*) to him as Caliph, offered the prime example of the powers (theoretically) granted to the early Islamic community. Abū Bakr is reported to have said to the gathered community: "I have been given authority over you, but I am not the best of you. If I do well, help me, and if I do wrong, then put me right.... Obey me as long as I obey God and His apostle, and if I disobey them you owe me no obedience."[32] Abū Bakr's attitude toward his authority was contingent upon his obedience to God and the Prophet, and he felt himself accountable to the Muslim community. These factors checked his powers as Caliph, but he encouraged these limits as appropriate and necessary. Similarly, ʿUmar is reported to have said: "those who fear God should conduct their affairs in consultation."[33] Thus, the authority of the Islamic community in concert with, and sometimes over, that of the Caliphs reemerged during the time of the first Caliphs as a consequence of the supra-tribal character of early Islamic *umma*.

What has been labeled the tribal model of authority consisted of a distribution of powers between a group's leader and his community whereby the community assumed (or was symbolically granted) a certain amount of authority in relation to the leader. This institutional configuration of authority rested on a belief in the connection between the leadership of and the collective survival or success of the communal group. During the pre-Islamic and early Islamic eras, the size of the tribe or *umma* allowed for the balance of powers to remain a matter informally negotiated between persons. As a result, there were no official statutes that regulated the relationship.

The latter part of ʿUmar's reign witnessed the beginning of the transformation of the tribal model of leadership. This process would not be completed until the fall of the Umayyad dynasty nearly one hundred years later. Although tribal motivations and social structures continued to dominate early Islamic culture, the spectacular success of the conquests indelibly changed the character of Islamic society and with it the character of its leadership. With the borders of the Islamic empire stretching from North Africa to Central Asia, and the populations of these territories comprising large numbers of non-Arabs and non-Muslims, the personal style of leadership adopted by Abū Bakr and ʿUmar became difficult, if not impossible, to emulate, as did maintaining the unity of the Muslims strewn across the vastness of the empire. As Islamic society grew and became more complex, more formalized prescriptions for the allocation of powers between the Imām and his community developed. It comes as no surprise that in the fractious days of the Umayyad era, these notions were elaborated along sectarian lines.

Communal Authority in Umayyad and Early Khārijite Thought

The early Khārijite era provided another potent precedent for medieval Ibāḍī conceptions of the role of the community, insofar as the early Khārijite view toward guaranteeing the effectiveness of their Imām was believed to be a continuation of the principles that had animated the early caliphates of Abū Bakr and 'Umar, and a systematization of the conception of efficacious leadership that was present in the Qur'ān (along with the role of the community that this conception implied). The Umayyad Caliphs also viewed their institutions of authority as an extension of Qur'ānic and early Islamic conceptions and institutions of authority. However, while the Khārijites and Umayyads shared a belief in the role of the Imām in relation to his community, they had disparate notions about the recognition of an efficacious Imām. These differences arose from the dissimilar ways in which the Umayyads and Khārijites viewed how an Imām was chosen: either by divine sanction or by communal verification of their efficacy. Consequently, the Khārijites and Umayyads instituted different conventions regarding the nature of the relationship between the community and the Imām.

The first Khārijite articulation of communal success in connection with leadership comes from early Ibāḍī sources. As one of the earliest Ibāḍī texts, the first letter of Ibn Ibāḍ testifies to an early Ibāḍī expression of the notion of the importance of the Imām to the community.[34] It mentions that there are but two types of Imāms: the Imām of guidance (*imām al-hudā*) and the Imām of misguidance (*imām al-ḍalāla*). The Imām of guidance follows what has been revealed from God and acts in accordance with the proper *sunna*.[35] The Imām of misguidance follows his whims (*ahwā'*) and the whims of those who went before him. Ibn Ibāḍ's letter makes it clear that the choice of Imām affects the chooser: the Imām that one follows remains one's Imām "in this world and the next."[36] Similarly, another early piece of Ibāḍī writing, the second/eighth-century epistle of Sālim b. Dhakwān, discusses the ramifications of the choice of an Imām.[37] Sālim warns: "it is by their Imām that God will call His servants on the Day of Resurrection,"[38] and then quotes 17:71 as proof of his statement. Sālim immediately thereafter admonishes his readers to give their allegiance only to God-fearing people (*awliyā'*) and to avoid the allies of Satan. Proper action leads to salvation in heaven, but Sālim advises "many people have been led by their whims to go separate ways, which took them to dead ends."[39] He states: "it is for you to follow the good path and the conduct (*sīra*) approved in Islam."[40] Sālim's epistle makes it is clear that all Muslims must choose their leader wisely, as the wrong choice has repercussions in the afterlife.

In addition, al-Kindī preserves a piece of Abū 'Ubayda's Qur'ānic interpretation of 17:71, whereby Abū 'Ubayda takes the phrase "with their Imām" to mean "with those whom they followed, and whom they made their model" (*billadhī aqtadū bihi wa ja'alūhu imāman*).[41] Although al-Kindī acknowledges other interpretations of the phrase (for example, he comments that the phrase could also indicate that human beings will be called according to the record of their actions: their "book," *bi-kitābihim*), the import of Abū 'Ubayda's interpretation clearly indicates that some early Ibāḍī scholars believed the Imām to be a guide by which people would be judged on the Day of Judgment.

As the only surviving subsect of the *khawārij*, these Ibāḍī sources provide the most developed examples in early Khārijite literature of the implications of the choice of an Imām. However, evidence from other Khārijī subsects exists that likewise links the Imām to the community. The Muḥakkima, for example, in their attribution of disbelief (*kufr*) to ʿUthmān and ʿAlī implied that the choice of leader held consequences for the community. The term *kufr* carried strong connotations of damnation, as Qur'ān repeatedly promised perdition to the *kuffār* and *mushrikūn*. In a passage in al-Balādhurī, Abū Mikhnaf reports that the Muḥakkima branded ʿAlī's followers as *kuffār* for continuing to pay allegiance to ʿAlī after the arbitration agreement.[42] These associations between *kufr* and leadership strongly imply a connection between damnation and the choice of leader.

Likewise, Ibn Muljam's assassination of ʿAlī was believed to be an attempt to remove an unjust leader who, in the eyes of the Khārijites, threatened the well-being of the community.[43] According to the report of al-Wāqidī, the conspiracy of Khārijites who resolved to murder ʿAlī, Muʿāwiya and ʿAmr b. al-ʿĀṣ stated their goal as that of "ridding the land of the Imāms of misguidance (*ā'immat al-ḍalāla*)"[44] and returning the caliphate to righteousness.[45] The sources simultaneously portray the attack as retaliation for the killing of Ibn Muljam's fellow tribesman at Nahrawān. Both tribal and religious motives are plausible and not, ultimately, mutually exclusive. Al-Wāqidī's report in al-Ṭabarī mentions that Ibn Muljam witnessed tribesmen of the Taym b. Ribāb remembering ten of their members who were slain at al-Nahrawān. Nevertheless, the use of the term "Imams of misguidance" implied that ʿAlī's sin involved guiding the community to error. Because the Qur'ānic concept of guidance was deeply connected to the notion of salvation, it is difficult to miss the correlation between misguidance, damnation, and leadership.

In addition, al-Ashʿarī mentions the belief of a subsect of the Bayhasiyya Khārijites in the efficacy of their Imām: "A group of the Bayhasiyya believed that if the Imām becomes a disbeliever, his followers become disbelievers" (*idhā kafara al-imām fa-qad kafarat al-ra'iyya*).[46] This connection between the actions of the leader and the actions of his followers, coupled with the language of disbelief (the verb *kafara*) indicated, for this subsect of Bayhasī Khārijites, a belief in potential for the Imām to lead his community to either success or damnation.

It thus seems as if early Khārijite (especially early Ibāḍite) discussions of the efficacy of the Imām eschew any notion of divine sanction for the Imām, and present the actions of the Imām as the indicator of his value to the community. Consequently, the Khārijite community faced an important choice when it came to their leader: they had to be sure that they followed an Imām who had proven his value. Otherwise, the community would be directed by an unqualified leader who would (mis)guide them to their own doom.

Like the early Khārijites, the Umayyads and their supporters believed in the salvific role of the Umayyad Caliph. However, the Umayyads cultivated a belief in the divine sanction of their Caliphs that assumed their efficacy as leaders, and precluded the idea of a communal choice in leadership. This is not to imply that the Umayyads abandoned the concepts of leadership that they had inherited from Abū Bakr and 'Umar. Rather, a subtle shift occurred, beginning with 'Uthmān and becoming slowly more overt as the Umayyad era progressed. This shift involved a more authoritarian style of rule, bolstered by a belief in the Caliphs as divinely approved sources of guidance and protection. This trend began with 'Uthmān; whereas Abū Bakr instructed the community to disobey him if he disobeyed God, 'Uthmān viewed his caliphate as a divine endorsement that the community of Muslims should respect. When faced late in his tumultuous career as Caliph with the prospect of relinquishing the office, 'Uthmān is reported to have stated: "I will not shed the cloak [of the caliphate] in which God has clothed me."[47] Later Umayyad Caliphs likewise adopted a view toward their authority as divinely sanctioned. Umayyad poets, for example, never tired of recalling how the Caliphs were sources of guidance.[48] Like the poets, the Umayyad Caliphs believed themselves to be sources of divine guidance: the Caliph 'Abd al-Malik, for example, referred to Ibn al-Zubayr's rebellion as directed against the "Imāms of guidance" (*ā'immat al-hudā*).[49] As (presumed) sources of guidance, the Caliphs led the Muslims to the right path and thus became indispensable for the general welfare of the Islamic community. These descriptions of the Umayyad Caliph match Ibn Ibāḍ's description of the *imām al-hudā*, and closely resemble Sālim b. Dhakwān's conception of the Imām as a model for behavior. However, the efficacy of the Caliph in Umayyad sources is assumed, whereas for Ibn Ibāḍ and Ibn Dhakwān, an Imām could be an *imām al-hudā* or *imām al-ḍalāla*, depending on his actions.

Similarly, the Umayyad Caliphs were compared to the "rope of God" that is mentioned in 3:98: "And hold fast to the rope of God (*ḥabl Allāh*), together, and do not scatter." Mu'āwiya was described as a "firm rope for humankind"[50] and "a rope among the ropes of God" (*ḥabl min ḥibāl Allāh*).[51] God had "strengthened the strands of His rope" through His Caliphs according to the epistle of Walīd II.[52] By portraying the Umayyad Caliphs as identical to the rope of God, the Umayyads identified themselves as the instrument of God's guidance and will: they were the sole connection between community and God, and the community therefore had an obligation to follow them.

Ibāḍī use of the rope of God metaphor differs slightly, but importantly, from the Umayyad conception of the Caliph as the rope of God. Ibn Ibāḍ, in his first letter, claimed: "the Book of God is the rope of God that the believers were ordered to grasp." Ibn Ibāḍ then instructs ʿAbd al-Malik b. Marwān to "take refuge in the rope of God, oh ʿAbd al-Malik, and take refuge in God who will guide you to a straight path."[53] Although employing the metaphor of the rope of God, Ibn Ibāḍ makes the Qur'ān, not the Imām, the rope. The Ibāḍī Imām remains responsible (along with each member of his community) for following the dictates of God and the Qur'ān (that is, for grasping the rope of God). Guidance, and by implication the efficacy of the Ibāḍī Imām's leadership, was contingent upon the Imām's ability to follow the dictates of Islam, not, as implied by the Umayyad use of the metaphor of the rope of God, coterminous with it.

Unlike the Khārijite Imāms, the Umayyad Caliphs assumed their role vis-à-vis the community by arrogating to themselves grand moral qualities. Some Umayyad Caliphs regarded themselves as sources of guidance because they saw themselves as correctly guided (*mahdī*) and as refuges from error (*ʿiṣma* and *ḥiṣn*).[54] Muʿāwiya claimed, in a letter to ʿAlī, that ʿUthmān was a "correctly guided Caliph" (*khalīfatan mahdīyan*).[55] Likewise, Umayyad court poets described the Caliph Sulaymān as the *mahdī* "through whom God guides whoever is in fear of going astray."[56] The Umayyad poet Jarīr described Hishām as "the correctly guided one and the judge who follows the right path" (*al-mahdī wa al-ḥakam al-rashīd*), as well as "the *mahdī* in whom we seek refuge when frightened."[57] Although these references to the Caliphs as *mahdī* do not necessarily connote the eschatological overtones that would later become more commonly associated with the term *mahdī*, they do portray the Caliphs as essential sources of guidance for the community due to their being correctly guided. Implied by this usage of the term *mahdī* is the idea that the proper guidance of the Umayyad Caliphs (and thereby their legitimacy) was assured by God's divine sanction. As "correctly guided" leaders, the Caliphs also became associated with justice. Umayyad supporters described ʿUthmān and Muʿāwiya as just Imāms (*imām ʿādil*), and ʿAbd al-Malik and ʿUmar II received the title "the just Caliph" (*khalīfat al-ʿadl*). Although these pretensions to justice come primarily from Umayyad court poets, and may have little to do with the feelings of the majority of Muslims, they nonetheless establish the Umayyad self-conception of their rule. Regardless of whether the majority of Muslims looked to their Caliphs as sources of justice or guidance (and there is evidence that a significant portion of the Muslim population did not), the Caliphs regarded themselves as such and perpetuated this image.[58]

Closely related to the Umayyad idea of the Caliphs being correctly guided and just was the notion that the Umayyad Caliph was a refuge from error (*ʿiṣma*). Muʿāwiya was told: "God has made you a refuge (*ʿiṣma*) for His friends, and a source of injury for His enemies... through you, God, exalted be He, makes the blind to see and guides the enemies [to the truth]."[59] A poet commented, "through [Muʿāwiya] God protected (*ʿaṣama*) humankind from perdition."[60] The Caliph was also described as a fortress (*ḥiṣn*),[61] and a "cave in which you seek refuge."[62] In this manner, the Umayyad Caliphs became regarded (by their supporters) as a source of salvation for the community because they shielded the community from error and disunity. As with the other moral qualities claimed by the Umayyad Caliphs, their effectiveness as refuges from error was assumed. This notion of divine sanction and protection was absent from the Khārijite conception of the Imām. The Khārijites never assumed the efficacy of their Imāms as sources of communal salvation. For the Khārijites, the Imām possessed no guarantees of authority: only his actions proved his piety and moral rectitude, and thereby legitimated his rule.

These respective positions regarding the efficacy of the Imām entailed certain consequent stances regarding the role of the community in relation to the Imām. For the Khārijites, the need for the Imām to prove his efficacy implied an activist stance of the Khārijite community beyond simply choosing the right Imām. The Khārijite community monitored the Imām's actions and deposed the Imām if he did not fulfill the requirements of piety. Heresiographical texts testify to the Khārijite obligation to depose an unjust ruler. Al-Shahrastānī reports that all Khārijī subsects adhered to the view that "it is an obligatory duty to rebel against an Imām if he contravenes the *sunna*."[63] Similarly, al-Ash'arī reports that the Khārijites "do not accept [the imāmate of] an unjust Imām" (*lā yarūna imāmat al-jā'ir*).[64] Likewise, early Khārijite poetry testified to the duty to depose an unjust Imām: the Khārijite poet Abū al-Wāzi' al-Rāsibī reproached Nāfi' b. al-Azraq by singing: "Your tongue does no harm to the enemy; you will only gain salvation from distress by means of your two hands; so struggle against people who have fought God, and persevere."[65] 'Īsā b. Fātik al-Khaṭṭī intoned: "You obeyed the orders of a stubborn tyrant (*jabbār 'anīd*), but no obedience is due to oppressors."[66] Another early Khārijite poet, Ibn Abī Mayyās al-Murādī, referring to 'Alī, said: "We have dissolved his kingship (*mulk*)...by the blow of a sword, since he had become haughty and was tyrannical."[67] As is clear from these quotations, the Khārijite community assumed an activist posture toward Islamic leadership from a very early period of Khārijite history.

On the other hand, the Umayyads, concurrent with their belief in the divine sanction of their rule, encouraged a passive role for the community. Although the Umayyads embraced the notion that communal welfare required allegiance to the Caliph, they opposed the concomitant idea that the *umma* was therefore required to insure the legitimacy of the Caliph through resistance or rebellion. This disconnect between the notion of the success of the community and caliphal accountability to the community was achieved by encouraging fatalism in the face of the excesses and indiscretions of the leader.[68] Evidence for this view toward the caliphate exists in the *ḥadīth* corpus. However, due to the nature of *ḥadīth* redaction, expressions of Umayyad theology regarding the passive role of the community (and Umayyad expressions of theology in general) are less common. The major collections of *ḥadīth* were edited during the ʿAbbasid era, at a time when even the mentioning of former Umayyad rulers was dangerous; the ʿAbbasid Caliph al-Ma'mūn, for example, sent an announcer into the streets of Baghdād in order to publicize in the name of the Caliph that he refused his protection to anyone who mentioned Muʿāwiya in a favorable manner.[69] Although many *ḥadīth* related to the actions of Muʿāwiya probably existed during the Umayyad era, al-Bukhārī, one of the two redactors of *ḥadīth* whose collection is considered absolutely sound by the Sunnis, provides very few of them. In contrast, the ʿAbbasids encouraged the collection of *ḥadīth* that defamed the Umayyads.

Nevertheless, among the *ḥadīth* that denigrate the Umayyads, a type of *ḥadīth* exists that, even though it expresses the notion that the Umayyad Caliphs were sinful, exhorts Muslims to accept them as de facto rulers. Rebellion and disobedience, in these *ḥadīth*, are condemned as more sinful than the sins of the leaders. Alternately, these *ḥadīth* present the Umayyad rulers as a punishment for the Muslim community. This kind of *ḥadīth* strives to teach that an immoral government must nevertheless be obeyed and that it must be left to God to cause the downfall of rulers of whom He disapproves. It must be noted that these *ḥadīth* fundamentally accept the notion that the Umayyad Caliphs were chosen by God, and that success in religion came from obeying them: "He who disapproves of his ruler's actions, let him bear this in patience, for he who leaves obedience by even a span will die like a pagan";[70] "He who leaves the community by the distance of but one span, has cast away the rope of Islam" (*ḥabl al-islām*); "Obey your superiors and resist not, for to obey them is to obey God, and to rebel against them is to rebel against God"; "He who despises God's government (*sulṭān Allāh*) on earth, God will humble him"; "Al-Ḥajjāj is a punishment sent by God; do not meet God's punishment with the sword." Another *ḥadīth* states:

> Do not insult the regents because of actions of the representatives of the government which are against the *sunna*. If they are acting well they deserve God's reward and you must be grateful; it they act badly the sin rests with them and you must be patient; they are the whip with whom God punishes those he wishes to punish. Do not receive the scourge of God with anger and annoyance, but receive it with humility and subjection.[71]

These *ḥadīth* ran counter to the spirit of pious activism in the Qur'ān and turned the notion of communal responsibility for just leadership on its head through an inversion of communal duties toward government; the *umma*'s primary duty became obedience to a divinely sanctioned regime. Such a view obviously benefited the Umayyad Caliphs, and it is not difficult to see why they may have supported it. At the same time, belief in the divine endorsement of the Umayyad Caliphs (and the consequent pressure on the Islamic community to quietly accept the leaders whom God had chosen) ran counter to the spirit of accountability that animated the caliphates of Abū Bakr and ʻUmar.

In addition, the Umayyad move away from the personal style of leadership can be gauged symbolically by inspecting the changes to the mosques and prayer rituals. Because the Friday prayer service brought leader and community (at least those present in Damascus) together into one physical location, it represented a measure of the relationship between the two entities. Although introduced by Muʻāwiya, the changes to the Friday prayers were adopted by all subsequent Umayyad rulers and should be considered as symbolic of the Umayyad conception of their place in relation to the community: Muʻāwiya was the first Caliph to have bodyguards that accompanied him wherever he went in public, including the mosque. Muʻāwiya also, out of fear of assassination and in order to set himself off from the common Muslims, commanded the construction of separate boxes (*maqṣūra*) in the mosque for himself and his court.[72] He ordered that steps be added to the *minbar* so that the ruler might be set off from his subjects during the *khuṭba*.[73] Finally, the Umayyads changed the order of the *ʻīd* prayers so that the *khuṭba* preceded the *ṣalāt*; this change was so that the people would not disgrace the dignity of the Caliph by leaving before his *khuṭba*.[74] Thus, during prayers, the Umayyads set themselves off from the Islamic community, and took steps to deprive the community of the means to express their discontent with the regime. These changes portray the Umayyad desire to separate themselves from the community, as well as to control it.

The differences between the Umayyad and early Khārijite views toward the efficacy of the community's leader can be partially explained with reference to the size of their respective communities. The Khārijites were able to maintain a smaller, tribe-like social organization, and consequently they preserved more of a role for the community in assuring the efficacy of their leaders. The tribal character of many Khārijite groups was readily apparent. The Azāriqa and Najdāt, for example, possessed a dominant affiliation with the Ḥanīfa tribe of the Ḥijāz, and organized themselves into a separate "camps" (*dār*) that constituted the faithful. These groups resembled independent tribes, but were organized on the basis of sectarian affiliation.[75] Similarly, Shabīb b. Yazīd's roving Khārijite war party bore a resemblance to a Bedouin raiding party, as did the smaller groups of Khārijite rebels led by Qarīb, Zuḥḥāf, and Mirdās b. Udayya (Abū Bilāl). The size of Khārijite groups allowed them to maintain a more tribe-like structure, and consequently to preserve more of the constitution of the early caliphate: that is,

Khārijite leadership was able to remain on a personal (and informal) level. The Khārijite community, thereby, exercised checks on the authority of their Imām (insofar as they monitored and deposed or resisted the Imām) that were similar to those implemented by the pre-Islamic tribe, and granted (in theory) to the early Islamic community. The Umayyads, on the other hand, administered a large, impersonal empire, and consequently were not able to maintain the personal style of authority. Instead, they drifted toward an authoritarian method of leadership that relied on conceptions of divine sanction, and consequently required obedience from the community.

Necessity of the Imām in Khārijite Religious Thought

Another consequence of the belief in the efficacy of the Imām was that most Khārijite subsects held an Imām to be necessary for the functioning of the Islamic *umma*. While no systematic expression of this belief exists in early Khārijite sources, the prevalence of Imāms in the early Khārijite subsects tacitly presupposed the need for a leader. Like the early Caliphs, the Umayyads and early Khārijites selected and acknowledged leaders, thus implying their belief in the necessity of the institution. However, not all Khārijite groups accepted the notion that an Imām was required. Evidence from heresiographical sources explains that certain groups of Najdāt rejected the obligatory nature of the imāmate. However, this belief remained an exception applicable only to the later Najdāt. Moreover, it resulted from the unique historical circumstances of the later Najdāt, and cannot be considered typical of the Khārijites as a whole.

Sunni heresiography and histories confirm a general Khārijite commitment to acknowledgment of Imāms by pledge (*bayʿa*). The Muḥakkima first employed these concepts when they seceded from ʿAlī's army to Ḥarūrāʾ. There they declared their independence from ʿAlī and acknowledged Shabath b. Ribʿī al-Tamīmī as their leader in battle (*amīr al-qitāl*) and ʿAbdullāh b. al-Kuwwāʾ al-Yashkūrī as leader of prayers (*amīr al-ṣalāt*). The Muḥakkima considered these leaders temporary, and vowed to convene a council (*shūrā*) to establish a permanent leader. Until such time as they could select a permanent Imām, they declared their allegiance to God (*al-bayʿa lil-lāh*) on the condition that every soldier "command the good and forbid evil."[76] Similarly, after their return to Kūfa and subsequent disillusionment with ʿAlī, the Muḥakkima gathered at the house of ʿAbdullāh b. Wahb al-Rāsibī and, after some consideration, pledged their allegiance to him (*bāyaʿūhu*).[77] The Muḥakkima, despite their rejection of ʿAlī's authority, called upon themselves to "elect a leader (*amīr*) from among us—for there must be [a person who is] a support, a prop and a banner around whom you can rally, and to whom you can return."[78] This phrase represents one of the few examples of an overt declaration of the necessity of an Imām.

Likewise, heresiographical and historical sources contain scattered references to the acknowledgment of later Khārijite Imāms by pledge (*bay'a*): a subsect of the Azāriqa who followed 'Abd Rabbih al-Kabīr pledged their allegiance to him as Caliph (*fa-bāya'ūhu bi al-khilāfa*); a different subsect of Azāriqa pledged allegiance (*bāya'ū*) to Qaṭarī b. al-Fujā'a.[79] These Azraqite leaders adopted the title *amīr al-mū'minīn*, and used the *bay'a* to confirm their authority among their followers.[80] Similarly, heresiographers report that Najda b. 'Āmir al-Ḥanafī used the title *amīr al-mū'minīn*[81] as well as Imām[82] and was elected using the *bay'a*;[83] 'Aṭiyya b. al-Aswad informed Abū Fudayk that he had pledged allegiance to himself (that is, he declared himself the Imām);[84] the followers of Ṣāliḥ b. Musarriḥ pledged allegiance to Shabīb b. Yazīd after Ṣāliḥ's death;[85] and al-Ḍaḥḥāk b. Qays received allegiance from 120,000 soldiers, and from some Qurayshīs when he entered Kūfa.[86] Among the Omani Ibāḍīs, an early example of the use of *bay'a* comes from Abū Ḥamza, who swore allegiance to 'Abdullāh b. Yaḥya (Ṭālib al-Ḥaqq) in 129/745–746.[87] Moreover, succeeding leaders among the Azāriqa and Najdāt of Fars and Kirmān established their authority to the extent of being able to mint coins: the Najdite leader 'Aṭiyya b. al-Aswad al-Ḥanafī minted coins in his name between 72–76/691–695; and the Azraqite Imām Qaṭarī b. Fujā'a minted coins with the title "Commander of the Faithful" in Fars between the years 69 and 75/688 and 694.[88] Finally, al-Balādhurī reports that followers of the early Khārijite rebels Qarīb and Zuḥḥāf refused to fight without an Imām.[89] This refusal, likewise, illustrates the belief of these early Khārijites in the necessity for an Imām.

The exception to the conviction of the necessity of an Imām among the Khārijites was a group of the Najdāt, who shared the doctrine of the rejection of the obligatory nature of the Imām with certain Mu'tazilites, especially al-Aṣam, Ḥishām al-Fuwaṭī, al-Naẓẓām, 'Abbād b. Sulaymān, and the Mu'tazilite Ascetics (*ṣūfiyyāt al-mu'tazila*).[90] Islamic heresiographical sources clearly portray the Najdāt as rejecting the imāmate: "Zurqān relates from the Najdāt that they say that they do not need an Imām and that they are only obliged to act by the book of God in their dealings with each other";[91] "the Najdiyya of the Khārijites say that the *umma* does not need an Imām or anyone else, and that they and other people are only obligated to uphold the book of God in their dealings with one another";[92] "as for what the Najdāt of the Khawārij hold regarding the people not needing an Imām and only being obliged to uphold the book of God in their dealings with one another, that doctrine is worthless."[93]

Crone convincingly argues that the Najdite rejection of the obligatory nature of the Imām developed as a survival strategy among the later Najdāt, who lived in a state of secrecy.[94] Citing al-Mubarrad and al-Baghdādī's statements to the effect that Najdāt existed in later eras, Crone proposes that existing Najdāt modified their doctrines after the demise of their initial revolt; al-Mubarrad referred to the Najdāt with the comment that "many of them remain to this day";[95] al-Baghdādī broke the Najdāt into four groups, one of which, he claimed, "are the Najdāt today," implying the existence of Najdāt in the fifth/tenth century.[96] In addition, other historical sources hint at the continued existence of the Najdāt; despite the massacre of original Najdites in the Ḥijāz, Ibn al-Athīr mentions a Khārijite revolt in Bahrain and al-Yamāma in 106/724 by Masʿūd b. Abī Zaynab al-ʿAbdī, and by his successor Hilāl b. Mudlij, a mere thirty years after the downfall of the original Najdāt.[97] No other Ibāḍī or Sunni source refers to this revolt, which must be assumed to have Najdite inspiration. Given that the early Najdāt acknowledge Najda b. ʿAmr al-Ḥanafī as Imām, the rejection of the obligatory nature of the imāmate must have occurred among the later Najdāt.

The Najdite argument against the obligatory nature of the Imām from al-Shahrastānī's *Kitāb Nihāyat al-Iqdām* makes clear that the Najdāt based this doctrine on a rejection of *ijmāʿ* in favor of individual *ijtihād*.[98] Each Najdite was viewed as a *mujtahid* in his own right, capable and responsible for making the decisions that ultimately affected his salvation. It followed that no *ijtihād* should have preference over another, including the *ijtihād* of the Imām.[99] Moreover, as the Najdāt argued, the community had not reached consensus (*ijmāʿ*) on the imamate of Abū Bakr or any other Imām since Abū Bakr's time. Abū Bakr had certainly been the most qualified person (*al-afḍal*) to lead the Muslim community after the death of the Prophet, and yet the early community could not agree upon him. And if the early Companions could not agree on an Imām, it would be impossible for the community to do so now.[100] Thus, underlying this conception of authority was the view that the Imām was someone whose manifest superiority over others would make his choice as Imām obvious. At the same time, the Najdites believed that this type of Imām could not exist and that he was nothing more than a utopian ideal. Due to the impossibility of the Imām, the Najdāt contented themselves with a "quasi-Imam," or *raʾīs* whose authority rested solely on the Najdite community's approval of him.[101] The *raʾīs* defended the community, and maintained order in it, but enjoyed no special status or power.

As such, the later Najdāt presented something of an anomaly in Khārijite history; no other Khārijite groups blatantly rejected the obligatory nature of the imāmate, or the efficacy of the Imām in favor of the *ijtihād* of each individual. As shown above, most other Khārijite groups tacitly accepted the need for an Imām by repeatedly designating Imāms. In addition, the early Ibāḍiyya explicitly linked the success of the community with their leaders, a position that implied the need for an Imām.

The historical situation of the later Najdāt can account to a certain extent for the peculiar Najdite rejection of the obligatory nature of the Imām. First, it is possible that the Najdite dismissal of the necessity of the Imām reflects a doctrinal justification for the later Najdite's existence in a state of *taqiyya*, whereby an Imām proper remained impossible.[102] The later Najdāt did not establish political entities such as those of the Ibāḍiyya and Ṣufriyya in Basra, Oman, and North Africa. Thus, they were unable to declare an imāmate, and may have developed their doctrine to justify this situation. Second, the small, homogeneous communities in which the Najdāt undoubtedly persisted lent themselves to informal modes of leadership, such as the *ra'īs*. This state of affairs differed little from the condition of the quietist Khārijite communities in Basra, or the post-Rustumid Ibāḍī communities in North Africa. In both situations, the Ibāḍī community effectively functioned without an Imām; the scholars who ruled during the formative period of Ibāḍism in Basra were only later dubbed Imāms, and the North African Ibāḍī *'ulamā'* never claimed to be Imāms, only to rule by dispensation in the Imām's stead. Thus, the later Najdāt may have simply made overt what other groups, especially the Ibāḍiyya, took pains to explain as exceptions in legal texts.

The Balance of Authority in the Medieval Ibāḍī Imāmate

The medieval Ibāḍī imāmate ideal, as it is preserved in both western and eastern Ibāḍī sources, institutionalized the balance of powers between the Ibāḍī Imām and the community (that is, the *ulamā'* as the representatives of the community) that was based upon a conviction in the communal duty to insure the efficacy of the Ibāḍī Imām. This balance of powers comprised, on the one hand, the necessity and integrity of the Imām whereby an Imām was considered an absolutely requirement for the proper functioning of the *umma*, and the community could not curtail certain aspects of his authority. On the other hand, the Ibāḍī community retained the duty to select an Imām, to monitor his behavior, and to depose him if he committed a major infraction of Islamic law. Under certain conditions, the Ibāḍī *'ulamā'* assumed more powers in relation to the Imām: in Oman they imposed consultation on "weak" and *difā'ī* Imāms and, as shown to be the case in North Africa, they assumed full control of the community in the absence of an Imām.

The early Ibāḍī belief in the efficacious role of the Imām became a standard feature of later Ibāḍī thought, and medieval Ibāḍī jurisprudence preserved the notion that the Imām functioned as a guide for his followers, and thereby affected their collective welfare. Al-Kindī provides the example of the Prophet Muhammad as the "Imām of all people" (*imām al-khalā'iq*), because God had sent him as a model for all to follow. The Prophet Muhammad thus became the preeminent Imām and religious guide. Likewise, al-Kindī quotes the Prophetic *ḥadīth* that states: "He who dies and does not know the Imām of his age dies a death of ignorance"; and "Seeing the just Imām is an act of worship."[103] These *ḥadīth* imply the necessity of an Imām for the success of the Islamic community. Similarly, al-Kudamī notes: "like [the Prophets], the Imām has his recompense (*lahu ajrahu*), and [there is] reward for those who pursue obedience to him... so long as he is just."[104] Al-Kindī notes that the Imām is called the Imām because "he is [a source of] order to the people; he is a source of imitation for them; he is a pattern whose word they follow; they follow his example by his command."[105] It is clear that these jurists regard the Imām as someone who affects the destiny of his followers by the fact that he provides a model for behavior, and that by virtue of his ability to command obedience and action, he affects the actions of his followers. This is an obvious continuation of the earlier Ibāḍī notion of the Imām as source of succor for the community.

The Ibāḍī belief in the efficacy of the Imām was not simply a pious phrase repeated by legal scholars in books; it possessed important ramifications for the subsequent institutional structure of the medieval Ibāḍī imāmate. Among the consequences of this belief was the consequent conviction that the Ibāḍī community required an Imām. Al-Kindī, synthesizing the views of earlier Ibāḍī scholars, declares that the acknowledgment of an Imām is a duty (*farḍ*) incumbent upon the Muslim community, and produces Qur'ānic verses as evidence for his assertion.[106] Similarly, al-Bisyānī establishes the necessity of the Imām on the basis of "the book of God, the *sunna* of the Prophet, and the consensus (*ijmāʿ*) of the community."[107] As if responding to the Najdite attack on the consensus over Abū Bakr's caliphate, al-Kindī notes that although the early community could not agree upon who should properly assume the leadership of the community, there was no dissention over the fact that the community should have an Imām.[108] Moreover, as proof of the necessity of the imāmate, Abū Mundhir argues that only the Imāms can apply Islamic legal penalties (the *ḥudūd*).[109] This reference to the application of *ḥudūd* is not accidental; the executive powers of the Imām remained an essential element of the establishment of Islamic justice. Although disputed, a majority of Ibāḍī jurists held that no just social order existed, theoretically, without the enforcement of Islamic law by a qualified Imām. By enforcing the *ḥudūd*, the Ibāḍī Imām became an indispensable institution that rendered the laws of God applicable in the world, and executed the Islamic responsibility of creating the just society on earth.

The same conviction in the efficacy of the Imām protected, to a certain extent, the integrity of his authority. The paramount necessity of an Imām to the Ibāḍī community implied certain amount of authority independent from the community. The basic principles behind the integrity of the powers of the Imām were laid down very early in Ibāḍī history by the second Basran Imām al-Rabīʿ b. Ḥabīb al-Farāhidī, who ruled as head of the Ibāḍī community during the second half of the second/eighth century. Al-Farāhidī, who pronounced on questions surrounding the election of the second Rustumid Imām ʿAbd al-Wahhāb, adjudged that there could be no conditions imposed on the Imām (*lā sharṭ ʿalā al-imām*):

> It is not fitting that the Imām should submit to conditions and act only in accordance with a regular assembly. The imāmate is truth and conditions are falsehood. To impose conditions on the Imām... is to impede the [application of] punishments, to suppress judgment, and to destroy the truth. If the powers of the *jamāʿa* are such that the Imām cannot condemn a thief and cut off his hand without consulting them, nor have a adulterer stoned or flogged without consulting them, or if he can not make war upon the enemy and put a stop to disorder, such a state is inadmissible.[110]

Thus, the integrity of the Imām's authority was protected, to a certain extent, from communal interference.

Nevertheless, al-Farāhidī's prohibition of the imposition of conditions on the Imām did not rule out the possibility that the Imām could voluntarily consult with the Muslims. In fact, consultation with the Muslims (especially with the Ibāḍī *ʿulamāʾ*) was a highly recommended practice for an Imām. Al-Kindī, for example, declares: "It is appropriate for the Imām to consult with the people of legal opinion (*ahl al-raʾy*) in religion."[111] Among the North African Ibāḍiyya, ʿAbd al-Raḥmān b. Rustum, as the representation of the ideal Imām, was portrayed as consulting the Muslims over seemingly trivial matters; for example, Ibn al-Ṣaghīr and Abū Zakariyya narrate how ʿAbd al-Raḥmān consulted his *ʿulamāʾ* as to whether he should accept a monetary gift from two Basran Ibāḍī visitors.[112] Thus, while consultation was not required of the Imām, it was highly recommended.

Just as medieval Ibāḍī jurisprudence protected the integrity of the Imām's decision-making capabilities from interference from the Ibāḍī community, so it also shielded, to a certain extent, the integrity of the Imām's office. According to al-Kudamī, as long as the Imām acted according to the standards of justice, communal obedience became a qualified duty: "the people are required to obey the just Imāms insofar as [the Imāms] obey God and His messenger, and act by His Book, and do not change its interpretation, and do not demand obedience to something sinful."[113] Likewise, al-Ṣāʾighī warns, "the fundamental principle involved is that since the *imāma* is a divine obligation, the Imām may not be deposed or abdicate without good reason (*ʿudhr*)." The grounds for removal involve sin, mental incapacity, or a refusal to discharge the responsibilities incumbent upon the Imām; in all other cases the Imām must be obeyed.[114] This type of qualified obedience allowed the Imām to operate, to a certain extent, independently from the influence of the community.

On the other hand, the Ibāḍī *'ulamā'* were granted limited powers in relation to the Imām. These powers included the duty to choose, monitor and, possibly, to depose the Imām. In the selection of an Imām, the communal aspects of authority became apparent in the requirement for a council to pick an Imām, as well as in the transformation of the practice of *bay'a* into a qualified pledge. Among the Ibāḍiyya, the practice of *shūrā* is well documented, and became an essential aspect of the medieval institution of the Imām. Ibāḍī sources present Omani Ibāḍī Imāms as elected by a council of Ibāḍī *shaykh*s. Regarding the election of the first Omani leader, al-Wārith b. Ka'b al-Kharūṣī, Ibn Qaḥṭān reports, "[the Muslims] gathered and chose for themselves an Imām."[115] Likewise, al-Kindī, Abū Mu'thir, and Ibn Baraka hold consultation (*mashwara*) in the choice of an Imām to be required, even if only two of the *'ulamā'* are present (six are preferred, in emulation of the council established by the Caliph 'Umar to select his successor).[116] Abū Isḥāq requires at least six men of knowledge to establish an Imām.[117] In North Africa, the first Imām, 'Abd al-Raḥmān b. Rustum, was elected by a council of Berber tribal leaders, after which leadership in the Rustumid dynasty became hereditary.[118]

The authority of the community was symbolically acknowledged during the pledge of allegiance (*bay'a*) to the Imām. Al-Kindī preserves examples of the ways in which the followers of the Imām might pledge their allegiance to him: the pledge is qualified with the promise to follow "obedience to God, and to His Prophet Muhammad, to act by His Book, and by the *sunna* of His Prophet Muhammad, and to command the good and forbid evil."[119] Although generalized, such conditions transformed the *bay'a* into an instrument of potential control on behalf of those pledging allegiance. The followers of the Imām claimed a right against him to refuse obedience and depose him if he should fail to uphold the standards of Islam. Such latent authority on behalf of the Imām's subjects clearly demonstrated the limiting authority of the Ibāḍī community in the application of the *bay'a*.

Medieval Ibāḍī jurisprudence further institutionalized the activist communal posture of the Ibāḍiyya by requiring the community to monitor and depose an unjust ruler. Ibn Maḥbūb argues that the application of the *ḥudūd* becomes meaningless unless the Imām is just; therefore it is imperative for the Imām to be just.[120] Al-Kindī, representing a general view among Ibāḍī jurors, explains that an unjust Imām, or an Imām who persists in sin, must be removed, by force if necessary, from the position of Imām unless he repents.[121] In resisting an unjust Imām, al-Kindī argues, the community is not required to establish another Imām before rebelling, and is only compelled to rebel if it has the capacity to succeed. Al-Kindī cites the example of 'Uthmān's killing to justify his ruling that the community may depose a leader before establishing a new leader.[122] Likewise, al-Kudamī requires the community to depose an Imām if he does not maintain the standards of Islamic behavior: "If [the Imāms] sin against God, then the people owe them no obedience—on the contrary, the people are [then] required to depose them, and fight them until they return to the ruling of the Book of God, and the *sunna* of His Prophet Muhammad."[123] This activist stance of the Ibāḍī community in relation to their leaders necessarily limited the authority of Ibāḍī leaders, making the scope of the Imām's authority similar (at least in theory) to the restricted authority of Abū Bakr and 'Umar.[124]

In actual fact, the Ibāḍiyya rarely deposed their leaders on the basis of sin. In a third/ninth-century epistle, Ibn Qaḥṭān gives a candid view of some of the misdeeds of the Imāms. His description was meant to prove a point in the controversy surrounding the replacement of the Imām al-Ṣalt b. Mālik by a rival faction of the Julanda tribe. Ibn Qaḥṭān argues that although earlier Imāms acted in a manner that was inconsistent with the strict requirements of justice, these Imāms nonetheless maintained their authority as Imāms. As examples, Ibn Qaḥṭān discusses the Imām 'Abd al-Mālik b. Ḥumayd who went insane and had to be confined to his palace, yet was not deposed. Similarly, Ibn Qaḥṭān relates how two of the most prominent Omani scholars secretly dissociated from the Omani Imām al-Muhannā' b. Jayfar because of his tyrannical behavior, and yet he nevertheless retained the position of Imām.[125]

Even so, medieval Ibāḍī jurisprudence theoretically balanced the authority of the Ibāḍī Imām with certain powers that it reserved for the Ibāḍī "community." This need for an Imām who could exercise the responsibilities of an Islamic leader simultaneously guaranteed that the community did not interfere overmuch in the imāmate, at least under ideal conditions. However, in extreme cases, the Ibāḍī community might have to forgo the requirement for an Imām if the existence of the community was threatened. If, for example, the Ibāḍiyya did not possess the ability to effectively resist an unjust Imām, the community entered a state of concealment (*kitmān*) and the imāmate became dispensable.[126] This state of concealment and consequent lack of Imām remained a special dispensation (*rukhṣa*), while the ultimate duty to establish and support an Imām persisted.[127] Thus, while it is formally correct to say that the Ibāḍī Imām is dispensable, it is only so in exceptional situations involving the potential annihilation of the Ibāḍī community. In all other cases the *imāma* was required.

In North Africa, the special conditions that allowed for the Ibāḍī community to enter a state of *kitmān* and thereby to dispense with their Imām have persisted until the present day, and the Ibāḍīs there have evolved novel institutions of authority for the state of *kitmān* on the basis of leadership by the Ibāḍī *'ulamā'*. Nevertheless, the North African Ibāḍī *'ulamā'* upheld the duty of the community to possess an Imām. Al-Malshūṭī, a fifth/eleventh century Berber Ibāḍī theologian who lived in southern Tunisia and al-Warjlān (in present-day Algeria) during the time of *kitmān*, wrote: "We consider the contract of the Imām a duty" (*'aqd al-imāma farīḍa 'andanā*).[128] Thus, while the North African Ibāḍīs have practically replaced the institution of the Imām with other forms of communal governance, the necessity of an imāmate has remained as an ideal.

Medieval Ibāḍī jurisprudence also recognized the possibility of accepting a restricted Imām, that is, Imāms who governed either for a limited time or for the purposes of defending the Ibāḍī community. As we have seen, such an Imām was called a "defensive" Imām (*al-imām al-difā'ī* or *al-imām 'alā al-difā'*), and was allowable when the community entered into a defensive posture vis-à-vis its enemies.[129] Although this institution remained hypothetical in North Africa, the Omani Ibāḍiyya developed it along practical lines: the Ibāḍī community elected the defensive Imām on the provision that he could be removed after a fixed time or after the conclusion of hostilities.[130] When the defensive Imām was appointed for a fixed period of time, he became, in the words of al-Bisyānī, like a trustee (*wakīl*) of the community. Ibāḍī scholars provide the example of 'Abdullāh b. Wahb al-Rāsibī and the Imām Muḥammad b. Abī 'Affān (who briefly ruled in Oman in 178–180/794—796) as prototypes for the "defensive" Imāms.[131] Concurrently, Omani Ibāḍī scholars established the notion of the "weak" Imām (*al-imām al-ḍa'īf*); if the Ibāḍī community feared it would not survive, a powerful but unqualified person may be given the oath of a weak Imām on condition that he consult with the Ibāḍī *'ulamā'*.[132] This consultation applied to the use of the treasury, appointing administrators (*walī/awliyā'*), raising an army, and judging in matters of the *sharī'a*. Weak Imāms, according to al-Bisyānī, may only be elected during times of dire necessity (*ḍarūra*).[133] Thus, the notion of a defensive or weak Imām presents another case where the Ibāḍī community claimed an increased amount of authority over the Imām beyond that already granted to them in the case of a strong Imām. As Wilkinson notes, defensive and weak Imāms were limited to periods of imperfect Ibāḍī rule, especially during the collapse of the third Ibāḍī imāmate in Oman (fifth/eleventh through the sixth/twelfth centuries), when the concepts of the defensive and weak Imām were increasingly developed.[134] Thus, the Ibāḍī *imāma* presents a case whereby medieval Ibāḍī jurisprudence only recognized an expanded authority for the community when the *imāma* was threatened with annihilation. Although the potential for the Ibāḍī community to dominate the Imām increased with the establishment of defensive or weak Imāms, Ibāḍī scholars took great pains to discourage the use of weak and defensive Imāms, stressing their contingent and limited natures.

The balance of powers that ideally existed between the Ibāḍī Imām and their community, as it is preserved in medieval Ibāḍī legal and historical texts, established the necessity of the Imām, as well as the powers granted to the *'ulamā'* in relation to selecting, monitoring, and deposing the Imām. This institutional structure was based on an underlying conviction in the efficacy of the Imām, and in the need for the community to assure their own success by insuring that the Imām performed in a manner befitting his position. These institutional features of the medieval Ibāḍī *imāma* were based on earlier precedents: the powers assumed by Arabian tribes in relation to the pre-Islamic *sayyid*, and the authority granted to the community during the caliphates of Abū Bakr and 'Umar. Likewise, the Qur'ān implied a soteriological role for the Prophet as leader of the community, and hinted at a possible role for the community in monitoring temporal institutions of authority. Although the early Khārijites and Umayyads shared a belief in the efficacy of their leaders, they reached different conclusions regarding the subsequent powers of the community in relation to the Imām. The early Khārijites maintained a balance of powers much closer to what had existed during the pre-Islamic and early Islamic era. The Umayyads, on the other hand, based their theory of the leader's efficacy on the divine sanction of their Caliphs, and consequently tended toward authoritarianism.

The pre-Islamic and early Islamic precedents for the balance of authority between Ibāḍī Imām and Ibāḍī *'ulamā'* ultimately became incorporated into medieval Ibāḍī institutions of authority in numerous institutional forms: on the one hand, in the necessity of the Imām, and in the protection of certain of his powers; on the other hand, the authority of the Ibāḍī community to select, monitor, and depose an Imām based upon the criterion of righteousness. Moreover, the Ibāḍī community assumed extra authority in the case of a *ḍa'īf* or *difā'ī* Imām, or in the special case of the state of *kitmān*, when an Imām became dispensable. These special conditions, however, did not overrule the belief in the ultimate necessity of the Imām, or in the integrity of the office of the Imām.

Conclusion

The importance of the Ibāḍiyya for Islamic studies, and for the study of sectarianism in general, lies in their uniqueness as the only remaining subsect of a significant sectarian grouping in early Islamic history, the Khārijites. And although it is true that the Ibāḍiyya have developed well beyond their early manifestations in Basra, and only vaguely resemble their cousins among the Khārijites, they nevertheless do represent a distinctive—the Ibāḍīs would say a truer—interpretation of what it means to be a Muslim. As such, the historical study of the Ibāḍiyya offers a means by which scholars can gain a fresh perspective on the course of Islamic history by sidestepping the usual Sunni and Shi'ite accounts and assumptions. This endeavor has been greatly facilitated by the recent publications of the Ibāḍī textual corpus, which offers a wealth of newly available resources for the scholar.

Yet the uniqueness of the Ibāḍiyya—and of their distant relatives the Khārijites—must not be overstated. Sunni (and occasionally Shi'ite) heresiographers, who mapped the sectarian geography of their eras in an attempt to establish the one "true" and "saved" Islamic sect, separated all other groups as heretical by accentuating their doctrinal and practical differences. The isolation of the Khārijite subsects was the predictable result of these polemics, whereby heresiographers treated any group not deemed appropriately orthodox as exceptional. Likewise, the well-known historical sources for early Islamic history accentuate the tendency to view the Khārijites and their subsects as deviants from the emerging Sunni norm. Not only did the compilers of the great

Muslim annals live many decades after the events that their sources described but they also inherited and contributed to a historical tradition that was rarely written by Khārijites and often hostile to them.[1] In the near absence of primary materials from the Khārijites, modern scholars, Muslim and non-Muslim alike, have relied heavily on heresiographical and historical texts for their information on the Islamic sects. These sources have bequeathed to scholarship on the Khārijites a tendency to view them as exceptional, isolated, and unique.

Because the question of Islamic sectarian identity is intimately tied to conceptions of proper politicoreligious authority, the development of the Ibāḍī imāmate theory offers a means to reassess the uniqueness of Ibāḍī sectarian identity. This study has attempted to correct the common scholarly misperception of the Khārijites and Ibāḍiyya as anomalous cases in Islamic history by locating historical precedents for the Ibāḍī imāmate in the broader Islamic currents out of which they developed. A central assumption has been that the historical, regional, and internal complexities of the medieval Ibāḍī imāmate suggest a correspondingly complex evolutionary process that produced them. Such an assumption is not uniquely appropriate to the Ibāḍiyya; al-Māwardī, for example, built upon, systematized and expanded the views of his predecessors regarding the caliphate, exercising his judgment as required to adapt the inherited tradition of the caliphate to the circumstances of his day.[2] In such a way, the Sunni caliphate. as articulated by al-Māwardī became the product of several different layers of historical precedent rationalized into a single vision of the caliphate. Likewise, the medieval Ibāḍī imāmate ideal is the product of multiple institutions of authority that were inherited from earlier eras via the early Basran Ibāḍiyya. Various historical conceptions and institutions of authority were passed on to the early Basran Ibāḍīs, who unified them into a somewhat coherent theory of authority for the Ibāḍiyya, and then subsequently passed this theory on to the Ibāḍiyya in North Africa and Oman, where historical circumstances obliged scholars of the imāmate traditions to adapt the *imāma* according to regional considerations. Thus the medieval North African imāmate ideal recognizes four distinct types of Imām, which match up with four different conditions of the community, while the Omani imāmate theory acknowledges four types of Imāms, who correspond to two different states of the community. This study has illustrated how the Ibāḍī vision of the imāmate, to the extent that it can be reconstructed from a comparison of later medieval Ibāḍī theories, built upon, systematized, and expanded the concepts and earlier institutions of authority that they inherited from the formative period of Ibāḍism in Basra, the early Khārijite era, the Madīnan caliphate, the Qur'ān and the Prophetic model of leadership, and also the pre-Islamic era.

Specifically, it has shown how ideas of personal merit shaped, to a certain extent, the pre-Islamic institution of the *sayyid*, but that the advent of Islam redefined the merits appropriate to leaders along the lines of Islamic piety. This conception of piety and moral rectitude as a legitimate aspect of authority achieved, in the eyes of Muslims, its most perfect expression under the leadership of the Prophet as the ultimate example of a moral leader; the examples of Abū Bakr and 'Umar follow in importance. Using the Prophet and early Islamic caliphates as their model, the early Khārijites adopted notions of piety and moral rectitude that were perceived to be a part of the early Madīnan caliphate of Abū Bakr and 'Umar, and incorporated these principles into their own institutions of authority. The Ibāḍiyya, in turn, adapted the Khārijite institutions of authority to their own institution of the *ẓuhūr* Imām: the type of Imām who represented the optimal leader, and who ruled under ideal conditions.

Yet the early Khārijites and Ibāḍiyya often found themselves in less than optimal situations. In the most extreme cases, like that of *kitmān*, where the very survival of the sect seemed in jeopardy, the Ibāḍīs suspended the requirements of the imāmate while turning to the scholars of their community for leadership and guidance. In this condition, the possession of knowledge, in addition to piety, legitimated the *'ulamā'*'s assumption of authority. This situation also had its precedents, for like piety, conceptions of knowledge as a characteristic expected of leaders circulated during the pre-Islamic era, and continued into the Islamic era as the belief in divinely inspired knowledge as a fundamental element of the office of Prophet. After the Prophet Muhammad's death, the early Madīnan Caliphs were subsequently assumed to have *'ilm* (defined after the coming of Islam as knowledge of religion), and the possession of knowledge became a requirement for the caliphate. The Khārijites systematized the trait of knowledge, like the quality of piety, into their conception of legitimate authority, and made the possession of knowledge a requirement for the imāmate. However, the experience of living in a state of secrecy (*kitmān*), in which no Imām existed, thrust the informal leadership of the Khārijite community onto the *'ulamā'*. In such a way, the possession of *'ilm* became a requisite for the Imām, as well as for those who assumed limited authority over the Khārijite community when the imāmate was limited or rendered impossible. Later medieval Ibāḍī institutions of the *imām al-difā'*, the *imām al-ḍa'īf*, and the largely fictive institution of the *imām al-kitmān* reflect, in their own ways, this concern for knowledgeable leaders as well as the ideological need to create, in the case of the *imām al-kitmān*, an "institution" that served to bolster the Ibāḍī claims to an unbroken line of Imāms (and their *'ilm*) reaching back to the Prophet Muhammad.

Next, this study turned to the *shārī* Imām, a truly unique aspect of Ibāḍī imāmate theory. Unlike piety and knowledge, the notion of *shirā'* did not originate as a concept of authority, nor did it necessarily originate in the pre-Islamic era. *Shirā'*, under the earliest Khārijites, described an indigenous, Khārijite interpretation of the Qur'ānic and early Islamic concepts and institutions of *jihād* and martyrdom (*shahāda*). In the early Islamic period, the practice of *shirā'* created a pantheon of Khārijite heroes and martyrs (*shurāt*), whose stories possessed tremendous potential as propaganda. In such a way, the practice of *shirā'* posthumously conferred an authority on the Khārijite *shurāt* and created an informal "institution" of martyrs and heroes. The Basran Ibāḍiyya adopted the Iraqi narratives of the early Khārijite martyrs and heroes in order to assimilate their mantle and bolster the popular appeal of the Ibāḍī sect. Furthermore, by posthumously raising the early Iraqi heroes and martyrs to the status of Imāms, the Ibāḍiyya established the precedent for the medieval Ibāḍī institution of the *imām al-shirā'*. However, medieval Ibāḍī jurists tempered the revolutionary potential of this institution by encasing it in a set of juridical regulations. In effect, the institutionalization of *shirā'* tamed its revolutionary potential, and brought it safely under the purview of the scholars.

Finally, this study examined how a belief in the efficaciousness of the leader empowered the Ibāḍī community (represented by the *'ulamā'*) with the duty to select, monitor, and potentially depose the Imām. It argued that this conception of communal authority, balanced by the conviction in the necessity and ultimate integrity of the Imām, has precedents in the pre-Islamic conception of tribal survival and communal authority; furthermore, it is implied by the Qur'ān, and by the way in which the early Caliphs encouraged the tribal-Islamic model of balanced powers between leader and community during the Madīnan period. While the early Umayyad Caliphs moved toward a more authoritarian model of authority, the early Khārijites perpetuated the tribal-Islamic model of communal authority, a model that eventually provided the precedent for the role of the community in relation to the medieval Ibāḍī Imām.

Having examined these four aspects of medieval Ibāḍī imāmate theory, it should be noted that the deconstruction of the imāmate institution into four different institutions corresponding to four underlying aspects of authority is a somewhat subjective exercise, even if the institutions can be found in medieval Ibāḍī imāmate writings. In fact, attention to piety, knowledge, bravery, and the need for the community to insure that the Imām abides by all three are concerns that permeate every aspect of the North African and Omani imāmate institutions to some degree. Likewise, distinctions between the *imām al-ẓuhūr*, *imām al-shirā'*, *imām al-difā'*, and *imām al-kitmān* are not nearly as clear as post-medieval Ibāḍī imāmate theorists (and the non-Ibāḍī scholars who rely on them) would have us believe. Nevertheless, it is a helpful exercise to separate and focus on the different facets of the Imām's authority in order to highlight the different institutional features of the imāmate across regional, sectarian, and historical boundaries. By so doing, the deconstruction of the Imām's authority serves as a means to examine the similarities underlying the various subinstitutions that comprise the North African and Omani theories of the imāmate.

Moreover, by focusing on the constituent parts of the Ibāḍī imāmate, this study has been able to illuminate its correspondences with earlier Islamic, that is, proto-Sunni, as well as early Shi'ite and (non-Ibāḍī) Khārijite, models of authority. Thus, analysis of the historical precedents of the Ibāḍī imāmate ideal highlights the importance of the persistence of tribal models of authority into the early Islamic period, and how these tribal understandings of authority functioned as precedents for the early Khārijite, as well as the medieval Ibāḍī institutions of authority. However, it must be stressed that so-called "tribal" paradigms of authority must be understood in relation to the whole of Islamic society's development, and not simply restricted to the pre-Islamic era. That is, the early Madīnan period of Islamic history remained grounded in "tribal" models of social structure and authority insofar as tribal ideals continued to animate the decisions of those in positions of power, even when they were thoroughly anchored in the urban milieu of Makka and Madīna. Therefore, it is not enough to observe, as Watt does, that the Khārijites attempted to reconstitute on an Islamic basis the small groups they had been familiar with in the desert.[3] Islamic society was already steeped in a tribal ethos that shaped its conceptions of legitimate authority; the Khārijites simply systematized (albeit selectively) tribal notions of authority that underpinned the Madīnan caliphate itself. Watt's statement on the authority of the Khārijite Imām turns out to be partially helpful, and partially misleading: the authority of the Khārijite Imām remained primus inter pares, like the Arab *sayyid*, but only because the Khārijites modeled their institutions of authority on Abū Bakr and 'Umar, whose authority remained, like the Arab *sayyid*, the first among equals. In the final analysis, the Khārijite political theories were no more or less "tribal" than their proto-Sunni or Shi'ite counterparts, all of which sprang from a similar Arabian context. For this reason, the supposed exceptionalism of the Khārijite (and thereby Ibāḍī) case must be viewed with caution.

By looking at the areas of convergence between Ibāḍī and non-Ibāḍī conceptions of leadership, a clearer idea of what constitutes their differences also arises. Despite their emergence from and debt to the Arabian context from which they developed, there is no denying that the Sunni, Shi'ite, and Ibāḍī paths toward their own understanding of legitimate authority began to diverge at an early period. Thus, though the proto-Sunnis, Khārijites, and Ibāḍiyya share a concern for the moral probity of their leaders, only the Khārijites and Ibāḍiyya clung to and later incorporated this belief into the very structure of the imāmate institution. Likewise, while the Khārijites, Ibāḍiyya, and early Shi'ites found themselves arrayed against the Umayyads as part of what has been called the "pious opposition," Khārijite, Ibāḍī, and Shi'ite notions of what constituted knowledge fundamentally differed. Further, only the Ibāḍiyya developed the particularly Khārijite institution of *shirā'* into the *shārī* Imām, despite the popularity and proliferation of Shi'ite martyrdom narratives. And only the Khārijites and Ibāḍiyya maintain the formal role of the community (via the *'ulamā'*) as a stopgap against the excesses of their leaders, even though such a relationship exists informally among the Sunni *'ulamā'*, and after the disappearance of the twelfth Imām, the same could be said for the twelver Shi'ite *'ulamā'* at certain points in their long history.

Finally, in tracing the internal developments of the Ibāḍī imāmate theory, this study has offered a model for understanding how a religious institution develops, even across geographical boundaries, into an integral aspect of religious identity. The Ibāḍī institution of the Imām, and its constituent parts, has been shown as a complex institution with an equally multifaceted history that stretches back to the early periods of Islamic history and beyond. Such a model for conceptualizing institutions looks to several sources for mapping the accumulation of historical development. Most important, this model looks beyond sectarian definitions of the Ibāḍiyya (which were established after the formative period of Ibāḍism) toward the areas where Ibāḍī, Khārijite, proto-Sunni, and proto-Shi'ite doctrines, practices, and thereby identities comingled.

It is hoped that this study will serve as a stepping stone for further investigation. Ibāḍī studies remain very much in their infancy, and plenty of work remains to be done. While this study focused on the processes and influences that worked to shape the Ibāḍiyya from within the Islamic fold, another inquiry should attend to the influences of non-Islamic contexts and sources on the Khārijites and Ibāḍiyya. The Khārijites did, after all, emerge in Iraq into an era saturated with Christian, Jewish, Zoroastrian, and "pagan" traditions. In particular, the time has come for a reassessment of Morony's insights into the Assyrian Christian influences on early Mesopotamian Khārijites and other aspects of Khārijite religious thought in light of now accessible Ibāḍī texts.[4] While Ibāḍī resources offer a glimpse into a world of religious ideas that exists parallel to the Sunni and Shi'a, they may also suggest a means to cross the dividing line between Muslims, Christians, Jews, and other religious groups of the late antique to early medieval period.

In addition, much work remains to be done on the actual functioning of the imāmate, especially as it was practiced in Oman at various times. This study has concerned itself with the imāmate ideal as it has been articulated primarily in legal works and idealized histories. As such, the imāmate ideal presented in those works and reflected in this study does not necessarily correspond to how Ibāḍī Imāms have, in reality, been selected, maintained, or deposed. It is hoped that this study might provide a reference point for such research.

The increased availability of Ibāḍī materials, both early and medieval, has enabled a reassessment of the origins and development of the Ibāḍī imāmate ideal and allowed a modification of certain entrenched notions about the Khārijite attitude toward authority in general. As the distant relative and, in some senses, the sole remaining representative of the movement that was known as Khārijism, the Ibāḍiyya and their texts provide a rare opportunity for scholars of Islam to step outside of the typical Sunni-Shiʿa–dominated frames of reference. Such perspective offers a welcome opportunity to view the history of Islam from a fresh angle.

Notes

Introduction

1. According to a *ḥadīth* (which survives in many variants), Muhammad is reported to have said: "the Jews are divided into seventy-one sects, and the Christians into seventy-two, but my community will be divided into seventy-three sects." Only one of these sects would be the "saved sect" (*al-firqa al-nājiyya*), leaving seventy-two to be damned. See 'Abd al-Qāhir b. Ṭāhir al-Baghdādī, *al-Farq Bayn al-Firaq* (Beirut: Dār al-Afāq al-Jadīda, 1987), 4.
2. Wilferd Madelung, *The Succession to Muḥammad* (Cambridge: Cambridge University Press, 1997), 1.
3. Wellhausen, for example, used the Sunni sources available to him in his 1901 work *Die Religios-Politischen Oppositionsparteien im Alten Islam*, and accordingly he provides only the barest details about the Ibāḍiyya. Relevant passages may be found in Julius Wellhausen, *The Religio-Political Factions in Early Islam* (New York: American Elsevier, 1975), 45; 85–88. Likewise, Salem's treatment of the Khārijite Imāmate relies overwhelmingly on evidence from Sunni sources. He cites only the Ibāḍī authors available to him in 1956: al-Shammākhī, Abū Zakariyya, Ibn Rāziq, and Ibn Ṣaghīr. See Elie Adib Salem, *Political Theory and Institutions of the Khawārij* (Baltimore: Johns Hopkins University Press, 1956), 47–67.
4. Ennami's edited Arabic texts may be found in his PhD dissertation, published as 'Amr K. Ennami, *Studies in Ibadism (Edition of Ibāḍī texts)* (Tripoli, Libya: Publications of the University of Libya Faculty of Arts, 1972).
5. Patricia Crone and Fritz Zimmerman, trs. and eds., *The Epistle of Sālim Ibn Dhakwān* (New York: Oxford University Press, 2001).

6. Lewicki, whose familiarity with the Ibāḍī manuscript collection in the Krakow library and insights into the early Ibāḍī imāmate of Basra and North Africa remain unsurpassed, nevertheless accepts the portrayal of Ibāḍī history given in the texts themselves. Similar criticism may be leveled at Ennami and other modern Ibāḍī historians such as Aṭfayyish, al-Ḥārithī, and Mu'ammar, as well as the Jordanian scholar Khulayfāt and UAE scholar Ghubash.
7. Montgomery Watt, *The Formative Period of Islamic Thought* (Oxford: Oneworld, 1998), 1–6; Keith Lewinstein, "The Azāriqa in Islamic Heresiography," *BSOAS* 54 (1991); Lewinstein, "Making and Unmaking a Sect: the Heresiographers and the Ṣufriyya," *SI* 76 (1992); Lewinstein, "Notes on Eastern Ḥanafite Heresiography," *JAOS* 114 (1994).
8. Levy claims that the Khārijites "disputed any need at all for any imām, or head of the State, as long as the divine law was carried out." See Reuben Levy, *The Social Structure of Islam* (Cambridge: Cambridge University Press, 1957), 279. Likewise, Salem maintains: "if the people can, without any superior authority, exercise [the application of the *sharī'a*], then there is no need for an Imām." See *Political Theory*, 51.
9. Hamid Dabashi, *Authority in Islam* (New Brunswick, N.J.: Transaction, 1989), 125.
10. For a discussion of scholarship on the Khārijites, see Hussam S. Timani, *Modern Intellectual Readings of the Kharijites* (New York: Peter Lang, 2008); Adam Gaiser, "Source Critical Methodologies in Recent Scholarship on the Khārijites," *Historical Compass* 7/5 (2009): 1376–1390.
11. Watt, *Formative Period*, 36–37.
12. Salem, for example, opts to describe the Khārijite political organization as a nomocracy—a system ruled by the Word of God (the Qur'ān) and enforced by the Khārijite community, which only grudgingly accepted a human authority out of practical need for a strong leader. See *Political Theory*, 48–50. In a similar vein, Bernard Lewis characterized the Khārijites as "an aggressive anarchist opposition acknowledging no authority but that of a Caliph whom they themselves selected and whom they could, and frequently did, at any time reject." See *The Arabs in History* (New York: Harper and Row, 1966), 73–74. Likewise, Dabashi argues that the Khārijites substituted the "radical puritanism" of the Khārijite community as a surrogate for meaningful government. See *Authority in Islam*, 124.
13. Salem, *Political Authority*, 49–50. Similarly, Watt acknowledges the importance of leadership to the Khārijite movement, but nevertheless locates soteriological efficacy in the Khārijite's supposed "charismatic community." See *Formative Period*, 37.
14. Dabashi writes: "Political authority stripped of any significant sacred or metaphysical significance" was the "sole attribute of any Muslim leader." See *Authority in Islam*, 7.
15. Dabashi claims that the Khārijite's "radical democracy, along with the lack of institutional order to regulate it" made positions of authority precarious. See *Authority in Islam*, 128. Von Grunebaum finds that the "moral absolutism" of the Khārijites precluded the possibility of building a state. See Gustav Von Grunebaum, *Classical*

Islam: A History 600–1258 (New York: Barnes and Noble Books, 1970), 62. Lambton views the arbitrariness of the Khārijite's methods of deciding on the legitimacy of their Imām as an inherent aspect of the Khārijite community's willingness to depose their Imām on moral grounds, and an indicator of the failing of the Imām's authority. See Ann Lambton, *State and Government in Medieval Islam* (Oxford: Oxford University Press, 1981), 24. Wellhausen also believes that the Khārijites acted "recklessly" on their duty to insure moral rectitude in leadership: their "extreme observance of the principles of Islam" led them to depose their Imām over "trivial" indiscretions and resulted in their splitting up into sects "over minor differences." See *Religio-Political Factions*, 22.

16. Patricia Crone, *God's Rule: Government and Islam* (New York: Columbia University Press, 2004), 57.
17. Crone, *God's Rule*, 59.
18. Elizabeth Savage, *A Gateway to Hell, A Gateway to Paradise: The North African Response to the Arab Conquest* (Princeton: Princeton University Press, 1997), 43–61.
19. For a description of some of the adaptations to the Omani Ibāḍī *imāma* after its formal establishment, see John C. Wilkinson, *The Imamate Tradition of Oman* (Cambridge: Cambridge University Press, 1987), 149–175.
20. Abū Zakariyya was a member of the North African Ibāḍī generation (*tabaqa*) that dates from the end of the fourth/tenth and beginning of the fifth/eleventh centuries. His quote regarding the stages of religion is the first comprehensive statement on the *masālik al-dīn*. See Abū al-'Abbās Aḥmad b. Sa'īd al-Darjīnī, *Kitāb Ṭabaqāt al-Mashāyikh bī al-Maghrib* (Algiers: Alger-Constantine, n.d.), 2:364. For a medieval North African description of the stages, see Abū Zakariyya Yaḥyā Ibn Abī Khayr al-Jannāwanī (d. sixth/twelfth century), *Kitāb al-Waḍ'* (Muscat: Maktabat al-Istiqāma, n.d.), 29.
21. al-Kindī, *al-Muṣannaf* (Muscat: *WTQwTh*, 1984), 10:53–54. Only since the revival of Ibāḍism in the tenth/sixteenth century have the four stages become a permanent fixture of western/North African and eastern/Omani Ibāḍī descriptions of the imāmate. See Adam Gaiser, "The Ibāḍī 'Stages of Religion' Re-examined: Tracing the History of the *Masālik al-Dīn*," *BSOAS* 73/2 (2010): 207–222. For a description of the modern Ibāḍī *imāma*, see Ḥusayn 'Ubayd Ghānim Ghubāsh, *'Umān: al-Dīmuqrāṭiyya al-Islāmiyya Taqlīd al-Imāma* (Beirut: Dār al-Jadīd, 1997), 68; Ghubash, Hussein, *Oman—The Islamic Democratic Tradition*, tr. Mary Turton (New York: Routledge, 2006), 33–35.
22. See the fourth/tenth-century scholar Abū al-Ḥasan 'Alī b. Muḥammad al-Bisyānī (var. al-Bisyawī) in Abū Bakr Aḥmad b. 'Abdullāh b. Mūsā al-Kindī, *Kitāb al-Ihtidā'* (Muscat: *WTQwTh*, 1985), 162; al-Kindī, *al-Muṣannaf*, 10:85.
23. For a discussion of the *muḥtasib* Imām, see Wilkinson, *Imamate Tradition*, 162.
24. al-Kindī, *al-Muṣannaf*, 10:61, 65, 69.
25. P. J. Wolf, "Authority: Delegation," in *International Encyclopedia of the Social & Behavioral Sciences*, eds. Neil J. Smelser and Paul P. Baltes (New York: Elsevier, 2001), 973.
26. John Wansbrough, *The Sectarian Milieu* (Oxford: Oxford University Press, 1978), 70.

27. John Wilkinson, "Early Development of the Ibāḍī Movement in Basra," in *Studies on the First Century of Islamic Society*, ed. G.H.A. Juynboll (Carbondale: Southern Illinois University Press, 1982), 125.
28. As Ennami observes, the state of *shirā'* and *kitmān* may exist simultaneously, because those who make a pact to sell themselves in service to God may exist separately from those who choose to remain in hiding. See 'Amr Ennami, *Studies in Ibadism (al-Ibāḍīyah)* (Tripoli, Libya: Publications of the University of Libya Faculty of Arts, 1972), 231.
29. al-Kindī, *al-Muṣannaf*, 10:69.
30. For an example of Ibāḍī heresiography, see the relevant portions of al-Qalhātī's *al-Kashf wa al-Bayān*, published as: Abū Sa'īd Muḥammad b. Sa'īd al-Azdī al-Qalhātī, *al-Firaq al-Islāmiyya min Khilāl al-Kashf wa al-Bayān*, ed. Muḥammad Ibn 'Abd al-Khalīl, (Tunis: Markaz al-Dirasāt wa al-Abḥāth al-Iqtiṣādiyya wa al-Ijtima'iyya, 1984).
31. I will focus here on published works. However, much text still remains in manuscript form. For a helpful list and analysis of Omani epistles, for example, see al-Salimi, Abdulrahman S., "Identifying the Ibāḍī/Omani *Siyar*," *Journal of Semitic Studies* 55/1 (2010); al-Salimi, "Themes of the Ibāḍī/Omani *Siyar*," *Journal of Seminitic Studies* 54/2 (2009).
32. Jābir's legal opinions (known as the *Jawābāt*) and his *Kitāb al-Nikāḥ* have been published in the arrangement of the Omani scholar Sa'īd b. Khalaf al-Kharūṣī: see *Min Jawābāt al-Imām Jābir b. Zayd* (Muscat: *WTQwTh*, 1992).
33. The sixth/twelfth-century Maghribī scholar Abū Ya'qūb Yūsuf b. Ibrāhīm al-Wārjlānī arranged these *aḥādīth* into their present form; they are published as Abū Ya'qūb al-Wārjlānī, *al-Jāmi' al-Ṣaḥīḥ Musnad lil-Imām al-Rabī' b. Ḥabīb Ibn 'Umar al-Azdī al-Baṣrī* (Muscat: Maktabat Musqat, 1994); see also Wilkinson's analysis and dating of this material in Wilkinson, "Ibāḍī Ḥadīth: An Essay in Normalization," *Der Islam* 62/2 (1985).
34. Abū 'Ubayda Muslim Ibn Abī Karīma, *Risālat Abī Karīma fī al-Zakāt* (Muscat: *WTQwTh*, 1982).
35. The first letter of Ibn Ibāḍ (purportedly to the Caliph 'Abd al-Malik) is preserved in two versions: the western (North African) version in Abū al-Faḍl b. Ibrahīm al-Barrādī, *Kitāb al-Jawāhir* (Cairo: n.p.,1885), 156–167; see also an edited version in 'Āmir al-Najjār, *al-Ibāḍiyya wa Madā Silatihā bi al-Khawārij* (Cairo: Dār al-Ma'ārif, 1993), 129–137 (hereafter cited as Ibn Ibāḍ); and the eastern (Omani) version in Sayyida Ismā'īl Kāshif, ed., *al-Siyar wa al-Jawabāt li-'Ulamā' wa Ā'immat 'Umān* (Muscat: *WTQwTh*, 1989), 2:325–345. The second letter (to an unnamed Shi'ite) has recently been published in Sirḥān b. Sa'īd al-Izkawī (attrib.), *Kashf al-Ghumma al-Jāmi' li-Akhbār al-Umma* (Beirut: Dār al-Bārūdī, 2006), 1:600–608. For a critical discussion of these epistles, see Michael Cook, *Early Muslim Dogma: A Source-Critical Study* (Cambridge: Cambridge University Press, 1981). Cook argues, quite convincingly, that the first letter might well come from Jābir b. Zayd.
36. Kāshif, *al-Siyar*, 2:346–383.
37. Kāshif, *al-Siyar*, 1:229–249.

38. Kāshif, *al-Siyar*, 2:223–268.
39. Ibn Salām, *Kitāb Ibn Salām al-Ibāḍī*, ed. R. F. Schwartz and Sālim b. Ya'qūb (Beirut: Dār Iqra', 1985).
40. Ibn al-Ṣaghīr, *Kitāb Akhbār al-Ā'imma al-Rustumiyyīn*, ed. Muḥammad Nāsir and Ibrāhīm Biḥḥāz (Algiers: Dār al-Gharb al-Islāmī, 1986).
41. Abū Mu'thir's *sīra* in Kāshif, *al-Siyar*, 2:269–319; Ibn Qaḥṭān's *sīra* in Kāshif, *al-Siyar*, 1:81–148.

Chapter 1

1. In Oman, the terms *'alāniyya* and *kitmān* were employed informally and interchangeably. See, for example, the *sīra* of Abū Qaḥṭān Khālid b. Qaḥṭān in Kāshif, *al-Siyar*, 1:92, 109, where *ẓuhūr* (used in the verbal form *aẓhara da'watahu*) and *'alāniyya* are used. See also Abū 'Abdullāh Muḥammad b. Maḥbūb's *sīra* in Kāshif, *al-Siyar*, 2:259.
2. The principle of "no conditions on the Imām" was first laid down by the Basran Imām al-Rabī' b. Ḥabīb al-Farāhidī in a letter supporting the second Rustumid Imām, 'Abd al-Wahhāb b. 'Abd al-Raḥmān b. Rustum: "To impose conditions on the Imām is to suppress justice, abolish authority, and destroy judgment and the law." See Abū Zakariyya, *Kitāb Siyar al-Ā'imma wa Akhbārihim*, 90–91.
3. al-Jannāwanī, *Kitāb al-Waḍ'*, 29.
4. al-Kindī, *al-Muṣannaf*, 10:63, 85.
5. An Imām who did not possess *'ilm* was thereby considered a "weak" Imām who should only be appointed out of necessity (*ḍarūra*). See al-Kindī, *al-Muṣannaf*, 10:69. The Omani scholar Ibn Maḥbūb implies that the *imām al-shārī* is of a higher degree than the *mudāfi'* Imām. See al-Kindī, *al-Muṣannaf*, 10:83–85.
6. The term "piety" serves here as a rough translation of the Qur'ānic concept of *taqwā*. Used in connection with the notion of moral rectitude, this term will partially remedy the deficiency of English to fully capture the many nuances of the notion of *taqwā*.
7. Ignaz Goldziher, *Muslim Studies* (Chicago: Aldine, 1967), 1:22; Watt, *Muhammad at Mecca* (Oxford: Oxford University Press, 1953), 20.
8. Toshihiko Izutsu, *God and Man in the Koran* (Kuala Lumpur: Islamic Book Trust, 2002), 39–40.
9. Izutsu, *God and Man*, 222–231.
10. Montgomery Watt, *Islamic Political Thought* (Edinburgh: Edinburgh University Press, 1968), 35.
11. Syed Husein Mohammed Jafri, *The Origins and Early Development of Shi'a Islam* (Oxford: Oxford University Press, 2000), 6.
12. Jafri, *Origins and Early Development*, 5.
13. Watt, *Islamic Political Thought*, 35.
14. Patricia Crone, "Quraysh and the Roman Army: Making Sense of the Meccan Leather Trade," *BSOAS* 70/1 (2007): 63.
15. Watt, *Muhammad at Mecca*, 9.

16. Abū ʿAbdullāh Muḥammad Ibn Saʿd, *al-Ṭabaqāt al-Kubrā*, ed. Edward Sachau (Beirut: Dār Ṣādr, 1957), 5:7.
17. 27:34.
18. Each *sūra* of the Qur'ān (except the ninth, *sūrat al-tawba*) opens with the *basmalla*, the verse: "In the Name of God the Compassionate, the Merciful." Muslim exegetes often explain this repetition as an indicator of the extreme mercifulness and compassion of God. See, for example, ʿImād al-Dīn Ismāʿīl b. ʿUmar Ibn Kathīr, *Tafsīr al-Qur'ān al-ʿAẓīm*, ed. Ḥasan al-Jibālī (Riyad: International Ideas Home, 1999), 26–27.
19. 2:173, 182, 192, 199, 218, 225, 226, 235.
20. 16:90.
21. 2:30; 5:7; 6:165.
22. 33:72.
23. 7:179.
24. 95:5–6.
25. 91:7–8.
26. 22:52; 17:53. As Rahman notes, not even the prophets are immune from the temptations of the devil. See Fazlur Rahman, *Major Themes of the Qur'ān* (Minneapolis: Bibliotheca Islamica, 1994), 18.
27. 16:64.
28. 3:104, 110, 114; 7:157; 9:67, 71; 22:41.
29. 5:2–3; 40:9, 45; 52:27; 76:11.
30. Izutsu, *God and Man*, 258–259.
31. Rahman, *Major Themes*, 28–29.
32. 5:2.
33. 2:3–5.
34. 49:13.
35. 33:21.
36. 93:7.
37. Badīʿuzzamān Furūzānfar, *Aḥādīth-i Mathnawī* (Tehran: University of Tehran, 1955), no. 459.
38. Quoted in Annemarie Schimmel, *And Muhammad Is His Messenger* (Chapel Hill: University of North Carolina Press, 1985), 57.
39. Schimmel, *And Muhammad Is His Messenger*, 56. Schimmel's definition is preferred over "infallibility" because it implies that the source of Muhammad's protection was not intrinsic to him, but came from without (i.e., from God), as Muslims hold.
40. ʿAbd al-Mālik Ibn Hishām, *al-Sīra al-Nabawiyya*, ed. Ibrāhīm al-Abyārī, Muṣṭafā al-Saqā, and ʿAbd al-Ḥafīẓ Shabalī (Beirut: Dār al-Khayr, 1997), 1:132ff. See also Abū Nuʿaym al-Iṣbahānī, *Dalā'il al-Nubuwwa* (Hyderabad: Dairatul Maarif, 1950), 117; Alfred Guillaume, *The Life of Muhammad* (London: Oxford University Press, 1970), 72.
41. Abū Nuʿaym, *Dalā'il al-Nubuwwa*, 175–176.
42. 3:32.
43. 3:132.
44. Shiʿite Imāms were believed to be, like the Prophet Muhammad, protected from error. See Abdulaziz Sachedina, *The Just Ruler in Shiʿite Islam* (Oxford: Oxford University

Press, 1988), 98, 101. Also, certain Sufi writers believed that the practitioner of the Sufi path could attain a level or moral and spiritual perfection equal to the Prophet Muhammad. See Annemarie Schimmel, *Mystical Dimensions of Islam* (Chapel Hill: University of North Carolina Press, 1975), 98–99.

45. Sachedina, *The Just Ruler*, 95.
46. Sunni and Ibāḍī sources preserve the well-known *ḥadīth* in which the Prophet ordered Abū Bakr to lead the prayers during his sickness. In the body of the *ḥadīth*, 'Ā'isha protests that the people will not be able to hear Abū Bakr over the cries of lamentation, and that the Prophet should allow 'Umar to lead the prayers, but the Prophet again orders Abū Bakr to lead the prayers. For an Ibāḍī version of this well-known *ḥadīth*, see al-Warjlānī, *al-Jāmi' al-Ṣaḥīḥ*, 57 (no. 211). It was not uncommon for the Prophet to deputize someone to lead the prayers in his absence, but owing to his impending death, the selection of Abū Bakr assumed added purpose to those who regarded Abū Bakr as the legitimate successor to Muhammad. Some sources make it clear that they regarded the choice of Abū Bakr to lead prayers as designation by Muhammad himself, rather than as the result of an election on the porch of the Banū Sā'ida. See Madelung, *Succession to Muḥammad*, 54.
47. Abū al-Ḥasan 'Alī b. Muḥammad b. Ḥajīb al-Māwardī, *Aḥkām al-Sulṭāniyya* (Beirut: Dār al-Kutub al-'Ilmiyya, 1985), 6.
48. Ibn Hishām, *al-Sīra al-Nabawiyya*, 4:230; Muḥammad b. Jarīr al-Ṭabarī, *Tārīkh al-Rusul wa al-Mulūk*, ed. M. J. de Goeje (Leiden: Brill, 1879), 1:1837–1845; Madelung, *Succession to Muḥammad*, 44.
49. So inglorious was Abū Bakr's "election" that 'Umar later admitted it to be a rushed and unexpected deal (*falta*). See Ibn Hishām, *al-Sīra al-Nabawiyya*, 4:229; Madelung, *Succession to Muḥammad*, 33.
50. Ibn Sa'd, *Ṭabaqāt*, 2:185. Crone argues that this tradition "voices Sunnī quietism, not Khārijite egalitarianism." See Patricia Crone, "Even an Ethiopian Slave: The Transformation of a Sunni Tradition," *BSOAS* 57 (1994), 60–61. While the tradition may have been used to foster quietism, its import lies in placing merit, as measured by one's piety, above descent.
51. 'Umar, 'Uthmān, and 'Alī were also included in this group. See Abū al-Faḍl Ibn Ḥajar al-'Asqalānī, *Fatḥ al-Bārī bi-Sharḥ Ṣaḥīḥ al-Bukhārī* (Riyad: International Ideas Home, 1999), 2:1658; Abū 'Abdullāh Muḥammad b. Ismā'īl al-Bukhārī, *Kitāb al-Jāmi' al-Ṣaḥīḥ* (hereafter *Ṣaḥīḥ*), 62.5.3674; see also Martin Lings, *Muḥammad: His Life Based on the Earliest Sources* (Rochester: Inner Traditions International, 1983), 329.
52. al-'Asqalānī, *Fatḥ al-Bārī*, 2:1672; al-Bukhārī, *Ṣaḥīḥ*, 62.5.3698. For a sympathetic overview of the life of 'Uthmān, see Abū al-Qāsim 'Alī b. al-Ḥasan Ibn 'Asākir, *Tārīkh Madīnat Dimashq: 'Uthmān b. 'Affān*, ed. Sukayna al-Shihābī (Damascus: Majma' al-Lugha al-'Arabiyya, 1984), 45–70.
53. Madelung, *Succession to Muḥammad*, 78–79.
54. The *khawārij* and Ibāḍiyya unambiguously regard 'Uthmān's *aḥdāth* as sins (*dhunūb*). See Ibn Ibāḍ in al-Najjār, *al-Ibāḍiyya wa Madā Ṣilatiha bī al-Khawārij*, 129.
55. Ibn Sa'd, *Ṭabaqāt*, 3:44.

56. Aḥmad b. Yaḥya al-Balādhurī, *Ansāb al-Ashrāf*, (Beirut: Dār al-Fikr, 1996), 6:173.
57. Abū Dharr also criticized then governor Mu'āwiya b. Abī Sufyān's extravagant spending on his palace in Damascus. See al-Balādhurī, *Ansāb al-Ashrāf*, 6:166–167.
58. al-Balādhurī, *Ansāb al-Ashrāf*, 6:161.
59. Madelung, *Succession to Muḥammad*, 84.
60. Ibn Ibāḍ in al-Najjār, *al-Ibāḍiyya wa Madā Ṣilatiha bī al-Khawārij*, 131.
61. al-Ṭabarī, *Tārīkh*, 1:2979.
62. al-Ṭabarī, *Tārīkh*, 1:2977. 'Uthmān's later repudiation of this repentance occurred only a few days before his death.
63. al-Balādhurī, *Ansāb al-Ashrāf*, 5:173–231; Madelung, *Succession to Muḥammad*, 113–140.
64. On the term *fitna*, see Abdulkader Tayob, "Fitnah: The Ideology of Conservative Islam," *Journal of Theology for Southern Africa* 69 (1989), 65–71.
65. For a discussion of the Qur'ānic precedents to the Shi'ite conception of legitimate succession, see Madelung, *Succession to Muḥammad*, 10–12.
66. Like the Prophet Muhammad, Ithnā 'Asharī ("twelver") Shi'ites considered their Imāms to be *ma'ṣūm*; see Sachedina, *The Just Ruler*, 98.
67. 'Imād al-Dīn Ismā'īl b. 'Umar Ibn Kathīr, *al-Bidāya wa al-Nihāya* (Cairo: Maṭba'at al-Sa'āda, 1932), 5:209.
68. For those who saw no exceptional claim for 'Alī's leadership, the term *mawlā* merely expressed close relation, or friendship without the connotations of political authority: "Whoever is my friend, 'Alī is their friend." This has become the standard Sunni interpretation of the *ḥadīth*.
69. Ibn Qutayba (attrib.), *al-Imāma wa al-Siyāsa* (Beirut: Dār Kutub al-'Ilmiyya, 1997), 104.
70. Mu'āwiya's army also had their *qurrā'*. Similarly, sources mention the *quṣāṣ*, who specialized in reciting the Qur'ānic stories of the Prophets (*qiṣṣa*): see Hāshim Ja'īṭ, *al-Fitna* (Beirut: Dār al-Ṭalī'a, 1991), 97. On the term *qurrā'*, see T. Nagel, "Ḳurrā'," in *EI2*, ed. Bernard Lewis, Charles Pellat, and Joseph Schacht (Leiden: Brill, 1965), 499–500; G.H.A.Juynboll, "The Qurrā' in Early Islamic History," *Journal of the Economic and Social History of the Orient* 26 (1973): 113–129, and "The Qur'ān Reciter on the Battlefield and Concomitant Issues," *Zeitschrift der Deuthschen Morganlandischen Gesellschaft* 125 (1975), 11–27.
71. Wilkinson, "Ibāḍī Ḥadīth," 250.
72. al-Shahrastānī, *al-Milal wa al-Niḥal* (Beirut: Dār al-Fikr, n.d.), 114–118; al-Baghdādī, *al-Farq Bayn al-Firaq*, 56–62; al-Ḥasan Ibn Mūsā al-Nawbakhtī, *Kitāb Firaq al-Shī'a* (Istanbul: Maṭba'at al-Dawla, 1931), 6; Shafūr Ibn Ṭāhir al-Isfarā'inī, *al-Tabṣīr fī al-Dīn wa Tamyīz al-Firqa al-Nājiyya 'an al-Firaq al-Hālikīn* (Cairo: Maktabat al-Azhar lil-Turāth, 1940), 38–42; Abū Ḥusayn Muḥammad b. Aḥmad al-Malaṭī, *al-Tanbīh wa al-Radd 'alā Ahl al-Ahwā' wa al-Bid'a* (Cairo: Maktabat al-Azhar lil-Turāth, 1993), 49–51; in early Ibāḍī sources, see Crone and Zimmerman, *Epistle*, 94–99; al-Qalhātī, *al-Firaq al-Islāmiyya*, 66–73; in Western sources, see Watt, *Formative Period*, 12–15; Wellhausen, *Religio-Political Parties*, 1–2.

73. The arbitration itself is sometimes referred to as the *taḥkīm*, but in the interest of reducing confusion the term *taḥkīm* will only be used for the phrase *lā ḥukm illā lil-lāh*.
74. 6:57; 12:40, 67.
75. 52:48; 68:48; 76:24.
76. al-Ṭabarī, *Tārīkh*, 1:3338–3339; al-Balādhurī, *Ansāb al-Ashrāf*, 3:110, 112; a variant in al-Shahrastānī credits al-Ḥajāj b. 'Ubaydullāh with the *taḥkīm*: "Have you judged over God's religion?! There is no judgment but God's! So let us judge by what God decrees in the Qur'ān"; al-Shahrastānī, *al-Milal wa al-Niḥal*, 117–118.
77. al-Shahrastānī, *al-Milal wa al-Niḥal*, 118.
78. Crone and Zimmerman, *Epistle*, 92–93.
79. Crone and Zimmerman, *Epistle*, 96–97.
80. al-Ṭabarī, *Tārīkh*, 1:3360–3361. Abū Mikhnaf's account in al-Ṭabarī matches al-Zuhrī's account in al-Balādhurī, suggesting a similar source. See al-Balādhurī, *Ansāb al-Ashrāf*, 3:129.
81. Abū Mikhnaf's report, whence this quote comes, synthesizes two divergent accounts of the *munāẓara*, one of which likely incorporates some materials of Khārijite (possibly Ibāḍī?) origin. The Khārijite material is set off by its use of the words *qālat al-khawārij: qulnā*, "the Khārijites said: we said . . ." preceding the quotation. Abū Mikhnaf's other source simply uses *qālat al-khawārij*, "the Khārijites said." Comparison of these two accounts yields different attitudes toward the *ḥakam al-ḥakamayn*. In the Khārijite materials, the Khārijites are convinced of the impropriety of the arbitration. In the other account, the Khārijites are not assured of their position; they ask 'Alī, "Do you think it fair to establish human beings as judges in [a matter] of blood?" To which 'Alī replied: "We have not set up human beings to judge, but have set up the Qur'ān to judge—but it is a lined piece of parchment between two flaps, and it does not speak, but people speak for it." Thus, in Abū Mikhnaf's second account, 'Alī answers a question about the propriety of human judgment with a statement of the necessity of human judgment. The necessity of human judgment was not the Khārijite's concern, suggesting that Abū Mikhnaf's second account might have been written or edited by a pro-'Alīd author. See al-Ṭabarī, *Tārīkh*, 1:3350–3353.
82. al-Balādhurī, *Ansāb al-Ashrāf*, 3:134. Most non-Ibāḍī sources maintain that the Khārijites initially forced 'Alī to accept the arbitration, only to later renege and demand that 'Alī resume the fight; al-Ṭabarī, *Tārīkh*, 1:3330, 3353.
83. Ibn Qutayba, *al-Imāma wa al-Siyāsa*, 104.
84. al-Ṭabarī, *Tārīkh*, 1:3360; al-Balādhurī, *Ansāb al-Ashrāf*, 3:129–130; Jamāl al-Dīn 'Abd al-Raḥmān b. 'Alī Ibn al-Jawzī, *Talbīs Iblīs*, ed. Muḥammad al-Ṣabbāḥ (Beirut: Manshurāt Dār Maktabat al-Ḥayāt, 1989), 137.
85. An area outside of Kūfa; another term for the Khārijites—Ḥārūriyya—comes from those who gathered at Ḥarūrā'. See Abū al-Ḥasan 'Alī b. Ismā'īl al-Ash'arī, *Kitāb Maqālāt al-Islāmiyyīn* (Beirut: Maktabat al-'Aṣriyya, 1999), 1:207.
86. al-Ṭabarī, *Tārīkh*, 1:3353 (on the authority of Abū Mikhnaf); see variant in al-Balādhurī, *Ansāb al-Ashrāf*, 3:123 (also on the authority of Abū Mikhnaf).
87. al-Ash'arī, *Maqālāt*, 1:204.

88. al-Balādhurī, *Ansāb al-Ashrāf*, 3:141.
89. al-Ṭabarī, *Tārīkh*, 1:3353; see variants in al-Balādhurī, *Ansāb al-Ashrāf*, 3:123; Abū al-ʻAbbās Muḥammad b. Yazīd al-Mubarrad, *al-Kāmil: Bāb al-Khawārij* (Damascus: Dār al-Ḥikma, n.d.), 24.
90. Crone and Zimmerman, *Epistle*, 96–97.
91. al-Ṭabarī, *Tārīkh*, 1:3363–3365; al-Balādhurī, *Ansāb al-Ashrāf*, 3:135; Ibn Qutayba, *al-Imāma wa al-Siyāsa*, 113–114; al-Mubarrad, *al-Kāmil: Bāb al-Khawārij*, 7; Ibn Qaḥṭān in Kāshif, *al-Siyar*, 1:107.
92. al-Ṭabarī, *Tārīkh*, 1:3365.
93. al-Balādhurī, *Ansāb al-Ashrāf*, 3:133; al-Ṭabarī, *Tārīkh*, 1:3365; both al-Ṭabarī and al-Balādhurī use Abū Mikhnaf's account of al-Rāsibī's appointment. Ibn Qutayba identifies al-Rāsibī as one of the *qurrā'*, but is the only source to do so. See Ibn Qutayba, *al-Imāma wa al-Siyāsa*, 104.
94. Al-Shahrastānī notes that one of the identifying characteristics of the Muḥakkima was that they allowed the Imām to be from a tribe other than the Quraysh: al-Shahrastānī, *al-Milal wa al-Niḥal*, 116; al-Ashʻarī, *Maqālāt*, 1:204.
95. al-Balādhurī, *Ansāb al-Ashrāf*, 3:145.
96. al-Balādhurī, *Ansāb al-Ashrāf*, 3:121–122.
97. al-Shahrastānī, *al-Milal wa al-Niḥal*, 115.
98. al-Baghdādī, *al-Farq Bayn al-Firaq*, 55; see also al-Ashʻarī, *Maqālāt*, 1:167, 204.
99. al-Ashʻarī, *Maqālāt*, 1:170, 174–176; al-Baghdādī, *al-Farq Bayn al-Firaq*, 62–70; al-Shahrastānī, *al-Milal wa al-Niḥal*, 118–125.
100. al-Ashʻarī, *Maqālāt*, 1:184–185; al-Shahrastānī, *al-Milal wa al-Niḥal*, 134; Crone and Zimmerman, *Epistle*, 68–69.
101. See Crone and Zimmerman, *Epistle*, 198–203.
102. For a discussion of the term *qawm*, see Crone and Zimmerman, *Epistle*, 34.
103. Abū Mu'thir in Kāshif, *al-Siyar*, 2:292ff., 308; al-Bisyānī in Kāshif, *al-Siyar*, 2:126; epistles of Maḥbūb b. al-Raḥīl and Ḥārūn b. al-Yamān in Kāshif, *al-Siyar*, 1:273–336; al-Jannāwanī, *Kitāb al-Waḍʻ*, 17–18.
104. al-Baghdādī, *al-Farq Bayn al-Firaq*, 68.
105. al-Baghdādī, *al-Farq Bayn al-Firaq*, 69; al-Shahrastānī, *al-Milal wa al-Niḥal*, 124.
106. On Abū Ḥamza, see Charles Pellat, "al-Mukhtār b. ʻAwf al-Azdī," in *EI2*, ed. Bernard Lewis, Charles Pellat, and Joseph Schacht (Leiden: Brill, 1965).
107. Ibn Qutayba, *ʻUyūn al-Akhbār*, ed. Yūsuf ʻAlī Ṭawīl (Beirut: Dār Kutub al-ʻIlmiyya, 1998), 2:271–272; Abū ʻUthmān ʻAmr b. Baḥr al-Jāḥiẓ, *al-Bayān wa al-Tabyīn*, ed. Muwaffaq Shahāb al-Dīn (Beirut: Dār Kutub al-ʻIlmiyya, 1998), 2:79–82; ʻIzz al-Dīn ʻAbd al-Ḥamīd Ibn Abī al-Ḥadīd, *Sharḥ Nahj al-Balāgha*, ed. M.A.F. Ibrāhīm (Cairo, ʻIsā al-Bābi al-Ḥalabī, 1965), 5:117–119; see also a translation in Patricia Crone and Martin Hinds' *God's Caliph: Religious Authority in the First Centuries of Islam* (Cambridge: Cambridge University Press, 1986), 129–132.
108. For a discussion of the necessity for obedience in Sunni Islamic thought, see Khaled Abou El Fadl, *Rebellion and Violence in Islamic Law* (Cambridge: Cambridge University Press, 2001), 239.
109. Crone and Zimmerman, *Epistle*, 140–141.

110. Ibn al-Jawzī, *Talbīs Iblīs*, 140.
111. For a discussion of the sources of Ibāḍī *ḥadīth*, see Wilkinson, "Ibāḍī Ḥadīth."
112. al-Wārjlānī, *al-Jāmi' al-Ṣaḥīḥ*, 18–19 (nos. 44–49); 205 (nos. 817–820).
113. al-Ṭabarī, *Tārīkh*, 2:986.
114. Abū Ṭāhir Ismā'īl b. Mūsā al-Jiṭālī, *Kitāb Qawā'id al-Islām*, ed. Balkī 'Abd al-Raḥmān b. 'Umar (Muscat: Maktabat al-Istiqāma, 1992), 1:66–67.
115. Abū Sa'īd Muḥammad b. Sa'īd al-Kudamī, *al-Istiqāma* (Muscat: *WTQwTh*, 1985), 1:63.
116. al-Kindī, *al-Ihtidā'*, 237; see also al-Kindī, *al-Jawhar al-Muqtaṣir* (Muscat: *WTQwTh*, 1983), 138.
117. al-Kindī, *Bayān al-Shar'*, 3:270–271.
118. Nūr al-Dīn 'Abdullāh b. Aḥmad al-Sālimī, *Tuḥfat al-'Ayān bī-Sīrat Ahl 'Umān* (Cairo: Dār al-Kitāb al-'Arabī, 1961), 1:85.
119. Ibn Qaḥṭān specifically refers to Abū Bakr and 'Umar as "just Imāms" (*ā'immat al-'adl*); Ibn Qaḥṭān in Kāshif, *al-Siyar*, 1:93.
120. al-Kindī, *al-Muṣannaf*, 10:55; for a North African equivalent, see al-Shammākhī, *Muqaddimat al-Tawḥīd*, 98; al-Barrādī, *Kitāb al-Jawāhir* (also known as *al-Jawhar al-Muntaqāt*), citing Ibn Baraka, 34.
121. al-Kudamī, *al-Istiqāma*, 2:119.
122. al-Bisyānī, *al-Jāmi' Abī al-Ḥasan al-Bisyānī* (Muscat: *WTQwTh*, 1984), 1:261.
123. al-Kudamī, *al-Mu'tabar* (Muscat: *WTQwTh*, 1984), 2:161.
124. al-Kindī, *al-Muṣannaf*, 10:55. Al-Kindī cites the Umayyad Caliph 'Umar b. 'Abd al-'Azīz as an example of a just non-Ibāḍī leader to whom limited obedience was due.
125. Abū Isḥāq Ibrāhīm Ibn Qays, *Mukhtaṣar al-Khiṣāl* (Muscat: *WTQwTh*, 1983), 194.
126. al-Bisyānī in al-Kindī, *al-Muṣannaf*, 10:60, 72. Lane defines *war'* as "piety" and as "abstinence from unlawful things:" William Edward Lane, *Arabic-English Lexicon* (London: Williams and Norgate, 1863), 8:3051.
127. Savage, *Gateway to Hell*, 50.
128. Great personal beauty is ascribed to 'Abd al-Raḥman, such that Abū 'Ubayda was forced to "hang a curtain between himself and his fellow students lest they be distracted from their work." See Abū Zakariyya, *Kitāb Siyar al-Ā'imma*, 56. Savage speculates that this reference to 'Abd al-Raḥmān's personal beauty might be inserted into the narrative as an allusion to his past royal heritage and future role as Imām; Savage, *Gateway to Hell*, 49. Ibāḍī historians trace his heritage to the Sāsānian leader Rustum b. Bahrām b. Shābūr b. Bābak Dhū al-Aktāf, who was defeated by the Muslims at the Battle of al-Qādisīyya. See Abū al-'Abbās Aḥmad b. Sa'īd al-Shammākhī, *Kitāb al-Siyar*, ed. Aḥmad b. Sa'ūd al-Siyābī (Muscat: *WTQwTh*, 1987), 1:124; al-Darjīnī, *Kitāb Ṭabaqāt al-Mashayikh*, 1:19–20; Abū Zakariyya, *Kitāb Siyar al-Ā'imma*, 54; al-Barrādī, *Kitāb al-Jawāhir*, 174.
129. Abū Zakariyya, *Kitāb Siyar al-Ā'imma*, 83; Ibn al-Ṣaghīr, *Akhbār al-Ā'imma al-Rustumiyyīn*, 29.
130. Ibn al-Ṣaghīr, *Akhbār al-Ā'imma al-Rustumiyyīn*, 29.
131. Abū Zakariyya, *Kitāb Siyar al-Ā'imma*, 84.

132. Ibn al-Ṣaghīr, *Akhbār al-Ā'imma al-Rustumiyyīn*, 28. This reference to 'Abd al-Raḥmān's ease of access recalls the early caliphates of Abū Bakr and 'Umar, who also remained accessible to the people of Madīna. It might also be intended to contrast with the popular image of the Umayyads as removed from their constituents by their boxes (*maqsūra*) in the mosque: see al-Ṭabarī, *Tārīkh*, 2:70.
133. Abū Zakariyya, *Kitāb Siyar al-Ā'imma*, 83.
134. Ibn al-Ṣaghīr, *Akhbār al-Ā'imma al-Rustumiyyīn*, 28, 32.
135. Ibn al-Ṣaghīr, *Akhbār al-Ā'imma al-Rustumiyyīn*, 28; Abū Zakariyya, *Kitāb Siyar al-Ā'imma*, 84.
136. al-Shammākhī, *Muqaddimat al-Tawḥīd*, 69–70.
137. For Omani examples, see al-Kindī, *al-Muṣannaf*, 10:44–48; Abū al-Ḥawārī Muḥammad Ibn al-Ḥawārī, *Jāmi' Abī al-Ḥawārī* (Muscat: *WTQwTh*, 1985), 1:71, 73ff.; al-Kudamī, *al-Istiqāma*, 1:213ff.
138. Ibn Qaḥṭān in Kāshif, *al-Siyar*, 1:97.
139. Ibn Maḥbūb in Kāshif, *al-Siyar*, 1:125.
140. Abū Mu'thir in Kāshif, *al-Siyar*, 2:303.
141. al-Qalhātī, *al-Firaq al-Islāmiyya*, 76.
142. Ibāḍī tradition maintained that God made his judgment of Mu'āwiya's cause clear in *sūra* 49:9: "And if two parties fall to fighting, then make peace between them. And if one party does wrong to the other, fight the one that does wrong until they return to the command of God; then, if they return, make peace between them justly and act fairly. Surely God loves the equitable." See al-Qalhātī, *al-Firaq al-Islāmiyya,* 76.
143. al-Qalhātī, *al-Firaq al-Islāmiyya*, 73, 82; al-Kudamī, *al-Istiqāma*, 1:59–61.
144. While the actions of Abū Bakr and 'Umar became sources of *sunna* to the Ibāḍīyya, the actions of 'Alī did not. However, one notable exception to this rule concerns the legal status and treatment of rebels (*bughāt*). Although not explicitly stated, Ibāḍī jurisprudence is deeply indebted to 'Alī for their *aḥkām al-bughāt*. See Abou El Fadl, *Violence and Rebellion*, 320.
145. al-Qalhātī, *al-Firaq al-Islāmiyya*, 252.
146. al-Kindī, *al-Muṣannaf*, 10:57; al-Bisyānī, *al-Jāmi'*, 1:261.
147. In fact, al-Kindī prefers (but does not require) the rule of a pure Qurayshī over the Ibāḍī community; see *al-Muṣannaf*, 10:79.

Chapter 2

1. Abū Zakariyya, *Kitāb Siyar al-Ā'imma*, 82, 99 (on the *'ilm* of the Rustumids); Abū Mu'thir in al-Kindī, *al-Muṣannaf*, 10:63, (quoting al-Bisyānī) 65.
2. The term *ma'rifa* would later take on specialized meanings in the mystical traditions, but in the early period it did not yet have those connotations.
3. D. MacDonald, "'Ilm," in *EI2*, ed. Bernard Lewis, V. L. Menage, Charles Pellat, and Joseph Schacht (Leiden: Brill, 1968), 1133.
4. al-Rāghib al-Iṣfahānī, *Mufradāt Alfāẓ al-Qur'ān* (Damascus: Dār al-Qalam, 1997), 642–643.

5. R. Stephen Humphreys, *Islamic History: A Framework for Inquiry* (Princeton: Princeton University Press, 1991), 187. For the distinction between "in authority" and "an authority," see Richard E. Flathman, *The Practice of Political Authority: Authority and the Authoritative* (Chicago: University of Chicago Press, 1980).
6. al-Bisyānī in al-Kindī, *al-Muṣannaf*, 10:60–61.
7. In medieval Omani texts, there are but two recognized states of communal existence: *ẓuhūr* and *kitmān*. The medieval Omani Ibāḍiyya recognized *shārī* and *difā'ī* Imāms, but did not consider *shirā'* and *difā'* to be modes of being (that is, *masālik al-dīn*) for the Ibāḍī community until, at the very earliest, the beginning of the Ibāḍī "renaissance" in the tenth/sixteenth century, and more likely in the thirteenth/nineteenth century. See Gaiser, "The Ibāḍī 'Stages of Religion Re-examined."
8. Tadeusz Lewicki, "Ḥalḳa," in *EI2*, ed. Bernard Lewis, V. L. Menage, Charles Pellat, and Joseph Schacht (Leiden: Brill, 1971).
9. Abū 'Ammār 'Abd al-Kāfī b. Abī Ya'qūb al-Tanwātī, *Arā' al-Khawārij al-Kalāmiyya: Al-Mujaz li-Abī 'Ammār 'Abd al-Kāfī al-Ibāḍī*, ed. 'Ammār al-Ṭālibī (Algiers: Sharikat al-Waṭaniyya lil-Nashar wa al-Tawzī', n.d.), 2:238.
10. al-Sālimī, *Tuḥfat al-A'yān*, 1:362; Ibn Baṭūṭa, *Riḥlat Ibn Baṭūṭa* (Beirut: Dār al-Kutub al-'Ilmiyya, 2002), 274.
11. al-Kindī, *al-Muṣannaf*, 10:26. Later Ibāḍī historical texts acknowledged a leader dubbed the *muḥtasib* Imām, who is described as an *'ālim* who led the community until such time as they could select a permanent Imām. See al-Sālimī, *Tuḥfat al-A'yān*, 1:104; Wilkinson, *Imamate Tradition*, 162.
12. For North African examples, see al-Shammākhī, *Muqaddimat al-Tawḥīd*, 74; al-Jannāwanī, *Kitāb al-Waḍ'*, 29, and Abū Ya'qūb Yūsuf b. Ibrāhīm al-Warjlānī, *al-Dalīl wa al-Burhān* (Muscat: *WTQwTh*, 1983), 3:200. For Omani examples, see Abū Mu'thir in Kāshif, *al-Siyar*, 2:314–315; al-Kindī, *al-Ihtidā'*, 237; and al-Kindī, *Bayān al-Shar'*, 3:271.
13. Wilkinson, *Imamate Tradition*, 162.
14. Jawād 'Alī, *al-Mufaṣṣal fī Tārīkh al-'Arab Qabl al-Islām* (Baghdad: Maktabat al-Nahḍa, 1970), 5:312–316.
15. For an early Islamic interpretation of how the *kāhin* received inspiration, see al-Bukhārī, *Ṣaḥīḥ*, 65.34.4800.
16. Muḥammad Ibn Sallām al-Jumāḥī, *Ṭabaqāt Fuḥūl al-Shu'arā'*, ed. Maḥmūd Muḥammad Shākir (Cairo: Maṭba'at al-Midanī, 1973), 24.
17. Ibn Qutayba, *'Uyūn al-Akhbār*, 2:200.
18. T. Fahd, "Shā'ir," in *EI2*, ed. C. Bosworth, E. Van Donzel, W. P. Heinrichs, and Charles Pellat (Leiden: Brill, 1995), 225.
19. al-Jumāḥī, *Ṭabaqāt*, 1:52, 71.
20. Bosworth, "Sayyid," 115.
21. Ibn Sa'd, *Ṭabaqāt*, 1:286.
22. E. Tyan, "Ḥakam," in *EI2*, ed. Bernard Lewis, Charles Pellat, and Joseph Schacht (Leiden: Brill, 1965).
23. Fahd, "Shā'ir," 225.
24. 12:76; also 8:60. See also Ibn Kathīr, *Tafsīr*, 896.

25. 5:109; 72:26.
26. al-Rāghib al-Iṣfahānī, *Mufradāt*, 580.
27. 55:1–2.
28. 72:26–27.
29. 20:114.
30. 18:65–66. See Ibn Kathīr, *Tafsīr*, 1057.
31. Ibn Kathīr, *Tafsīr*, 1334.
32. On the finality of prophethood, see, for example, al-Bukhārī, *Ṣaḥīḥ*, 61.18.3534 and 3535. Several "false prophets" claiming to receive revelation did, in fact, arise in the Arabian Peninsula after the death of the Prophet Muhammad.
33. 58:11.
34. al-'Asqalānī, *al-Fatḥ al-Bārī*, 1:323; al-Bukhārī, *Ṣaḥīḥ*, 3.10.
35. Aḥmad Abū 'Abdullāh Ibn Ḥanbal, *al-Musnad* (Riyad: International Ideas Home, 1998), 1.35.232; Ibn Kathīr, *Tafsīr*, 1693.
36. al-Bukhārī, *Ṣaḥīḥ*, 62.1. He defines the companions (*ṣaḥāba*) as those who "accompanied (*ṣaḥiba lahu ṣuḥba*) the Prophet or saw him (*rāhu*)."
37. M. Muranyi, "Ṣaḥāba," in *EI2*, ed C. Bosworth, E. Van Donzel, W. P. Heinrichs, and M. Lecompte (Leiden: Brill, 1995), 827.
38. Al-Bukhārī considers al-Ḥasan and al-Ḥusayn companions. See al-Bukhārī, *Ṣaḥīḥ*, 62.22.3746–3753; as well as Mu'āwiya. See al-Bukhārī, *Ṣaḥīḥ*, 62.28.3764–3766.
39. al-Māwardī, *Aḥkām al-Sulṭāniyya*, 6; Crone, *God's Caliph*, 48.
40. Sachedina, *The Just Ruler*, 32, 62.
41. Abū 'Abdullāh Muḥammad al-Ḥārithī al-Baghdādī al-Mufīd, *Kitāb al-Irshād*, tr. I.K.A. Howard (London: Balagha Books, 1981), 20.
42. al-Mufīd, *al-Irshād*, 22.
43. al-Māwardī, *Aḥkām al-Sulṭāniyya*, 7; Lambton, *State and Government*, 98.
44. Crone, *God's Caliph*, 48.
45. For a discussion of the *qurrā'*, see Juynboll, "The Qur'ān Reciter on the Battlefield and Concomitant Issues."
46. Abū Mikhnaf's account in al-Ṭabarī, *Tārīkh*, 1:3330.
47. Several other prominent early Khārijites supposedly belonged to the *qurrā'*: Abū Mikhnaf includes Zayd b. Ḥisn al-Ṭā'ī and Mis'ar b. Fadakī al-Tamīmī among their number. See al-Ṭabarī *Tārīkh*, 1:3330; Ibn Qutayba mentions 'Abdullāh b. Wahb al-Rāsibī. See Ibn Qutayba, *al-Imāma wa al-Siyāsa*, 104.
48. Ibn Qutayba, *al-Imāma wa al-Siyāsa*, 104.
49. al-Ṭabarī, *Tārīkh*, 2:20–21.
50. al-Baghdādī, *al-Farq Bayn al-Firaq*, 69; al-Ash'arī, *Maqālāt*, 1:176 (does not have the reference to *ijtihād*).
51. 'Abd al-Karīm al-Shahrastānī, *Nihayat al-Iqdām fī 'Ilm al-Kalām* (Cairo: Maktabat al-Mutanabbī, 1980), 483; Crone and Zimmerman, *Epistle*, 206–210.
52. al-Mubarrad, *al-Kāmil: Bāb al-Khawārij*, 59–67.
53. al-Ṭabarī, *Tārīkh*, 2:881.
54. al-Baghdādī, *al-Farq Bayn al-Firaq*, 89; on the possible forgery of the relationship between Ṣāliḥ and Shabīb, see Chase F. Robinson, *Empire and Elites and Elites after the Muslim Conquest* (Cambridge: Cambridge University Press, 2000), 117–118.

55. Crone and Zimmerman, *Epistle*, 140–141.
56. For a discussion of the concept of caliphal law during the Umayyad period, see Crone and Hinds, *God's Caliph*, 43–57.
57. Ibn Sa'd, *Ṭabaqāt*, 5:43.
58. Ibn Sa'd, *Ṭabaqāt*, 5:224.
59. Ibn Sa'd, *Ṭabaqāt*, 5:226.
60. al-Ṭabarī, *Tārīkh*, 2:1843.
61. Jarīr b. 'Aṭiyya b. al-Khaṭafā, *Diwān* (Dār al-Ma'ārif bī Maṣr, 1969), 390; see Crone and Hinds, *God's Caliph*, 44.
62. 'Abd al-Razzāq b. Hammām al-Ṣan'ānī al-Himyarī, *al-Muṣannaf*, ed. Ḥabīb al-Raḥmān al-A'zamī (Beirut: al-Majlas al-'Ilmī, 1970), 10:18829 (hereafter cited as 'Abd al-Razzāq).
63. Abū al-Qāsim 'Abd al-Raḥmān b. 'Abdullāh Ibn 'Abd al-Ḥakam, *Futūḥ Maṣr wa Akhbāruhā*, ed. Charles C. Torrey (New Haven: Yale University Press, 1920), 155.
64. 'Abd al-Razzāq, 7:13385.
65. Sachedina, *The Just Ruler*, 32–35.
66. Jafri, *Origins and Early Development*, 289–291.
67. Wilfred Madelung, "Hishām b. al-Ḥakam," in *EI2*, ed. Bernard Lewis, V. L. Menage, Charles Pellat, and Joseph Schact (Leiden: Brill, 1971), 497; al-Nawbakhtī, *Kitāb Firaq al-Shī'a*, 66. According to al-Yamān b. Ribāb's report in al-Mas'ūdī, Hishām shared a store in Kūfa with an Ibāḍī, 'Abdullāh b. Yazīd. See al-Mas'ūdī, *Murūj al-Dhahab*, 5:442–445. It is unclear whether this Yazīd is the same Yazīd who established the Ibāḍī sect of the Yazīdiyya. On the Ibāḍī Yazīdiyya, see al-Ash'arī, *Maqālāt*, 1:184. On Hishām b. al-Ḥakam, see also al-Ash'arī, *Maqālāt*, 1:106–108, 116–117; al-Baghdādī, *al-Farq Bayn al-Firaq*, 47–49; al-Shahrastānī, *al-Milal wa al-Niḥal*, 184–185; Ibn Qutayba, *'Uyūn al-Akhbār*, 2:166, 169.
68. al-Malaṭī, *Tanbīh*, 24–25.
69. al-Malaṭī, *Tanbīh*, 25.
70. Abū 'Amr 'Umar b. 'Abd al-'Azīz Kashshī, *Ikhtiyār Ma'rifat al-Rijāl* (Mashhad: Daneshgah-i-Mashhad, 1964), 209; Sachedina, *The Just Ruler*, 32.
71. al-Ṭabarī, *Tārīkh*, 2:516–520; al-Mubarrad, *al-Kāmil: Bāb al-Khawārij*, 105; al-Shahrastānī, *al-Milal wa al-Niḥal*, 121–122; al-Baghdādī, *al-Farq Bayn al-Firaq*, 63; al-Ash'arī, *Maqālāt*, 1:169–170; see variant on the *tafrīq* in al-Balādhurī, *Ansāb al-Ashrāf*, 3:114–115.
72. The quietist Khārijites might have cited 9:122 to justify their disavowal of *khurūj* and subsequent embrace of quietism: "Nor should the believers all go forth together: if a contingent from every expedition remained behind they could devote themselves to studies in religion, and admonish the people when they return to them that thus they [may learn] to guard themselves [against evil]." This verse, while offering an eloquent justification for quietism, simultaneously refers to the need for the study of religion. If the quietists of Basra found inspiration for their quietism in this verse, they may also have taken the reference to religious learning as a command. See Savage, *Gateway to Hell*, 19.

73. Abū Zakariyya, *Kitāb Siyar al-Ā'imma*, 40–41.
74. As Lewinstein has shown, the term "Ṣufrī" rarely refers to a distinct Khārijite sect, and caution must be exercised when the word is encountered in historical narratives. See Keith Lewinstein, "Making and Unmaking a Sect: the Heresiographers and the Ṣufriyya," *SI* 76 (1992): 75–96.
75. Ibn Ḥajar al-'Asqalānī, *Tahdhīb al-Tahdhīb* (Hyderabad: Majlis al-Ma'ārif al-Niẓāmiyya al-Kā'ina fī al-Hind, 1907), 2:219.
76. al-Ash'arī, *Maqālāt*, 1:188.
77. Wilkinson, "Early Development," 132. Wilkinson refers to these quietists as "unitarians" on the basis of their refusal to break with the wider unity of Muslims and their use of the term *jamā'at al-muslimīn* to refer to themselves.
78. Wilkinson, *Imamate Tradition*, 162.
79. Wilkinson labels this era the "proto-Ibāḍite" period. I prefer "quietist Khārijite" period because it eschews any reference to Khārijite subsects. Wilkinson, "Early Development," 136.
80. Sachedina, *The Just Ruler*, 32; Humphreys, *Islamic History*, 187.
81. At the same time, the Umayyad state did appoint the *'ulamā'* to offices of authority, such as the office of *qāḍī* (judge); thus it is not completely accurate to say the *'ulamā'* were absolutely bereft of positions of authority.
82. al-Jannāwanī, *Kitāb al-Waḍ'*, 29; al-Darjīnī, *Kitāb Ṭabaqāt al-Mashāyikh*, 2:205; al-Shammākhī, *al-Siyar*, 1:67.
83. Wilkinson, "Ibāḍī Ḥadīth," 252.
84. al-Ash'arī, *Maqālāt*, 1:188.
85. Wilkinson, "Early Development," 133–134.
86. Ibn Sa'd, *Ṭabaqāt*, 7:181–182.
87. Abū 'Abdullāh Shams al-Dīn al-Dhahabī, *Kitāb Tadhkirat al-Ḥuffāẓ* (Hyderabad: Maṭba'at Dā'irat al-Ma'ārif al-Niẓāmiyya, 1915), 1:72.
88. Ibn Ḥajar al-'Asqalānī, *Tahdhīb al-Tahdhīb*, 2:219.
89. Ennami, *Studies in Ibadism (al-Ibāḍīyah)*, 35.
90. Ibn Ḥajar al-'Asqalānī, *Tahdhīb al-Tahdhīb*, 2:61; al-Dhahabī, *Tadhkirat al-Ḥuffāẓ*, 1:73; al-Shammākhī, *al-Siyar*, 1:67–68.
91. Ibāḍī sources give Ibn 'Abbās credit for defending the Muḥakkima after verbally sparring with them at Ḥarūrā'. According to al-Qalhātī, Ibn 'Abbās refused to fight against the Muḥakkima at Nahrawān and abandoned 'Alī before the battle. See al-Qalhātī, *al-Firaq al-Islāmiyya*, 84. Later Ibāḍī sources refer to Ibn 'Abbās as *ḥabr al-umma* (the "learned man of the community") and *al-baḥr* (the "sea") because of his vast knowledge. This reconstruction of Ibn 'Abbās in Ibāḍī sources resulted from the need to provide him with Ibāḍī credentials. The student-teacher relationship between Ibn 'Abbās and Jābir, combined with Jābir's place as founder of the sect, meant that the *'ilm* transmission required the proper sectarian qualifications. By making Ibn 'Abbās sympathetic to the Khārijite/Ibāḍite cause his *'ilm* became acceptable as authoritative.
92. Ibn Sa'd, *Ṭabaqāt*, 7:179–180; al-Dhahabī, *Kitāb Tadhkirat al-Ḥuffāẓ*, 1:62; Ibn Ḥajar al-'Asqalānī, *Tahdhīb al-Tahdhīb*, 2:38; al-Shammākhī, *al-Siyar*, 1:67.

93. al-Dhahabī, *Kitāb Tadhkirat al-Ḥuffāẓ*, 1:73; variant in al-Shammākhī, *al-Siyar*, 1:68.
94. Ibn Midād in Ennami, *Studies in Ibadism (al-Ibāḍīyah)*, 36.
95. al-Baghtūrī in Ennami, *Studies in Ibadism (al-Ibāḍīyah)*, 36.
96. al-Darjīnī, *Kitāb Ṭabaqāt al-Mashāyikh*, 2:206–207; al-Shammākhī, *Siyar*, 1:69.
97. al-Shammākhī, *Siyar*, 1:69–70.
98. Anonymous Ibāḍī manuscript, quoted in Ennami, *Studies in Ibadism (al-Ibāḍīyah)*, 38.
99. Ibn Sa'd, *Ṭabaqāt*, 7:180.
100. al-Shammākhī, *Siyar*, 1:70; al-Darjīnī, *Kitāb Ṭabaqāt al-Mashāyikh*, 2:211. Nevertheless, Jābir maintained a relationship with Yazīd b. Abī Muslim, a secretary (*kātib*) under al-Ḥajjāj. See al-Shammākhī, *Siyar*, 1:70.
101. al-Shammākhī, *Siyar*, 1:71.
102. al-Shammākhī, *Siyar*, 1:71.
103. Jābir b. Zayd in Ennami, *Studies in Ibadism (al-Ibāḍīyah)*, 45.
104. al-Baghdādī, *al-Farq Bayn al-Firaq*, 82; al-Shahrastānī, *al-Milal wa al-Niḥal*, 134; al-Isfarā'inī, *al-Tabṣīr fī al-Dīn*, 48; al-Qalhātī, *al-Firaq al-Islāmiyya*, 294; al-Malaṭī, *Tanbīh*, 52 (some of these sources give the name as Ibāḍ b. 'Amr).
105. al-Qalhātī, *al-Firaq al-Islāmiyya*, 294.
106. al-Baghdādī, *al-Farq Bayn al-Firaq*, 84.
107. al-Shahrastānī, *al-Milal wa al-Niḥal*, 134.
108. Abū Muḥammad 'Alī b. Aḥmad Ibn Ḥazm, *Kitāb al-Fisal fī al-Milal wa al-Ahwā' wa al-Niḥal* (Beirut: Dār al-Kutub al-'Ilmiyya, 1999), 3:124.
109. Wilkinson, "Early Development," 132.
110. Ibn Fatḥ in Ennami, *Studies in Ibadism (al-Ibāḍīyah)*, 5; see also Cook, *Early Muslim Dogma*, 182, n. 104.
111. Wilferd Madelung, "Abd Allāh Ibn Ibāḍ and the Origins of the Ibāḍiyya," in *Authority, Privacy and Public Order in Islam*, ed. Barbara Michalak-Pikulska and Andrzej Pikulski (Leuven: Dudley, 2006), 51–57.
112. al-Darjīnī, *Kitāb Ṭabaqāt al-Mashāyikh*, 2:214; al-Shammākhī, *Siyar*, 1:72–73. For a modern rationalization of the place of Ibn Ibāḍ in early Islamic history, see Ennami, *Studies in Ibadism (al-Ibāḍīyah)*, 4.
113. al-Qalhātī, *al-Firaq al-Islāmiyya*, 294.
114. For a critical assessment of the letters of Ibn Ibāḍ, see Cook, *Early Muslim Dogma*, 51–67.
115. al-Shammākhī, *Siyar*, 1:74–76; al-Darjīnī, *Kitāb Ṭabaqāt al-Mashāyikh*, 2:232–233.
116. al-Shammākhī, *Siyar*, 1:81–83; al-Darjīnī, *Kitāb Ṭabaqāt al-Mashāyikh*, 2:246–247.
117. For a description of these early *'ulamā'* as Imāms, see Abū Mu'thir in Kāshif, *al-Siyar*, 2:314–315; al-Shammākhī mentions Suḥār al-'Abdī as one of the "Imāms of the Muslims": *al-Siyar*, 1:76.
118. al-Shammākhī, *Siyar*, 1:78. Al-Jāḥiẓ reports that he was the *mawla* of 'Urwa b. Udaya, the brother of Abū Bilāl. See al-Jāḥiẓ, *al-Bayān wa al-Tabyīn*, 3:167.
119. al-Baghtūrī in Ennami, *Studies in Ibadism (al-Ibāḍīyah)*, 57.
120. al-Darjīnī, *Kitāb Ṭabaqāt al-Mashāyikh*, 2:238.

121. al-Shammākhī, *Siyar*, 1:84; al-Darjīnī, *Kitāb Ṭabaqāt al-Mashāyikh*, 2:249–250.
122. al-Darjīnī, *Kitāb Ṭabaqāt al-Mashāyikh*, 2:250.
123. al-Shammākhī, *Siyar*, 1:81; al-Darjīnī, *Kitāb Ṭabaqāt al-Mashāyikh*, 2:247.
124. al-Darjīnī, *Kitāb Ṭabaqāt al-Mashāyikh*, 2:236, 254–255; Lewicki, "The Ibāḍites in Arabia," 70 (incorrectly gives the name Mu'āwiya b. Iyyās al-Muzanī). On al-Nahdī, see al-Shammākhī, *Siyar*, 1:89–90; al-Darjīnī, *Kitāb Ṭabaqāt al-Mashāyikh*, 2:257–258.
125. al-Darjīnī, *Kitāb Ṭabaqāt al-Mashāyikh*, 2:253; the sources also mention al-Naẓar b. Maymūn. See al-Shammākhī, *Siyar*, 1:87, 95.
126. al-Shammākhī, *Siyar*, 1:86.
127. al-Shammākhī, *Siyar*, 1:105.
128. al-Shammākhī, *Siyar*, 1:105.
129. al-Shammākhī, *Siyar*, 1:90–91, 113; Abū Zakariyya, *Kitāb Siyar al-Ā'imma*, 41–42.
130. al-Shammākhī, *Siyar*, 1:113–114.
131. al-Sālimī, *Tuḥfat al-A'yān*, 1:85.
132. al-Shammākhī, *Siyar*, 1:95; al-Darjīnī, *Kitāb Ṭabaqāt al-Mashāyikh*, 2:273ff.
133. al-Darjīnī, *Kitāb Ṭabaqāt al-Mashāyikh*, 2:273–276.
134. On the role of al-Rabī' in the collection of Ibāḍī *aḥadīth*, see Wilkinson, "Ibāḍi Ḥadīth," 231ff.
135. Sirḥān b. Sa'īd al-Izkawī (attrib.), *Kashf al-Ghumma al-Jāmi' li-Akhbār al-Umma*, ed. Aḥmad 'Ubaydalī (Nicosia: Dilmun, 1985), 254; al-Sālimī, *Tuḥfat al-A'yān*, 1:113.
136. al-Sālimī, *Tuḥfat al-A'yān*, 1:111–112.
137. Abū Zakariyya, *Kitāb Siyar al-Ā'imma*, 122.
138. Abū Sufyān Maḥbūb b. al-Raḥīl in Kāshif, *al-Siyar*, 1:326; al-Sālimī, *Tuḥfat al-A'yān*, 1:122.
139. al-Sālimī, *Tuḥfat al-A'yān*, 1:156.
140. Ibn 'Abd al-Ḥakam, *Futūḥ Maṣr*, 224.
141. Ibn 'Abd al-Ḥakam, *Futūḥ Maṣr*, 224–225.
142. Abū Zakariyya, *Kitāb Siyar al-Ā'imma*, 58.
143. Savage, *Gateway to Hell*, 54; Lewicki, "The Ibadites in Arabia and Africa," 89.
144. al-Shammākhī, *Siyar*, 1:121.
145. al-Shammākhī, *Siyar*, 1:124.
146. Ibn al-Ṣaghīr, *Akhbār al-Ā'imma al-Rustumiyyīn*, 26.
147. al-Shammākhī, *Siyar*, 1:91.
148. Abū al-Faraj Muḥammad Abū al-Faḍl Ibrāhīm al-Iṣfahānī, *Kitāb al-Aghānī* (Beirut: Dār Iḥyā al-Turāth al-'Arabī, 1985), 23:223.
149. Wilkinson, *Imamate Tradition*, 205.
150. al-Sālimī, *Tuḥfat al-A'yān*, 1:93.
151. For a list of the Omani *'ulamā'* during the time of al-Julanda b. Mas'ūd, see al-Sālimī, *Tuḥfat al-A'yān*, 1:88–89. For an example of al-Julanda's consultation with the *'ulamā'*, see al-Izkawī, *Kashf al-Ghumma*, 249–51.
152. al-Izkawī, *Kashf al-Ghumma*, 250.
153. al-Kudamī, *al-Mu'tabar*, 1:13–14.
154. al-Kudamī, *al-Jāmi' al-Mufīd min Aḥkām Abī Sa'īd*, (Muscat: *WTQwTh*, 1985), 1:5–6.

155. Ibn Qays, *Mukhtaṣar al-Khiṣāl*, 194.
156. Abū Mu'thir in al-Kindī, *al-Muṣannaf*, 10:63.
157. al-Bisyānī in al-Kindī, *al-Muṣannaf*, 10:65.
158. Abū Zakariyya, *Kitāb Siyar al-Ā'imma*, 54–56.
159. Abū Zakariyya, *Kitāb Siyar al-Ā'imma*, 99.
160. Abū Zakariyya, *Kitāb Siyar al-Ā'imma*, 104; Savage, *Gateway to Hell*, 60.
161. Ibn 'Īsā in al-Kindī, *al-Muṣannaf*, 10:69.
162. al-Kindī, *al-Muṣannaf*, 10:69.
163. al-Bisyānī in al-Kindī, *al-Muṣannaf*, 10:60–61.
164. Ibn 'Īsā in Kāshif, *al-Siyar*, 1:400; also al-Kindī, *al-Muṣannaf*, 10:70.
165. al-Darjīnī, *Kitāb Ṭabaqāt al-Mashāyikh*, 1:6.
166. al-Kindī, *al-Muṣannaf*, 10:26.
167. al-Kindī, *al-Muṣannaf*, 10:26.
168. For a discussion of the role of the *ḥalqa* councils in the sociopolitical life of the North African Ibāḍī communities, see 'Awad Khulayfāt, *al-Niẓām al-Ijtima'iyya wa al-Tarbawiyya 'and al-Ibāḍiyya fī Shamāl Ifriqiyya fī Marḥalat al-Kitmān* (Amman: Jāma'a al-Urduniyya, 1978).
169. Abū Zakariyya, *Kitāb Siyar al-Ā'imma*, 206; Lewicki, "Ḥalḳa," 95.
170. Lewicki, "Ḥalḳa," 97–98; Savage, *Gateway to Hell*, 140–141.
171. al-Tanwātī, *Arā' al-Khawārij al-Kalāmiyya*, 2:238.
172. al-Warjlānī, *Kitāb al-Dalīl wa al-Burhān*, 3:200.
173. al-Jannāwanī, *Kitāb al-Waḍ'*, 29; al-Shammākhī, *Muqaddimat al-Tawḥīd*, 74.
174. al-Kindī, *al-Ihtidā'*, 237.
175. Abū Mu'thir in Kāshif, *al-Siyar*, 2:314–315.
176. al-Qalhātī, *al-Firaq al-Islāmiyya*, 229, 294.
177. Wilkinson, "Early Development," 134; Wilkinson, *Imamate Tradition*, 162. Wilkinson (along with Savage, *Gateway to Hell*, 26, who cites Wilkinson as her source) claims that the sixth/twelfth-century North African theologian and jurist al-Warjlānī is the source for the notion of the *imām al-kitmān*. I have not been able to find specific references to such an institution in al-Warjlānī's *al-Dalīl wa al-Burhān*, though it contains numerous references to *kitmān* and, separately, to the Imām. Moreover, Abū Mu'thir, an Omani jurist from the third/ninth century, clearly precedes al-Warjlānī in his depiction of the early Basran *'ulamā'* as Imāms. See Abū Mu'thir in Kāshif, *al-Siyar*, 2:314–315.
178. For a description of the ascetic practices of the *'azzāba*, see the description of Abū 'Abdullāh Aḥmad b. Bakr in al-Darjīnī, *Kitāb Ṭabaqāt al-Mashāyikh*, 2:377–392; Lewicki, "Ḥalḳa," 95–98.

Chapter 3

1. Lane, *An Arabic-English Lexicon*, 4:1544. Higgins notes that the verb *sharā-yashrī* can be translated as either "sell" or "exchange." She prefers "exchange" because the English phrase "he sold his soul" has negative connotations (that is, of selling one's soul to the devil). This study will retain, for the most part, the only slightly more familiar translation of "selling." See Annie Higgins, "Faces of Exchangers, Facets of

Exchange in Early *Shurāt* (Khārijī) Poetry," *Bulletin of the Royal Institute for Inter-Faith Studies* 7/1 (2005): 31–32 (fn. 1).

2. 4:74, 2.207.
3. For examples of the appellation *shurāt* as a synonym for Khārijite, see al-Ash'arī, *Maqālāt*, 1:207; al-Malaṭī, *Tanbīh*, 47; and the Khārijī poetry collected in 'Abbās, *Shi'r al-Khawārij*, 31, 33, 51, 53 (has *bī' nafsī*) , 59 (*abī'*), 61–62, 70.
4. al-Shammākhī, *Muqaddimat al-Tawḥīd*, 73; al-Jannāwanī, *Kitāb al-Waḍ'*, 29; al-Darjīnī, *Kitāb Ṭabaqāt al-Mashāyikh*, 1:7.
5. For the example of al-Muhannā b. Jayfar, see al-Kindī, *al-Muṣannaf*, 10:84.
6. See Munīr b. Nayyar al-Ja'lānī's *sīra* to the second Omani Ibāḍī Imām Ghassān b. 'Abdullāh al-Yaḥmadī (r. 188–208/803–823), in Kāshif, *al-Siyar*, 1:235–236.
7. The separation of the institution of the Imām and of the institution of *shirā'* in Omani jurisprudence is apparent in the different pledges (*bay'a*) for the *imāma* and for the practice of *shirā'*. For examples, see al-Kindī, *al-Muṣannaf*, 10:83. Mūsā b. Abī Jābir refused to make Muḥammad al-Ma'alī the Imām because he would not take the pledge of *shirā'*. See al-Kindī, *al-Muṣannaf*, 10:84; al-Sālimī, *Tuḥfat al-A'yān*, 1:111.
8. al-Shammākhī, *Muqaddimat al-Tawḥīd*, 73.
9. al-Shammākhī, *Muqaddimat al-Tawḥīd*, 73–74.
10. For a discussion of the many aspects of *jihād* in Qur'ānic and early Islamic thought, see James Johnson and John Kelsay, eds., *Cross, Crescent, and Sword* (Westport, Conn.: Greenwood, 1990).
11. 4:77. The reference to "withholding one's hands" apparently refers to an early command to avoid hostilities with the pagan Makkans (Ibn Kathīr, *Tafsīr*, 445).
12. See also 8:39.
13. Abū al-Ḥusayn Muslim b. al-Ḥajjāj Muslim, *Ṣaḥīḥ Muslim* (Beirut: Dār Ibn Ḥazm, 1997), 1.8.35.
14. Muslim, *Ṣaḥīḥ*, 1.20.80.
15. Abū Dāwud Sulaymān b. al-Ash'ath al-Sijistānī, *Sunan Abī Dawūd* (Riyad: International Ideas Home, 2000), 36.17.4344.
16. Mehdi Abedi and Gary Legenhausen, eds., *Jihād and Shahādat: Struggle and Martyrdom in Islam* (Houston: Institute for Research and Islamic Studies, 1986), 2–3.
17. 2:143.
18. 57:19.
19. al-Bukhārī, *Ṣaḥīḥ*, 56.2.2786, 2787; Muslim *Ṣaḥīḥ*, 32.31.1884–1887; Abū 'Abdullāh Muḥammad b. Yazīd al-Qazwīnī Ibn Māja, *Sunan Ibn Māja* (Riyad: International Ideas Home, n.d.), 24.16.2798–2802; E. Kohlburg, "Shahīd," in *EI2*, edited by Clifford Bosworth, Charles Pellat, and Joseph Schact (Leiden: Brill, 1997), 204.
20. Ibn Hishām, *al-Sīra al-Nabawiyya*, 3:72.
21. Kohlburg, "Shahīd," 204.
22. al-Bukhārī, *Ṣaḥīḥ*, 23.74.1346, 64.26.4079; Ibn Ḥajar al-'Asqalānī, *Fatḥ al-Bārī*, 1:841.
23. Kohlburg, "Shahīd," 204; Ibn Ḥajar al-'Asqalānī, *Fatḥ al-Bārī*, 2:1805–1806.
24. Abedi and Legenhausen, *Jihād and Shahādat*, 137.

25. Abedi and Legenhausen, *Jihād and Shahādat*, 143.
26. al-Baghdādī, *al-Farq Bayn al-Firaq*, 61–62.
27. ʻAbbās, *Shiʻr al-Khawārij*, 31. Many of the translations of Khārijite poems are here adapted from Fred Donner, "Piety and Eschatology in Early Kharijite Poetry," in *Fī Miḥrāb al-Maʻrifah: Festschrift for Iḥsān ʻAbbās*, ed. Ibrāhīm As-Saʻāfīn (Beirut: Dār Sader, 1997), 13–19.
28. ʻAbbās, *Shiʻr al-Khawārij*, 59.
29. ʻAbbās, *Shiʻr al-Khawārij*, 31–32.
30. ʻAbbās, *Shiʻr al-Khawārij*, 33.
31. ʻAbbās, *Shiʻr al-Khawārij*, 51.
32. ʻAbbās, *Shiʻr al-Khawārij*, 73.
33. ʻAbbās, *Shiʻr al-Khawārij*, 61. Abū Bilāl's father was Ḥudayr, his mother Udaya; his name is more often given as Ibn Udaya, but sometimes Ibn Ḥudayr is employed.
34. ʻAbbās, *Shiʻr al-Khawārij*, 62.
35. ʻAbbās, *Shiʻr al-Khawārij*, 70.
36. ʻAbbās, *Shiʻr al-Khawārij*, 72.
37. ʻAbbās, *Shiʻr al-Khawārij*, 50.
38. ʻAbbās, *Shiʻr al-Khawārij*, 73.
39. Ibn Qutayba, *al-Maʻārif* (Beirut: Dār al-Kutub al-ʻIlmiyya, 1987), 232.
40. al-Mubarrad, *al-Kāmil: Bāb al-Khawārij*, 107; Wellhausen, *Religio-Political Factions*, 46–47.
41. Eric J. Hobsbawm, *Bandits* (New York: Pantheon, 1969), 17.
42. Hobsbawm, *Bandits*, 17.
43. Hobsbawm, *Bandits*, 18.
44. Marshall G. S. Hodgson, *The Venture of Islam* (Chicago: University of Chicago Press, 1977), 1:227–230; Khalid Yahya Blankinship, *The End of the Jihād State* (Albany: State University of New York Press, 1994), 1–11.
45. On the early sources for data on Islamic sects, see Watt, *Formative Period*, 1–2.
46. See, for example, the eulogies of ʻĪsā b. Fātik in ʻAbbās, *Shiʻr al-Khawārij*, 54; Kaʻb b. ʻUmayra, 61; al-Rahīn b. Sahm al-Murādī, 63; and ʻImrān b. Ḥattān, 140.
47. For eulogies to Ṣāliḥ, see the poetry of al-Ḥuwayrith al-Rāsibī in ʻAbbās, *Shiʻr al-Khawārij*, 177; al-Jaʻd b. Ḍumām al-Dūsī, 178; and al-Minhāl al-Shaybānī al-Baṣrī, 180. For eulogies to Shabīb, see the poetry of ʻAtbān b. Uṣayla al-Shaybānī ʻAbbās, *Shiʻr al-Khawārij*, 182; and ʻAbd al-Wāḥid al-Azdī, 184.
48. al-Balādhurī, *Ansāb al-Ashrāf*, 5:189.
49. For an account of ʻUrwa's actions at the Battle of Ṣiffīn, see Ibn Qutayba, *al-Maʻārif*, 231–232; al-Shammākhī, *Siyar*, 1:64–65; al-Darjīnī, *Kitāb Ṭabaqāt al-Mashāyikh*, 2:215–216; Wellhausen, *Religio-Political Factions*, 41.
50. al-Balādhurī, *Ansāb al-Ashrāf*, 5:189; Wellhausen, *Religio-Political Factions*, 40.
51. al-Darjīnī, *Kitāb Ṭabaqāt al-Mashāyikh*, 2:217; al-Ṭabarī, *Tārīkh*, 2:186–187.
52. For descriptions of Abū Bilāl's piety see al-Darjīnī, *Kitāb Ṭabaqāt al-Mashāyikh*, 2:214; al-Shammākhī, *Siyar*, 1:64.
53. al-Balādhurī, *Ansāb al-Ashrāf*, 5:189–190; Wellhausen, *Religio-Political Factions*, 40–42.

54. al-Mubarrad, *al-Kāmil: Bāb al-Khawārij*, 81; al-Shammākhī, *al-Siyar*, 1:61
55. al-Mubarrad, *al-Kāmil: Bāb al-Khawārij*, 83.
56. al-Mubarrad, *al-Kāmil: Bāb al-Khawārij*, 83; al-Darjīnī, *Kitāb Ṭabaqāt al-Mashāyikh*, 2:218–219; al-Shammākhī, *Siyar*, 1:64.
57. al-Balādhurī, *Ansāb al-Ashrāf*, 5:191.
58. Hobsbawm, *Bandits*, 52.
59. al-Balādhurī, *Ansāb al-Ashrāf*, 5:191–192.
60. al-Mubarrad, *al-Kāmil: Bāb al-Khawārij*, 85.
61. Hobsbawm, *Bandits*, 50.
62. al-Balādhurī, *Ansāb al-Ashrāf*, 5:192–193.
63. See al-Mubarrad, *al-Kāmil: Bāb al-Khawārij*, 87; al-Balādhurī, *Ansāb al-Ashrāf*, 5:193; al-Shammākhī, *al-Siyar*, 1:63; al-Darjīnī, *Kitāb Ṭabaqāt al-Mashāyikh*, 2:222.
64. al-Isfarā'inī, *al-Tabṣīr fī al-Dīn*, 45; Ibn Qutayba, *al-Ma'ārif*, 232.
65. al-Mubarrad, *al-Kāmil: Bāb al-Khawārij*, 52.
66. Milton Gold, tr., *The Tārīkh-e Sistān* (Rome: Instituto Italiano per il Medil ed Estremo Oriente, 1976), 123.
67. Gold, *Tārīkh-e Sistān*, 123.
68. Gold, *Tārīkh-e Sistān*, 124.
69. Gold, *Tārīkh-e Sistān*, 132–133.
70. Gold, *Tārīkh-e Sistān*, 135.
71. Hobsbawm, *Bandits*, 58.
72. Robinson, *Empire and Elites*, 117.
73. al-Ṭabarī, *Tārīkh*, 2:882.
74. al-Ṭabarī, *Tārīkh*, 2:881.
75. al-Baghdādī, *al-Farq Bayn al-Firaq*, 89.
76. Ibn Qutayba, *al-Ma'ārif*, 232.
77. al-Ṭabarī, *Tārīkh*, 2:917.
78. Quoted in Robinson, *Empire and Elites*, 120.
79. al-Ṭabarī, *Tārīkh*, 2:934.
80. Abou El Fadl, *Violence and Rebellion*, 32. Maḥmūd Shaltūt clearly states that once two groups of Muslims resort to violence, one group among them must be considered rebels. See Shaltūt in Rudolph Peters, *Jihad in Medieval and Modern Islam* (Leiden: Brill, 1977), 40.
81. Ali Rahnema, *An Islamic Utopian: A Political Biography of 'Ali Shari'ati* (New York: I. B. Tauris, 1998), 161.
82. It is reported that 'Ammār was one of 'Alī's earliest supporters (*shī'a*), and died fighting for 'Alī at the Battle of Ṣiffīn: al-Mufīd, *al-Irshād*, 2, 189; also Abū Ja'far Muḥammad b. al-Ḥasan al-Ṭūsī, *Rijāl al-Ṭūsī*, ed. Muḥammad Kāẓim (Najaf: Maktabat al-Maṭba'a, 1961), 46.
83. al-Ṭabarī, *Tārīkh*, 1:3317.
84. al-Qalhātī, *al-Firaq al-Islāmiyya*, 66.
85. al-Qalhātī, *al-Firaq al-Islāmiyya*, 68.
86. 49:9 reads: "If two parties among the Believers fall into a quarrel, then make peace between them: but if one of them transgresses beyond bounds against the other, then

fight against the one that transgresses until it complies with the command of God; but if it complies, then make peace between them with justice, and be fair: for God loves those who are fair."

87. al-Ja'lānī in Kāshif, *al-Siyar*, 1:235.
88. al-Kindī, *Bayān al-Shar'*, 3:271; al-Kindī, *Kitāb al-Ihtidā'*, 237.
89. Abū Mu'thir in Kāshif, *al-Siyar*, 2:313.
90. al-Ja'lānī in Kāshif, *al-Siyar*, 1:235.
91. al-Mubarrad, *al-Kāmil: Bāb al-Khawārij*, 71. Abu al-'Abbās's account in al-Mubarrad conflates the events of Nukhayla with those of Ḥarūrā', and presents the Khārijites at Nukhayla as those who engaged in debate (*munāẓara*) with Ibn 'Abbās.
92. al-Ṭabarī, *Tārīkh*, 2:9–10. Compare with al-Balādhurī, who mentions also 'Abdullāh b. Abī Ḥawsā' al-Kilābī and Hawthara b. Wadā' al-Asadī as leaders of the *ahl Nukhayla*. See al-Balādhurī, *Ansāb al-Ashrāf*, 5:169–172.
93. See also al-Baghdādī, *al-Farq Bayn al-Firaq*, 62.
94. al-Ṭabarī, *Tārīkh*, 2:10.
95. al-Mubarrad, *al-Kāmil: Bāb al-Khawārij*, 73. Al-Balādhurī preserves the same line of poetry, but attributes it to an anonymous companion of the Khārijite Shabīb b. Bajra al-Ashja'ī. See al-Balādhurī, *Ansāb al-Ashrāf*, 5:172.
96. al-Qalhātī, *al-Firaq al-Islāmiyya*, 89; Ibn Qaḥṭān in Kāshif, *al-Siyar*, 1:109.
97. al-Qalhātī, *al-Firaq al-Islāmiyya*, 89. Compare with the account in al-Balādhurī, where al-Ḥasan says to Mu'āwiya: "If I preferred to fight anyone from the People of the Qibla [that is, the Muslims], I would begin by fighting you, but I have abandoned that for the good of the *umma*." See al-Balādhurī, *Ansāb al-Ashrāf*, 5:169–170.
98. Ibn Qaḥṭān in Kāshif, *al-Siyar*, 1:109.
99. As Thompson notes, sects in the Umayyad period worked in concert more often than not, and only opposed one another when forced to do so by the Umayyad regime. See William Thomson, "Kharijitism and the Kharijites," in *The MacDonald Presentation Volume* (Princeton: Princeton University Press, 1933), 373–389. Evidence survives of early collaboration and interaction between the Khārijites and other Islamic sects and individuals. For example, al-Mubarrad preserves correspondence between Nāfi' b. al-Azraq and Najda b. 'Amr. See al-Mubarrad, *al-Kāmil: Bāb al-Khawārij*, 112–115. Likewise, Nāfi' and the (pro-'Alīd) Ibn Ṣurad of Kūfa seem to have aligned themselves together against the Umayyads (mentioned in Thompson, "Kharijitism and the Kharijites," 382). The Tha'āliba Khārijites of Khurasān became involved in revolutionary activity there and, under the direction of Shaybān b. Salama, raised an army of 30,000 consisting of Khurasānī and Basran Khārijites. Shaybān aligned himself, briefly, with Abū Muslim al-Khurasānī. See Wilferd Madelung, *Religious Trends in Early Islamic Iran* (Albany: Bibliotheca Persica, 1988), 60. In addition, the Omani jurist Abū Sa'īd deals with the question of a person who mistakes an Ibāḍī for a Shi'ite; such a mistake may be another indicator of their closeness. See Abū Sa'īd Muḥammad b. Sa'īd al-Kudamī, *al-Jāmi' al-Mufīd min Aḥkām Abī Sa'īd* (Muscat: *WTQwTh*, 1985), 1:33–34.
100. Kāshif, *al-Siyar*, 1:81, fn 1.
101. See Ibn al-Ṣaghīr, *Akhbār al-Ā'imma al-Rustumiyyīn*, 81.

102. al-Qalhātī, *al-Firaq al-Islāmiyya*, 252–275.
103. Abū Mu'thir in Kāshif, *al-Siyar*, 2:314.
104. al-Ja'lānī in Kāshif, *al-Siyar*, 1:234.
105. al-Ṭabarī, *Tārīkh*, 2:15–16; al-Balādhurī's account of Sahm and al-Khaṭīm's rebellion matches al-Ṭabarī's, suggesting a similar source. See al-Balādhurī, *Ansāb al-Ashrāf*, 5:179–181.
106. Ibn al-Athīr, *al-Kāmil fī al-Tārīkh*, 3:350. Similarly, al-Balādhurī's account claims that Sahm and al-Khaṭīm were the first to apply the concept of *kufr* to the Muslims. See *Ansāb al-Ashrāf*, 5:179.
107. al-Ṭabarī, *Tārīkh*, 2:73–74.
108. 'Abbās, *Shi'r al-Khawārij*, 46; al-Balādhurī, *Ansāb al-Ashrāf*, 5:180.
109. al-Ja'lānī in Kāshif, *al-Siyar*, 1:234–235.
110. al-Ṭabarī, *Tārīkh*, 2:90–91. Their full names are given in al-Baghdādī, *al-Farq Bayn al-Firaq*, 62, and al-Balādhūrī, *Ansāb al-Ashrāf*, 5:182.
111. al-Baghdādī, *al-Farq Bayn al-Firaq*, 62; al-Balādhūrī, *Ansāb al-Ashrāf*, 5:183.
112. al-Mubarrad, *al-Kāmil: Bāb al-Khawārij*, 79.
113. 'Abbās, *Shi'r al-Khawārij*, 60.
114. al-Ja'lānī in Kāshif, *al-Siyar*, 1:234.
115. Abū Mu'thir in Kāshif, *al-Siyar*, 2:314.
116. al-Darjīnī, *Kitāb Ṭabaqāt al-Mashāyikh*, 1:7.
117. al-Shammākhī, *Muqaddimat al-Tawḥīd*, 73.
118. For the Sunni versions of these narratives, see Wahb b. Jarīr's account in al-Ṭabarī, *Tārīkh*, 2:187; al-Balādhruī, *Ansāb al-Ashrāf*, 5:188–195; Abū Mikhnaf's account in al-Ṭabarī, *Tārīkh*, 2:391; Ibn al-Athīr, *al-Kāmil fī al-Tārīkh*, 3:428; al-Mubarrad, *al-Kāmil: Bāb al-Khawārij*, 81–86. For the Ibāḍī versions, see al-Darjīnī, *Kitāb Ṭabaqāt al-Mashāyikh,* 2:214–226; al-Shammākhī, *Siyar*, 1:61–67.
119. Abū Mu'thir in Kāshif, *al-Siyar*, 2:314.
120. al-Ja'lānī in Kāshif, *al-Siyar*, 1:234, 236.
121. al-Darjīnī, *Kitāb Ṭabaqāt al-Mashāyikh*, 1:7.
122. al-Shammākhī, *Muqaddimat al-Tawḥīd*, 73.
123. Abū Zakariyya in al-Darjīnī, *Kitāb Ṭabaqāt al-Mashāyikh,* 2:364; al-Jannāwanī, *Kitāb al-Waḍ'*, 29.
124. Abū Mu'thir in Kāshif, *al-Siyar*, 2:315. In addition, al-Ja'lānī includes 'Abdullāh b. Yaḥya, Abū Ḥamza al-Mukhtār b. 'Awf, and al-Julanda b. Mas'ūd among the "good examples" of early Ibāḍiyya to be followed. See al-Ja'lānī in Kāshif, *al-Siyar*, 1:234, 236–237; al-Kindī, *al-Ihtidā'*, 237.
125. Abū Hamza's speeches in Makka and Madīna have been preserved in Ibn Qutayba, *'Uyūn al-Akhbār*, 2:271–272; al-Jāḥiẓ, *al-Bayān wa al-Tabyīn*, 2:79–82; al-Darjīnī, *Kitāb Ṭabaqāt al-Mashāyikh*, 2:266–269; for a translation, see Crone, *God's Caliph*, 129–132.
126. al-Darjīnī, *Kitāb Ṭabaqāt al-Mashāyikh*, 2:258–272. See also Mahdī Ṭālib Hāshim, *al-Ḥaraka al-Ibāḍiyya fī al-Mashriq al-'Arabī* (London: Dār al-Ḥikma, 2001), 151–152.
127. al-Darjīnī, *Kitāb Ṭabaqāt al-Mashāyikh*, 2:258.

128. al-Sālimī, *Tuḥfat al-A'yān*, 1:88; Wilkinson, *Imamate Tradition*, 153.
129. al-Sālimī, *Tuḥfat al-A'yān*, 1:94.
130. al-Sālimī, *Tuḥfat al-A'yān*, 1:95–96.
131. Crone and Zimmerman, *Epistle*, 140–141.
132. al-Darjīnī, *Kitāb Ṭabaqāt al-Mashāyikh*, 2:478.
133. Wilkinson, "Ibāḍī Ḥadīth," 250–251.
134. al-Shammākhī, *Muqaddimat al-Tawḥīd*, 73.
135. al-Kindī, *al-Muṣannaf*, 10:83.
136. al-Shammākhī, *Muqaddimat al-Tawḥīd*, 73; Ennami, *Studies in Ibadism (al-Ibāḍīyah)*, 233.
137. al-Ja'lānī in Kāshif, *al-Siyar*, 1:238–239; Ennami, *Studies in Ibadism (al-Ibāḍīyah)*, 233.
138. al-Tanwātī, *Arā' al-Khawārij al-Kalāmiyya*, 2:238.
139. al-Kindī, *al-Muṣannaf*, 10:83.
140. al-Bisyānī in al-Kindī, *al-Muṣannaf*, 10:60.
141. al-Ja'lānī in Kāshif, *al-Siyar*, 1:236. As has been demonstrated, Ibāḍī historians portrayed Abū Bilāl as one of the first individuals to practice *shirā'*, and in many ways Abū Bilāl became the prototype for the practice of *shirā'*. This appropriation of the narrative of Abū Bilāl, of course, represents the creation of a fictive truth for the purposes of elucidating the practice of *shirā'*. Abū Bilāl may not have used the exact words, or conceived of his actions in the way in which this Ibāḍī historical account of his actions portray him as doing. Nevertheless, what is important is how the words and actions of Abū Bilāl as he appears in this account focused attention on *shirā'* as it was meant to be practiced by the contemporaries of the Ibāḍī historians who wrote about Abū Bilāl. Thus, when al-Ja'lānī presents Abū Bilāl's conditions for the practice of *shirā'* in the form of a speech that (al-Ja'lānī claims) Abū Bilāl gave to his prospective followers, this speech must be taken as relevant to (and therefore addressed to) the contemporaries of al-Ja'lānī.
142. al-Shammākhī, *Muqaddimat al-Tawḥīd*, 73.
143. Ibn Qays, *Mukhtaṣar al-Khiṣāl*, 193.
144. al-Shammākhī, *Muqaddimat al-Tawḥīd*, 73.
145. al-Shammākhī, *Muqaddimat al-Tawḥīd*, 74.
146. al-Tanwātī, *Arā' al-Khawārij al-Kalāmiyya*, 2:238.
147. al-Kindī, *al-Muṣannaf*, 10:83–84.
148. al-Bisyānī in al-Kindī, *al-Muṣannaf*, 10:60.

Chapter 4

1. For example, the *ulamā'* accepted and distributed the *zakāt* and alms (*ḥuqūq*) during the condition of *kitmān*, a responsibility reserved for the Imām during a state of *ẓuhūr*. See al-Jiṭālī, *Qawā'id al-Islām*, 2:428–432.
2. See Tabghūrīn b. Dāwūd b. 'Īsā al-Malshūṭī's *Kitāb Usūl al-Dīn* in Ennami, *Studies in Ibadism (Edition of Ibāḍī Texts)*, 37.
3. Watt, *Islamic Political Thought*, 35.

4. Watt, *Islamic Political Thought*, 41; see also Von Grunebaum, *Classical Islam*, 15.
5. Watt, *Islamic Political Thought*, 40.
6. Watt, *Muhammad at Mecca*, 8.
7. Ibn Hishām, for example, reports that the Prophet Muhammad's uncle, Waraqa b. Nawfal, was a Christian; see Ibn Hishām, *al-Sīra al-Nabawiyya*, 1:180.
8. 40:51 states: "We do indeed help Our Messengers, and the believers, in this life as well as on the Day when witnesses shall stand up." See also Rahman, *Major Themes*, 63.
9. 21:73.
10. Ibn Kathīr, *Tafsīr*, 1025.
11. 28:41.
12. 11:96–98. Most Qur'ān commentators take the term *wird* in verse 98 to indicate the act of entering the Fire: Ibn 'Abbās in al-Ṭabarī, for example, reads *wird* as *dukhūl*. See al-Ṭabarī, *Tafsīr al-Ṭabarī* (Beirut: Dār al-Kutub al-'Ilmiyya, 2005), 7:108. However, the word also indicates a watering hole, and the verb *awrada* (which is also used in verse 98) can mean "to lead to water." See al-Rāghib al-Iṣfahānī, *Mufradāt*, 865. Therefore the verse can be read as creating a metaphor whereby Pharaoh's people believe they are being led to a place of water, only to be led to the Fire. This interpretation is possible when the term *wird* in verse 98 is compared with 19:86: "And We shall drive the guilty to Hell, a weary herd," where those being led to Hell are compared to herd animals being driven to their watering place.
13. 2:124.
14. 21:73.
15. 32:24.
16. 38:26. The phrase "viceroy in the earth" recalls the trust (*amāna*) between God and humankind that established human beings as God's vice-regents on earth: "And when the Lord said to the angels, Lo! I am about to place a viceroy (*khalīfa*) in the earth" (2:30); see also 6:165; 10:14, 73; 35:39; 5:69, 74; 27:62.
17. 23:52.
18. 7:181.
19. 4:135.
20. 2:143.
21. 3:110.
22. 5:48.
23. 29:2–3.
24. 13:11.
25. 3:159.
26. 42:38; 2:233.
27. al-Kindī, *al-Muṣannaf*, 10:9.
28. 4:59.
29. As Madelung observes, a minority of Muslim scholars held that Abū Bakr was explicitly chosen by Muhammad as his successor, and that it was probably during the time of 'Umar that the prevalent view that Muhammad had named no successor gained prominence. See Madelung, *Succession to Muḥammad*, 54–55.

30. al-Ṭabarī, *Tārīkh*, 1:2771–2772.
31. al-Ṭabarī, *Tārīkh*, 1:2767–2768.
32. Ibn Hishām, *al-Sīra al-Nabawiyya*, 4:232; Ibāḍī variants of this speech can be located in al-Qalhātī, *al-Firaq al-Islāmiyya*, 204; al-Kudamī, *al-Istiqāma*, 2:120; *al-Mu'tabar*, 2:159.
33. al-Kindī, *al-Muṣannaf*, 10:7.
34. Cook convincingly argues that this letter was probably written toward the early part of the first half of the second/eighth century, but that the attribution to Ibn Ibāḍ is spurious. See Cook, *Early Muslim Dogma*, 67.
35. Ibn Ibāḍ, *al-Ibāḍiyya wa Madā Ṣilatiha bī al-Khawārij*, 136–137; see also Muḥammad b. Maḥbūb in Kāshif, *al-Siyar*, 2:259.
36. Ibn Ibāḍ, *al-Ibāḍiyya wa Madā Ṣilatiha bī al-Khawārij*, 136.
37. Crone and Zimmerman, *Epistle*, 266.
38. Crone and Zimmerman, *Epistle*, 48–49.
39. Crone and Zimmerman, *Epistle*, 50–51.
40. Crone and Zimmerman, *Epistle*, 48–49.
41. al-Kindī, *al-Muṣannaf*, 10:59.
42. al-Balādhurī, *Ansāb al-Ashrāf*, 3:121–122. Similarly, Abū Mikhnaf reports that when one of the Muḥakkima, Shurayḥ b. Awfā al-'Abasī, fled Kūfa he recited 28:21, explicitly comparing the people of Kūfa to the "wrongdoing folk" (*qawm al-ẓālimīn*) mentioned in the verse. See al-Ṭabarī, *Tārīkh*, 1:3365–3366; a variant in al-Balādhurī, *Ansāb al-Ashrāf*, 3:138, has Zayd b. Ḥisn instead of Shurayḥ. 28:21 reads: "So he escaped from thence, tearing, vigilant. He said: My Lord! Deliver me from a wrongdoing folk."
43. al-Ṭabarī, *Tārīkh*, 1:3457. This report also includes a story of Ibn Muljam resolving to murder 'Alī at the request of a woman with whom he had fallen in love. The woman, a member of the Taym b. Ribāb, demands that Ibn Muljam kill 'Alī in retaliation for her father and brother, who were slain at the Battle of Nahrawān, before she will marry him. These stories lead the reader to understand that tribally based revenge is the motive for the assassination of 'Alī. Similarly, the tribal concept of blood revenge is invoked by 'Alī after he receives his wound: "A life for a life—if I die, kill him as he killed me." See al-Ṭabarī, *Tārīkh*, 1:3461.
44. al-Ṭabarī, *Tārīkh*, 1:3457.
45. al-Mubarrad, *al-Kāmil: Bāb al-Khawārij*, 36.
46. al-Ash'arī, *Maqālāt*, 1:192; variant on 194.
47. al-Ṭabarī, *Tārīkh*, 1:2994. For an overview of 'Uthmān's reign, see Madelung, *Succession to Muḥammad*, 80–81.
48. Crone and Hinds, *God's Caliph*, 34–38.
49. al-Ṭabarī, *Tārīkh*, 2:743.
50. Crone and Hinds, *God's Caliph*, 39.
51. Aḥmad b. Muḥmmad Ibn 'Abd Rabbihi, *Kitāb al-'Iqd al-Farīd* (Beirut: Dār al-Arqam, 1999), 4:93; Crone and Hinds, *God's Caliph*, 39.
52. al-Ṭabarī, *Tārīkh*, 2:1758; see also the translation of the epistle of Walīd II in Crone and Hinds, *God's Caliph*, 120.

53. Ibn Ibāḍ, *al-Ibāḍiyya wa Madā Ṣilatiha bī al-Khawārij*, 134.
54. Crone and Hinds, *God's Caliph*, 36–38.
55. al-Ṭabarī, *Tārīkh*, 1:3277; Abū al-Faḍl Naṣar b. Muzāḥim b. Siyār al-Minqarī, *Waq'at Ṣiffīn*, ed. 'Abd al-Salām Muḥammad Hārūn (Cairo: Mu'assasat al-'Arabiyya al-Ḥadītha, 1962), 200.
56. al-Farazdāq, *Diwān*, 2:655.
57. Jarīr, *Diwān*, 147.
58. Crone and Hinds, *God's Caliph*, 37.
59. Crone and Hinds, *God's Caliph*, 38.
60. al-Iṣfahānī, *al-Aghānī*, 6:312.
61. Ghiyāth b. Ghawth al-Taghlībī al-Akhṭal, *Dīwān*, ed. A. Ṣalḥānī (Beirut: Imprimerie Catholique, 1891), 185.
62. al-Ṭabarī, *Tārīkh*, 2:75; Crone and Hinds, *God's Caliph*, 38.
63. al-Shahrastānī, *al-Milal wa al-Niḥal*, 115.
64. al-Ash'arī, *Maqālāt*, 1:204.
65. 'Abbās, *Shi'r al-Khawārij*, 69.
66. 'Abbās, *Shi'r al-Khawārij*, 55.
67. 'Abbās, *Shi'r al-Khawārij*, 35.
68. Goldziher, *Muslim Studies*, 2:90–91; on the title *khalīfat Allāh* see Crone and Hinds, *God's Caliph*, 21.
69. Goldziher, *Muslim Studies*, 2:54.
70. al-Bukhārī, *Ṣaḥīḥ*, 92.2.7053.
71. Goldziher, *Muslim Studies*, 2:94–95.
72. al-Ṭabarī, *Tārīkh*, 2:70; Goldziher, *Muslim Studies*, 2:50–51.
73. Aḥmad b. Abī Ya'qūb al-Ya'qūbī, *Tārīkh*, ed. M. T. Houtsma (Leiden: Brill, 1883), 2:283.
74. al-Ya'qūbī, *Tārīkh*, 2:265.
75. Though he overstates the case, Shaban claims: "[the Azraqite and Najdite] so-called Kharijite movement was in fact a major revolt in Arabia itself, led by a tribe with a long tradition of independence, which happened to be in alliance with the *khawārij* for the purposes of an Iraqi campaign." See M. A. Shaban, *Islamic History: A New Approach* (Cambridge: Cambridge University Press, 1971), 1:97.
76. al-Balādhurī, *Ansāb al-Ashrāf*, 3:114; al-Ṭabarī, *Tārīkh*, 1:3351–3354.
77. al-Ṭabarī, *Tārīkh*, 1:3365.
78. al-Ṭabarī, *Tārīkh*, 1:3365.
79. Patricia Crone, "The Khārijites and the Caliphal Title," in *Studies in Islamic and Middle Eastern Texts and Traditions in Memory of Norman Calder*, ed. G. R. Hawting, J. A. Mojaddedi, and A. Samely (Oxford: Oxford University Press, 2000), 85–91; al-Baghdādī, *al-Farq Bayn al-Firaq*, 65; Ibn Abī al-Ḥadīd, *Sharḥ Nahj al-Balāgha*, 4:130, 159.
80. al-Baghdādī, *al-Farq Bayn al-Firaq*, 65; al-Shahrastānī, *al-Milal wa al-Niḥal*, 120; al-Ash'arī, *Maqālāt*, 1:170–171. Al-Ash'arī uses the terms *'aqadat al-amr* and *astakhlafa* to describe the process of succession among the Azāriqa.
81. al-Shahrastānī, *al-Milal wa al-Niḥal*, 123.

82. al-Baghdādī, *al-Farq Bayn al-Firaq*, 67.
83. al-Baghdādī, *al-Farq Bayn al-Firaq*, 67; al-Shahrastānī, *al-Milal wa al-Niḥal*, 123; al-Ash'arī, *Maqālāt*, 1:174.
84. al-Ash'arī, *Maqālāt*, 1:176.
85. al-Baghdādī, *al-Farq Bayn al-Firaq*, 79; Ibn Abī al-Ḥadīd, *Sharḥ Nahj al-Balāgha*, 4:180.
86. Abū Muḥammad 'Alī b. Aḥmad Ibn Ḥazm, *Jamharat Ansāb al-'Arab*, ed. 'A. M. Hārūn (Cairo: Dār al-Ma'ārif, 1962), 322.
87. al-Ṭabarī, *Tārīkh*, 2:1942; Ibn al-Athīr, *al-Kāmil fī al-Tārīkh*, 5:267.
88. Madelung, *Religious Trends*, 57; Paul Walker, *A Catalogue of the Arab-Sassanian Coins* (London: Trustees of the British Museum, 1941), 111–113.
89. al-Balādhurī, *Ansāb al-Ashrāf*, 5:183.
90. Patricia Crone, "A Statement by the Najdiyya Khārijites on the Dispensability of the Imamate," *SI* 88 (1998): 56; the Nukkārī subsect of the Ibāḍiyya also reportedly adopted a belief similar to that of the Najdāt: see al-Jannāwunī, *Kitāb al-Waḍ'*, 23.
91. al-Ash'arī, *Maqālāt*, 1:205; variant in al-Shahrastānī, *al-Milal wa al-Niḥal*, 124.
92. al-Nawbakhtī, *Kitāb Firaq al-Shī'a*, 10.
93. al-Tanwātī, *Arā' al-Khawārij al-Kalāmiyya*, 2:233.
94. Crone and Zimmerman, *Epistle*, 208.
95. al-Mubarrad, *al-Kāmil*, 3:913.
96. al-Baghdādī, *al-Farq Bayn al-Firaq*, 69.
97. Ibn al-Athīr, *al-Kāmil fī al-Tārīkh*, 5:88.
98. al-Shahrastānī, *Kitāb Nihāyat al-Iqdām*, 481ff.; Crone, "A Statement," 75. Although the Najdite pieces of the argument must be distinguished from its Mu'tazilite pieces, the passage yields a coherent argument that was probably adapted from an original Khārijite source. See Crone, "A Statement," 66.
99. al-Shahrastānī, *Nihāyat al-Iqdām*, 482. There is evidence that a group of Najdites may have accorded Najda's *ijtihād* a higher priority over their own because of his status as Imām; see al-Baghdādī, *al-Farq Bayn al-Firaq*, 69; see also al-Ash'arī, *Maqālāt*, 1:176 (without the reference to Najda's *ijtihād*).
100. al-Shahrastānī, *Nihāyat al-Iqdām*, 482.
101. al-Shahrastānī, *Nihāyat al-Iqdām*, 484; Crone, "A Statement," 75.
102. Crone, "A Statement," 75–76.
103. al-Kindī, *al-Muṣannaf*, 10:4.
104. al-Kudamī in al-Kindī, *al-Muṣannaf*, 10:6.
105. al-Kindī, *al-Muṣannaf*, 10:59.
106. al-Kindī, *al-Muṣannaf*, 10:23–24; al-Kudamī, *al-Istiqāma*, 2:119; al-Bisyānī in Kāshif, *al-Siyar*, 2:175; Wilkinson, "The Ibāḍī Imāma," 535ff.
107. al-Bisyānī in Kāshif, *al-Siyar*, 2:175.
108. al-Kindī, *al-Muṣannaf*, 10:23.
109. Abū Mundhir in al-Kindī, *al-Ihtidā'*, 159.
110. Abū Zakariyya, *Kitāb Siyar al-Ā'imma*, 91. By the twelfth/eighteenth century, Omani jurists had reasserted their authority over the Imām to the point where

they could require consultation as a duty: al-Ṣā'ighī states in his *bāb al-imāma*: "Consultation is a duty and this may be imposed as an absolute duty (*farḍ wājib*), a condition of [the Imām's] tenure of office; if he fails in this then his *imāma* ceases and obedience from his flock is no longer obligatory." See al-Ṣā'ighī in Wilkinson, "The Ibāḍī Imāma," 539.

111. al-Kindī, *al-Muṣannaf*, 10:159.
112. Abū Zakariyya, *Kitāb Siyar al-Ā'imma*, 84; Ibn al-Ṣaghīr, *Akhbār al-Ā'imma al-Rustumiyyīn*, 30–31.
113. al-Kudamī, *al-Mu'tabar*, 2:159.
114. al-Ṣā'ighī in Wilkinson, "The Ibāḍī Imāma," 541.
115. Ibn Qaḥṭān in al-Sālimī, *Tuḥfat al-A'yān*, 1:114; varient in Kāshif, *al-Siyar*, 1:115.
116. al-Kindī, *al-Ihtidā'*, 165–166; *al-Muṣannaf*, 10:8–14; Abū Mu'thir in al-Kindī, *al-Muṣannaf*, 10:101; Ibn Baraka in al-Kindī, *al-Muṣannaf*, 10:100.
117. Ibn Qays, *Mukhtaṣar al-Khiṣāl*, 193.
118. Ibn al-Ṣaghīr, *Akhbār al-Ā'imma al-Rustumiyyīn*, 26–27; Savage, *Gateway to Hell*, 43.
119. al-Kindī, *al-Muṣannaf*, 10:105.
120. Muḥammad b. Maḥbūb in Kāshif, *al-Siyar*, 1:125.
121. al-Kindī, *al-Muṣannaf*, 10:127, 207–208, 215, 218.
122. al-Kindī, *al-Muṣannaf*, 10:49–50.
123. al-Kudamī, *al-Mu'tabar*, 2:159.
124. al-Kudamī, *al-Mu'tabar*, 2:159; *al-Istiqāma*, 2:120; al-Qalhātī, *al-Firaq al-Islāmiyya*, 204.
125. Ibn Qaḥṭān in Kāshif, *al-Siyar*, 1:115–118.
126. al-Tanwātī, *Arā' al-Khawārij al-Kalāmiyya*, 2:238; al-Darjīnī, *Kitāb Ṭabaqāt al-Mashāyikh*, 1:6; al-Kudamī, *al-Mu'tabar*, 2:161; al-Shammākhī, *Muqaddimat al-Tawḥīd*, 74.
127. al-Kindī, *al-Muṣannaf*, 10:24–25.
128. al-Malshūṭī in Ennami, *Studies in Ibadism (Edition of Ibāḍī Texts)*, 37.
129. al-Kindī, *al-Muṣannaf*, 10:60; al-Shammākhī, *Muqaddiamt al-Tawḥīd*, 70; al-Darjīnī, *Kitāb Ṭabaqāt al-Mashāyikh*, 1:6.
130. al-Kindī, *al-Muṣannaf*, 10:61; al-Shammākhī, *Muqaddiamt al-Tawḥīd*, 70.
131. al-Shammākhī, *Muqaddiamt al-Tawḥīd*, 70; al-Darjīnī, *Kitāb Ṭabaqāt al-Mashāyikh*, 2:364; al-Sālimī, *Tuḥfat al-A'yān*, 1:111 (who also notes that he agreed to *shirā'*).
132. al-Bisyānī in Kindī, *al-Muṣannaf*, 10:80.
133. al-Bisyānī in al-Kindī, *al-Muṣannaf*, 10:69.
134. Wilkinson, *Imamate Tradition*, 159–160.

Conclusion

1. Although it is true that heresiographers and later historians sometimes used Khārijite or Ibāḍī sources when compiling their works, they nevertheless edited the materials in such a way as to make it difficult to decipher what materials come from what

sources. For an excellent discussion of the problems of heresiographical literature, see Lewinstein, "The Azāriqa in Islamic Heresiography," 251–268.

2. H.A.R. Gibb, *Studies on the Civilization of Islam* (Lahore: Islamic Book Service, 1987), 153.
3. Watt, *Formative Period*, 36–37.
4. Michael Morony, *Iraq After the Muslim Conquest* (Piscataway, N.J.: Gorgias Press, 2005), 468–478. Sizgorich's study on Christian and Muslim modes of militant devotion in the late antique period contains an interesting chapter on the Khārijites, and provides a beginning for research in this direction. However, Sizgorich does not use Ibāḍī sources, and is not particularly interested in finding "horizontal influences" between Christians and Khārijites. His main concern is to contextualize the particular Khārijite modes of militant piety within the larger framework of Christian-Muslim articulations of violence and devotion. See Thomas Sizgorich, *Violence and Belief in Late Antiquity*, (Philadelphia: University of Pennsylvania Press, 2009), 196–230.

Bibliography

Primary Sources in Arabic

'Abbās, Iḥsān, ed. *Shi'r al-Khawārij: Jam' wa Taqdīm Iḥsān 'Abbās*. 3rd ed. Beirut: Dār al-Thaqāfa, 1974.

Abū Dawūd, Sulaymān b. al-Ash'ath al-Sijistānī. *Sunan Abī Dawūd*. Riyad: International Ideas Home, 2000.

Abū Zakarriya, Yaḥya b. Abī Bakr. *Kitāb Siyar al-Ā'imma wa Akhbārihim*, ed. Ismā'īl al-'Arabī. Algiers: Dār al-Maghrib al-Islāmī, 1979.

al-Akhṭal, Ghiyāth b. Ghawth al-Taghlībī. *Diwān*, ed. Antoine Ṣālḥānī. Beirut: Imprimerie Catholique, 1891.

al-Ash'arī, Abū al-Ḥasan. *Kitāb Maqālāt al-Islamiyyin wa Ikhtilāf al-Muṣallīn*. 2 vols. Beirut: Maktabat al-'Aṣriyya, 1999.

Aṭfayyish, Muḥammad b. Yūsuf. *Sharḥ Kitāb al-Nīl wa Sifā' al-'Alīl*. 17 vols. Beirut: Dār al-Fatḥ, 1972.

———. *Sharḥ Kitāb 'Aqīdat al-Tawḥīd*. Muscat: *WTQwTh*, 1983.

al-'Awtabī, Abu Mundhir Salama b. Muslim. *al-Ansāb*. 2 vols., ed. Muḥammad Iḥsān al-Naṣṣ. Muscat: Maṭba'at al-Alwān al-Ḥadītha, 2006.

———. *Kitāb al-Ḍiyā'*. 5 vols. Muscat: *WTQwTh*, 1991.

al-Baghdādī, 'Abd al-Qāhir b. Ṭāhir. *al-Farq Bayn al-Firaq*. Beirut: Dār al-Afāq al-Jadīda, 1987.

———. *Kitāb al-Milal wa al-Niḥal*. Beirut: Dar al-Machreq Editeurs, 1986.

———. *Kitāb Usūl al-Dīn*. Istanbul: Maṭba'āt al-Dawla, 1928.

al-Balādhurī, Aḥmad b. Yaḥyā. *Ansāb al-Ashrāf*. 13 vols, ed. Suhayl Zakkār and Riyāḍ Zarkalī. Beirut: Dār al-Fikr, 1996.

———. *Futuḥ al-Buldān*. Beirut: Dār al-Kutub al-'Ilmiyya, 1983.

al-Barrādī, Abū al-Faḍl (var. al-Qāsim) b. Ibrāhīm. *Kitāb al-Jawāhir*. Lithograph. Cairo: n.p., 1885.

al-Bisyānī (var. al-Bisyawī), Abū al-Ḥasan 'Alī b. Muḥammad. *al-Jāmi 'Abī al-Ḥasan al-Bisyānī*. 4 vols. Muscat: *WTQwTh*, 1984.

al-Bukhārī, Abū 'Abdullāh Muḥammad b. Ismā'īl. *Kitāb al-Jāmi' al-Ṣaḥīḥ*. 4 vols, ed. M. L. Krehl and T. W. Juynboll. Leiden: Brill, 1908.

Crone, Patricia, and Fritz Zimmerman, trans. and eds. *The Epistle of Sālim Ibn Dhakwān*. New York: Oxford University Press, 2001.

al-Darjīnī, Abū al-'Abbās Aḥmad b. Sa'īd. *Kitāb Ṭabaqāt al-Mashāyikh bī al-Maghrib*, 2 vols., ed. Ibrahim Tallay. Algiers: Alger-Constantine, n.d.

al-Dhahabī, Abū 'Abdullāh Shams al-Dīn. *Kitāb Tadhkirat al-Ḥuffāẓ*. 4 vols. Hyderabad: Maṭba'at Dā'irat al-Ma'ārif al-Niẓāmiyya, 1915.

Ennami, Amr K., ed. *Studies in Ibadism (Edition of Ibāḍī Texts)*. Tripoli, Libya: Publications of the University of Libya Faculty of Arts, 1972.

al-Farazdāq, Tammām b. Ghālib. *Diwān*, ed. 'Abdullāh Ismā'īl al-Ṣāwī. Cairo: al-Maktaba al-Tijāriyya al-Kubrā, 1936.

Fūrūzānfar, Badī'uzzamān. *Ahdāth-i Mathnawī*. Tehran: University of Tehran, 1955.

Gold, Milton, tr. *The Tārīkh-e Sistān*. Rome: Istituto Italiano per il Medio ed Estremo Oriente, 1976.

al-Ḥimyarī, 'Abd al-Razzāq b. Ḥammām al-Ṣan'ānī. *al-Muṣannaf*. 12 vols., ed. Ḥabīb al-Raḥmān al-A'zamī. Beirut: al-Majlas al-'Ilmī, 1970.

al-Ḥimyarī, Nashwān b. Sa'īd. *al-Ḥūr al-'Ayn*. Cairo: Maktabat al-Khānjā, 1948.

al-Ḥujwīrī, 'Alī b. 'Uthmān. *The "Kashf al-Maḥjūb," the Oldest Persian Treatise on Sufism by al-Hujwiri*, tr. Reynold A. Nicholson. London: Gibb Memorial Series, no. 11, 1959.

Ibn 'Abd al-Ḥakam, Abū al-Qāsim 'Abd al-Raḥmān b. 'Abdullāh. *Futūḥ Maṣr wa Akhbāruhā*, ed. Charles C. Torrey. New Haven: Yale University Press, 1920.

Ibn 'Abd Rabbihi, Aḥmad b. Muḥammad. *Kitāb al-'Iqd al-Farīd*. 6 vols., ed. Barkāt Yūsuf Habūr. Beirut: Dār al-Arqam, 1999.

Ibn Abī al-Ḥadīd, 'Izz al-Dīn 'Abd al-Ḥamīd. *Sharḥ Nahj al-Balāgha*. 10 vols., ed. M.A.F. Ibrahīm. Cairo: 'Isā al-Bābi al-Ḥalabī, 1965.

Ibn Abī Karīma, Abū 'Ubayda Muslim. *Risālat Abī Karīma fī al-Zakāt*. Muscat: *WTQwTh*, 1982.

Ibn 'Asākir, Abū al-Qāsim 'Alī b. al-Ḥasan. *Tārīkh Madīnat Dimashq: 'Uthmān b. 'Affān*, ed. Sukayna al-Shihābī. Damascus: Majma' al-Lugha al-'Arabiyya, 1984.

Ibn al-Athīr, 'Izz al-Dīn. *al-Kāmil fī al-Tārīkh*. 13 vols., ed. Carl Johan Tornberg. Leiden: Brill, 1851.

Ibn Baraka, Abū Muḥammad 'Abdullāh b. Muḥammad al-Bahlāwī. *Kitāb al-Jāmi'*. 2 vols. Muscat: *WTQwTh*, 1983.

Ibn Baṭūṭa. *Riḥlat Ibn Baṭūṭa*, ed. Ṭalāl Ḥarb. Beirut: Dār al-Kutub al-'Ilmiyya, 2002.

Ibn Fāris, Abū al-Ḥusayn b. Zakarīyya al-Rāzī. *Mu'jam Maqāyis al-Lugha*. Beirut: Dār al-Kutub al-'Ilmiyya, 1999.

Ibn Ḥajar al-'Asqalānī, Abū al-Faḍl Aḥmad b. 'Alī. *Fatḥ al-Bārī fī Sharḥ Ṣaḥīḥ al-Bukhārī*, 3 vols. Riyad: International Ideas Home, 1999.

———. *Tahdhīb al-Tahdhīb*. 12 vols. Hyderabad: Majlis al-Ma'ārif al-Niẓāmiyya al-Kā'ina fī al-Hind, 1907.

Ibn Ḥanbal, Aḥmad Abū 'Abdullāh. *al-Musnad*. Riyad: International Ideas Home, 1998.

Ibn al-Ḥawārī, Muḥammad. *Jāmi' Ibn al-Hawārī*. 5 vols. Muscat: *WTQwTh*, 1985.

Ibn Ḥazm, Abū Muḥammad 'Alī b. Aḥmad. *Jamharat Ansāb al-'Arab*, ed. 'A. M. Hārūn. Cairo: Dār al-Ma'ārif, 1962.

———. *Kitāb al-Fisal fī al-Milal wa Ahwā' wa al-Niḥal*. 3 vols. Beirut: Dār al-Kutub al-'Ilmīyya, 1999.

Ibn Hishām, 'Abd al-Mālik. *al-Sīra al-Nabawiyya*. 4 vols., ed. Ibrāhīm al-Abyārī, Muṣṭafā al-Saqā and 'Abd al-Ḥāfiẓ Shabalī. Beruit: Dār al-Khayr, 1996.

Ibn Ja'far, Abū Jābir Muḥammad. *al-Jāmi' Ibn Ja'far*. 6 vols. Muscat: *WTQwTh*, 1994.

Ibn al-Jawzī, Jamāl al-Dīn 'Abd al-Raḥmān b. 'Alī. *Talbīs Iblīs*, ed. Muḥammad al-Ṣabbāḥ. Beirut: Manshurāt Dār Maktabat al-Hiyāt, 1989.

Ibn Kathīr, 'Imād al-Dīn Ismā'īl b. 'Umar. *al-Bidāya wa al-Nihāya*. 14 vols. Cairo: Maṭba'at al-Sa'āda, 1932.

———. *Tafsīr al-Qur'ān al-'Aẓīm*, ed. Ḥasān al-Jibālī. Riyad: International Ideas Home for Publishing and Distribution, 1999.

Ibn Khaldūn. *Histoire des Berbères et des Dynasties Musulmanes de l'Afrique Septentrionale*. 4 vols., ed. William M. Slane. Algiers: Imprimerie du Gouvernment, 1852.

Ibn Khayyāṭ, Abū 'Amr Khalīfa. *Tārīkh Khalīfa b. Khayyāṭ*. Beirut: Dār al-Kutub al-'Ilmiyya, 1995.

Ibn Khamīs, Jumayyil. *Qamūs al-Sharī'a*. 16 vols. Muscat: *WTQwTh*, 1984.

Ibn Māja, Abū 'Abdullāh Muḥammad b. Yazīd al-Qazwīnī. *Sunan Ibn Māja*. Riyad: International Ideas Home, n.d.

Ibn Manẓūr, Abū Faḍl Jamāl al-Dīn Muḥammad b. Makram. *Lisān al-'Arab*. 15 vols. Beirut: Dār Sadar, 1882.

Ibn Qays, Abū Muḥammad Ibrāhīm. *Diwān al-Sayf al-Naqqād*. Muscat: *WTQwTh*, 1982.

Ibn Qays, Abū Isḥāq Ibrāhīm. *Mukhtaṣar al-Khiṣāl*. Muscat: *WTQwTh*, 1983.

Ibn Qutayba, Abū Muḥammad 'Abdallāh b. Muslim. *al-Ma'ārif*. Beirut: Dār al-Kutub al-'Ilmiyya, 1987.

———. *'Uyūn al-Akhbār*. 4 vols., ed. Yūsuf 'Alī Ṭawīl. Beirut: Dār al-Kutub al-'Ilmiyya, 1998.

Ibn Qutayba (attr.). *al-Imāma wa al-Siyāsa*. Beirut: Dār Kutub al-'Ilmiyya, 1997.

Ibn Sa'd, Abū 'Abdullāh Muḥammad. *Kitāb al-Ṭabaqāt al-Kubrā*. 15 vols., ed. Edward Sachau. Beirut: Dār Ṣādr, 1957.

Ibn al-Ṣaghīr. *Akhbār al-Ā'imma al-Rustumiyyīn*, ed. Muḥammad Nāsir and Ibrāhīm Biḥḥāz. Algiers: Dār al-Gharb al-Islāmī, 1986.

Ibn Salām. *Kitāb Ibn Salām al-Ibāḍī: al-Islām wa Tārīkhihi min Wijhat Naẓar Ibāḍī*, ed. R. F. Schwartz and Sālim b. Ya'qūb. Beirut: Dār Iqra', 1985.

al-Iṣbahānī, Abū Nu'aym. *Dalā'il al-Nubuwwa*. Hyderabad: Dairatul Maarif, 1950.

al-Iṣfahānī, Abu al-Farāj Muḥammad Abū al-Faḍl Ibrāhīm. *Kitāb al-Aghānī*. 24 vols. Beirut: Dār Iḥyā al-Turāth al-'Arabī, 1985.

al-Iṣfahānī, al-Rāghib. *Mufradāt Alfāẓ al-Qur'ān*. Damascus: Dār al-Qalam, 1997.

al-Israfā'inī, Shafūr Ibn Ṭāhir. *al-Tabaṣīr fī al-Dīn wa Tamyīz al-Firqa al-Nājiyya 'an al-Firaq al-Hālikīn*. Cairo: Maktabat al-Azhār lil-Turāth, 1940.

al-Izkawī, Sirḥān b. Sa'īd (attrib.). *Kashf al-Ghumma al-Jāmi' li-Akhbār al-Umma*, ed. Aḥmad 'Ubaydalī. Nicosa: Dilmun, 1985.

———. *Kashf al-Ghumma al-Jāmi' li-Akhbār al-Umma*. 2 vols., ed. Ḥasan Muḥammad 'Abdullāh al-Nābudih. Beirut: Dār al-Bārūdī, 2006.

al-Jāḥiẓ, Abū 'Uthmān 'Amr b. Baḥr. *al-Bayān wa al-Tabyīn*. 2 vols., ed. Muwaffaq b. Shahhāb al-Dīn. Beirut: Dār al-Kutub al-'Ilmiyya, 1997.

Jarīr b. 'Aṭiyya b. al-Khaṭafā. *Diwān Jarīr bi-Sharḥ Muḥammad b. Ḥabīb*, ed. Nu'mān Muḥammad Amīn Ṭaha. Cairo: Dar al-Ma'ārif bi-Maṣr, 1969.

al-Jannāwanī, Abū Zakariyya Yaḥya Ibn Abī Khayr. *Kitāb al-Waḍ'*. Muscat: Maktabat al-Istiqāma, n.d.

al-Jiṭālī, Abū Ṭāhir Ismā'īl b. Mūsā. *Kitāb Qawā'id al-Islām*. 2 vols., ed. Baklī 'Abd al-Raḥmān b. 'Umar. Muscat: Maktabat al-Istiqāma, 2003.

al-Jumāḥī, Muḥammad Ibn Sallām. *Kitāb Fuḥūl al-Shu'arā'*. 2 vols., ed. Maḥmūd Muḥammad Shākir. Cairo: Maṭba'at al-Midanī, 1973.

Kashīf, Sayyida Ismā'īl, ed. *al-Siyar wa al-Jawabāt li-'Ulamā' wa Ā'immat 'Umān*. 2 vols. Muscat: *WTQwTh*, 1989.

al-Kharūṣī, Sa'īd b. Khalaf. *Min Jawābāt al-Imām Jābir b. Zayd*. Muscat: *WTQwTh*, 1992.

al-Kindī, Abū 'Abdullāh Muḥammad b. Ibrahīm. *Bayān al-Shar'*. 72 vols. Muscat: *WTQwTh*, 1988.

al-Kindī, Abū Bakr Aḥmad b. 'Abdullāh b. Mūsa. *al-Jawhar al-Muqtaṣir*. Muscat: *WTQwTh*, 1983.

———. *al-Muṣannaf*. 44 vols. Muscat: *WTQwTh*, 1984.

———. *Kitāb al-Ihtidā'*. Muscat: *WTQwTh*, 1985.

al-Kudamī, Abū Sa'īd Muḥammad b. Sa'īd. *al-Istiqāma*. 3 vols. Muscat: *WTQwTh*, 1985.

———. *al-Jāmi' al-Mufīd min Aḥkām Abī Sa'īd*. 4 vols. Muscat: *WTQwTh*, 1985.

———. *al-Jāmi' al-Mufīd min Jawabāt Abī Sa'īd*. 4 vols. Muscat: *WTQwTh*, 1985.

———. *al-Mu'tabar*. 4 vols. Muscat: *WTQwTh*, 1985.

Madelung, Wilferd, and Paul E. Walker, eds. *An Ismaili Heresiography: The "Bāb al-Shayṭān" from Abū Tammām's Kitāb al-Shajara*. Leiden: Brill, 1998.

al-Malaṭī, Abū Ḥusayn Muḥammad b. Aḥmad. *Al-Tanbīh wa al-Radd 'alā Ahl al-Ahwā' wa al-Bid'a*. Cairo: Maktabat al-Azhar lil-Turāth, 1993.

al-Mas'ūdī, Abū al-Ḥasan 'Alī b. al-Ḥusayn. *Murūj al-Dhahab*. 5 vols., ed. Charles Pellat. Beirut: Publications of the University of Lebanon, 1966.

———. *al-Tanbīh wa al-Ashrāf*. Baghdad: Maktabat al-Muthannā, 1938.

al-Māwardī, Abū al-Ḥasan 'Alī b. Muḥammad b. Ḥajīb. *Aḥkām al-Sulṭāniyya wa al-Wilāyat al-Dīniyya*. Beirut: Dār al-Kutub al-'Ilmiyya, 1985.

al-Minqarī, Abū al-Faḍl Nasar b. Muzāhim b. Siyār. *Waq'at Ṣiffīn*, ed. 'Abd al-Salām Muḥammad Hārūn. Cairo: Mu'assisat al-'Arabiyya al-Ḥadītha, 1962.

al-Mubarrad, Abū al-'Abbās Muḥammad b. Yazīd. *al-Kāmil*. 2 vols., ed. M. J. de Goege and W. Wright. Leipzig: F. A. Brockhaus, 1874.

———. *al-Kāmil: Bāb al-Khawārij*. Damascus: Dār al-Ḥikma, n.d.

al-Mufīd, Abū 'Abdullāh Muḥammad al-Ḥārithī al-Baghdādī. *Kitāb al-Irshād: The Book of Guidance*, tr. I.K.A. Howard. London: Balagha Books, 1981.

Muslim, Abū al-Ḥusayn Muslim b. al-Ḥajjāj. *Ṣaḥīḥ Muslim*. Beirut: Dār Ibn Ḥazm, 1997.

al-Nāshi' al-Akbar (attr.). *Frühe Mu'tazilitische Häresiographie*, ed. J. Van Ess. Beirut: Kommission bei Franz Steiner Verlag, 1971.

al-Nawbakhtī, al-Ḥasan Ibn Mūsā. *Kitāb Firaq al-Shī'a*. Istanbul: Maṭba'at al-Dawla, 1931.

al-Nisā'ī, Abū 'Abd al-Raḥmān Aḥmad b. Shu'ayb b. 'Alī. *Sunan al-Nisā'ī*. Riyad: International Ideas Home, n.d. .

al-Qalhātī, Abū Sa'īd Muḥammad b. Sa'īd al-Azdī. *al-Firaq al-Islāmiyya min Khilāl al-Kashf wa al-Bayān*, ed. Muḥammad Ibn 'Abd al-Khalīl. Tunis: Markaz al-Dirasāt wa al-Abḥāth al-Iqtiṣādiyya wa al-Ijtima'iyya, 1984.

al-Qummī, Sa'd b. 'Abdullāh. *Kitāb al-Maqālāt wa al-Firaq*. Tehran: Mu'assasat Maṭbu'āt'ī Aṭā'ī, 1963.

al-Rāzī, Abū Ḥātim Aḥmad. *Kitāb al-Zīna*. In A. S. al-Sāmarrā'ī, *al-Ghuluww wa al-Firaq al-Ghāliya fi al-Ḥaḍāra al-Islāmiyya*. Baghdad: Dār al-Ḥuriyya, 1972.

al-Sālimī, Nūr al-Dīn 'Abdullāh b. Aḥmad. *al-Lu'ma al-Murḍiyya min Ash'at al-Ibāḍiyya*. Muscat: *WTQwTh*, 1981.

———. *Tuḥfat al-'Ayān bī-Sirat Ahl 'Umān*. 2 vols. Cairo: Dar al-Kitāb al-'Arabī, 1961.

al-Sam'ānī, 'Abd al-Karīm b. Muḥammad. *Kitāb al-Ansāb*. Leiden: Brill, 1912.

al-Shahrastānī, 'Abd al-Karīm. *al-Milal wa al-Niḥal*. Beirut: Dār al-Fikr, n.d.

———. *Nihāyat al-Iqdām fī 'Ilm al-Kalām*. Cairo: Maktabat al-Mutanabbī, 1980.

al-Shammākhī, Abū al-'Abbās Aḥmad b. Sa'īd. *Kitāb al-Siyar*. 2 vols., ed. Aḥmad b. Sa'ūd al-Siyābī. Muscat: *WTQwTh*, 1987.

———. *Muqaddimat al-Tawḥīd wa Shurūḥihā*. Muscat: Sulṭanat 'Umān, 1988.

al-Shammākhī, Abū Sākin 'Amr b. 'Alī. *Kitāb al-Iḍāḥ*. 4 vols. Beirut: Maṭba'at al-Watan, 1971.

al-Ṭabarī, Muḥammad b. Jarīr. *Tafsīr al-Ṭabarī*. 13 vols. Beirut: Dār al-Kutub al-'Ilmiyya, 2005.

———. *Tārīkh al-Rusul wa al-Mulūk*. 15 vols., ed. M. J. de Goeje. Leiden: Brill, 1879.

al-Tanwātī, Abū 'Ammār 'Abd al-Kāfī b. Abī Ya'qūb. *Arā' al-Khawārij al-Kalāmiyya: Al-Mūjaz li-Abī 'Ammār 'Abd al-Kāfī al-Ibāḍī*. 2 vols., ed. 'Ammār al-Ṭālibī. Algiers: Sharikat al-Waṭaniyya li al-Nashar wa al-Tawzī', n.d.

al-Tirmidhī, Abū 'Isā Muḥammad b. 'Isā. *Jāmi' al-Tirmidhī*. Riyad: International Ideas Home, n.d.

al-Ṭūsī, Abū Ja'far Muḥammad b. al-Ḥasan. *Ikhtiyār Ma'rifat al-Rijāl*, ed. Hassan Mosstafavi. Mashhad: University of Mashhad, 1964.

———. *Rijāl al-Ṭūsī*, ed. Muḥammad Kāẓim. Najaf: Maktabat al-Maṭba'a, 1961.

al-Wāqidī, Muḥammad b. 'Umar. *Kitāb al-Maghāzī*, ed. J. Wellhausen. Berlin: G. Reimer, 1882.

al-Warjlānī, Abū Ya'qūb Yūsuf b. Ibrāhīm. *al-'Adl wa al-Inṣāf fī Ma'rifat Usūl al-Fiqh wa al-Ikhtilāf*, 2 vols. Muscat: *WTQwTh*, 1984.

———. *al-Dalīl wa al-Burhān*. 2 vols. Muscat: *WTQwTh*, 1983.

———. *al-Jāmi' al-Ṣaḥīḥ Musnad lil-Imām al-Rabī' b. Ḥabīb Ibn 'Umar al-Azdī al-Baṣrī*. Muscat: Maktabat Musqat, 1994.

Yaḥyā b. Adam. *Kitāb al-Kharāj*, ed. T. W. Juynboll. Leiden: Brill, 1896.

al-Ya'qūbī, Aḥmad b. Abī Ya'qūb. *Kitāb al-Buldān*. 6 vols., ed. A.W.T. Juynboll. Leiden: Brill, 1860.

———. *Tārīkh al-Ya'qūbī*. 2 vols., ed. M. T. Houtsma. Leiden: Brill, 1883.

Ya'qūt, Shihāb al-Dīn b. 'Abdullāh al-Ḥamawī. *Mu'jam al-Buldān*. 5 vols. Beirut: Dār Sadar, 1955.

Secondary Sources in Arabic

'Abd al-Bāqī, Muḥammad. *al-Ru'ya al-Fanniya fī Shi'r al-Shī'a wa al-Khawārij*. Cairo: Maṭba'at al-Amāna, 1991.

'Abd Rabbih, al-Sayyid 'Abd al-Ḥāfiẓ. *al-Ibāḍiyya Madhhab wa Sulūk*. Cairo: al-Ṭab'a al-Thāniya, 1987.

'Abd al-Rāziq, Maḥmūd Ismā'īl. *al-Khawārij fī Bilād al-Maghrib ḥattā Muntasaf al-Qarn al-Rābi' al-Hijrī*. Cairo: Maktabat al-Ḥurriya al-Ḥadīth, 1986.

'Alī, Jawād. *al-Mufaṣṣal fī Tārīkh al-'Arab Qabl al-Islām*. 8 vols. Baghdad: Maktabat al-Nahḍa, 1970.

al-'Aqīlī, Muḥammad Rashīd. *al-Ibāḍiyya fī 'Umān wa 'Alāqatuha ma' al-Dawla al-'Abbāsiyya fī 'Aṣriha al-Awwal*. Muscat: *WTQwTh*, 1984.

al-'Aql, Nāsir b. 'Abd al-Karīm. *al-Khawārij: Awal Firqa fī Tārīkh al-Islām*. Riyad: Dār al-Qāsim, 1998.

Aṭfayyish, Abū Ishāq Ibrāhīm. *al-Farq bayn al-Ibāḍiyya wa al-Khawārij*. Muscat: Maktabat al-Istiqāma, 1980.

'Awājī, Ghālib bin 'Alī. *al-Khawārij: Tārīkhuhum wa Arā'uhum al-I'tiqādiyya wa Mawqif al-Islām minha*. Madina: Damnhur, 1997.

A'washt, Bakīr b. Sa'īd. *Dirasāt Islāmīyya fī al-Usūl al-Ibāḍiyya*. Cairo: Maktabat Waḥba, 1988.

Bājīyya, Ṣālih. *al-Ibāḍiyya bi al-Jarīd fī al-'Usūr al-Islāmiyya al-Uwla*. Tunis: Dār Bū Salāma lil-Ṭibā'a wa al-Nashr wa al-Tawzī'a, 1976.

al-Bakkay, Laṭīfa. *Ḥarakat al-Khawārij: Nash'atuha wa Taṭawwuruha li-Nihāyat al-'Ahd al-Umawī 37–132H*. Beirut: Dār al-Talī'a, 2001.

Bālī, Mirvat 'Izzat Muḥammad. *Namādhij min Madhāhib al-Firaq al-Islāmiyya*. Cairo: Maktabat al-Injalu al-Maṣriyya, 1991.

al-Būsa'īd, al-'Amīd al-Rukn Nizār. *Juthūr al-Shabāhat: Qira'āt fi Ḥarakāt al-Khawārij*. London: Dār al-Burāq, 1996.

Darwīsh, Aḥmad. *Jābir b. Zayd: Ḥayāt min Ajl al-'Ilm*. Muscat: Sulṭanat 'Umān, n.d. .

Fawzī, Farūq 'Umar. *Nash'at al-Ḥarakāt al-Dīniyya al-Siyāsiyya fī al-Islām*. Amman: Maktabat al-Ahliyya, 1999.

Ghubāsh, Ḥusayn 'Ubayd Ghanīm. *Umān: al-Dimuqrātiyya al-Islāmiyya Taqālīd al-Imāma wa al-Tārīkh al-Siyāsī al-Ḥadīth*. Beirūt: Dār al-Jadīd, 1997.

al-Ḥārithī, Mālik b. Ṣulṭān. *Naẓariyyat al-Imāma 'and al-Ibāḍiyya*. Muscat: Maṭba'at Musqat, 1991.

Ḥasan, Ibrāhīm Ḥasan. *Tārīkh al-Islām*. Beirut: Dār al-Jīl, 1991.

Hāshim, Mahdī Ṭālib. *al-Ḥaraka al-Ibāḍiyya fī al-Mashriq al-'Arabī*. London: Dār al-Ḥikma, 2001.

Ḥussayn, 'Abd al-Razzāq. *Shi'r al-Khawārij*. Amman: Dār al-Bashīr, 1986.

Ismāʿīl, Muḥammad Maḥmūd. *al-Ḥarakāt al-Sirriya fī al-Islām*. Beirut: Dār al-Qalam, 1973.

———. *al-Khawārij fī al-Maghrib al-Islāmī: Libya, Tūnis, al-Jazāʾir, al-Maghrib, Muritānya*. Beirut: Dār al-ʿAwda, 1976.

Jaʿīṭ, Hāshim. *al-Fitna: Jadaliyyat al-Dīn wa al-Siyāsa fī al-Islām al-Mubakkir*. Beirut: Dār al-Ṭalīʿa, 1991.

Jaffal, ʿAlī. *al-Khawārij: Tārīkhuhum wa Adabuhum*. Beirut: Dār al-Kutub al-ʿIlmiyya, 1990.

Jālī, Aḥmad. *Dirāsa ʿan al-Firaq fī Tārīkh al-Muslimīn: al-Khawārij wa al-Shīʿa*. Riyad: King Faisal Center for Islamic Research and Studies, 1988.

Kāmil, ʿUmar ʿAbdullāh. *al-Khawārij al-Judūd: al-Mutatarifūn*. Cairo: Maktabat al-Turāth al-Islamī, 1998.

Khulayfāt, ʿAwad. *Nashʾāt al-Ḥaraka al-Ibāḍiyya*. Amman: al-Jāmaʿa al-Urduniyya, 1978.

———. *al-Niẓām al-Ijtimaʿiyya wa al-Tarbuwiyya ʿand al-Ibāḍiyya fī Shamāl Ifriqiyya fī Marḥalat al-Kitmān*. Amman: al-Jāmaʿa al-Urduniyya, 1982.

———. *al-Tanẓimāt al-Siyāsiyya wa al-Idāriyya ʿand al-Ibāḍiyya fi Marḥalat al-Kitmān*. Muscat: Wizārat al-ʿAdl wa al-Awqāf wa Shuʿūn al-Islāmiyya, n.d.

———. *al-Usūl al-Ṭārīkhiyya lil-Firqa al-Ibāḍiyya*. Muscat: *WTQwTh*, 1988.

Mahrus, ʿAbdullāh. *al-Ẓāhira al-Adabiyya fī Shiʿr al-Khawārij*. Cairo: Maṭbaʿat al-Amāna, 1988.

Maʿrūf, Aḥmad Sulaymān. *Qirāʾa Jadīda fī Mawāqif al-Khawārij*. Damascus: Dār Talas li-Dirasāt wa al-Nashar, 1988.

———. *al-Ṭirimmāḥ Ibn Ḥākim: Bayn al-Khawārij wa bayn al-Shuʿarāʾ*. Damascus: Wizārat al-Turāth, 2004.

Maʿrūf, Nāyif. *Diwān al-Khawārij*. Beirut: Dār al-Masīra, 1983.

———. *al-Khawārij*. 4th edition. Beirut: Dār al-Talīʿa, 1994.

———. *al-Khawārij fī al-ʿAṣr al-Umawī*. Beirut: Dār al-Nafāʾis, 2006.

Muʿammar, ʿAlī Yaḥya. *al-Ibāḍiyya fī Mawkab al-Tārīkh*. Cairo: Maktabat Waḥba, 1964.

Muʿayṭa, Aḥmad. *al-Islām al-Khawārijī*. Latakia: Dār al-Ḥiwār, 2000.

al-Najjār, ʿĀmir. *al-Ibāḍiyya wa Madā Ṣilatiha bī al-Khawārij*. Cairo: Dār al-Maʿārif, 1993.

———. *al-Khawārij: ʿAqīdatan wa Fikran wa Falsafatan*. Beirut: Dār al-Maʿārif, 1988.

al-Qāḍī, Widād. *al-Kaysāniyya fī al-Tārīkh wa al-Adab*. Beirut: Dār al-Thaqāfa, 1974.

al-Saʿāwi, Nāṣir Ibn ʿAbdullāh. *al-Khawārij: Dirāsa wa Naqd li-Madhhabihim*. Riyad: Dār al-Maʿārij wa al-Dawliyya lil-Nashr, 1996.

al-Sabīʿī, Nāṣir b. Sulaymān b. Saʿīd. *al-Khawārij wa al-Ḥaqīqa al-Ghāʾiba*. Beirut: Dār al-Muntaẓar, 2000.

Shalqām, ʿAbd al-Raḥmān. *al-Dīn wa al-Siyāsa fī Tārīkh al-Islāmī*. Rome: Intergraph, 1991.

Waʿalī, Bakīr b. Balḥāj. *al-Imāma ʿand al-Ibāḍiyya bayn al-Naẓariyya wa al-Taṭbīq*. 2 vols. Ghardaya: Jamaʿiyyat al-Turāth, 2001.

Yūsuf, Sulaymān b. Dawūd. *al-Khawārij hum Anṣār al-Imām ʿAlī*. Qissnatina: Dār al-Baʿth, 1983.

Sources in English

Abedi, Mehdi, and Gary Legenhausen, eds. *Jihād and Shahādat: Struggle and Martyrdom in Islam.* Houston: Institute for Research and Islamic Studies, 1986.
Abou El Fadl, Khalid. *Rebellion and Violence in Islamic Law.* Cambridge: Cambridge University Press, 2001.
Allen, Calvin H. *Oman: The Modernization of the Sultanate.* Boulder: Westview, 1987.
Allen, James de Vere. *Swahili Origins: Swahili Culture and the Shungwaya Phenomenon.* Athens: Ohio University Press, 1993.
Alport, E. A. "The Mzab." *Journal of the Royal Anthropological Institute of Great Britain and Ireland* 84 (1954): 160–171.
Badger, George Percy, tr. *History of the Imâms and Seyyids of 'Omân, by Salîl Ibn Razîk.* London: Printed for the Hakluyt Society, 1871.
Bamyeh, Mohammed A. *The Social Origins of Islam: Mind, Economy, Discourse.* Minneapolis: University of Minnesota Press, 1999.
Batran, Aziz A. *Islam and Revolution in Africa.* Brattleboro, Vt.: Amana Books, 1984.
Bierschenk, Thomas. "Religion and Political Structure: Remarks on Ibadism in Oman and the Mzab (Algeria)." *SI* 68 (1988): 107–127.
Blankinship, Khalid Yahya. *The End of the Jihād State: The Reign of Hishām Ibn 'Abd al-Malik and the Collapse of the Umayyads.* Albany: State University of New York Press, 1994.
Bosworth, Clifford. *The New Islamic Dynasties: A Chronological and Genealogical Manuel.* Edinburgh: Edinburgh University Press, 1996.
———. *Sīstān under the Arabs, From the Islamic Conquest to the Rise of the Ṣaffārids (30–250/651–864).* Rome: Istituto Italiano per il Medio ed Estremo Oriente, 1968.
Brett, Michael, and Elizabeth Fentress. *The Berbers.* Oxford: Blackwell, 1996.
Brockelmann, Carl. *History of the Islamic Peoples.* London: Routledge and Kegan Paul, 1948.
Cook, Michael. *Commanding Right and Forbidding Wrong in Islamic Thought.* Cambridge: Cambridge University Press, 2000.
———. *Early Muslim Dogma: A Source-Critical Study.* Cambridge: Cambridge University Press, 1981.
Crone, Patricia. "'Even an Ethiopian Slave': The Transformation of a Sunni Tradition." *BSOAS* 57 (1994): 59–67.
———. *God's Rule: Government and Islam.* New York: Columbia University Press, 2004.
———. "The Khārijites and the Caliphal Title." In *Studies in Islamic and Middle Eastern Texts and Traditions in Memory of Norman Calder*, ed. G. R. Hawting, J. A. Mojaddedi, and A. Samely, 85–91. Oxford: Oxford University Press, 2000.
———. "Ninth-Century Muslim Anarchists." *Past and Present* 167 (2000): 3–28.
———. "Quraysh and the Roman Army: Making Sense of the Meccan Leather Trade." *BSOAS* 70/1 (2007): 63–88.
———. "A Statement by the Najdiyya Kharijites on the Dispensability of the Imamate." *SI* 88 (1998): 55–76.
Crone, Patricia, and Martin Hinds. *God's Caliph: Religious Authority in the First Centuries of Islam.* Cambridge: Cambridge University Press, 1986.

Custers, Martin H. *Al-Ibāḍiyya: A Bibliography*. 3 vols. Maastricht: Maastricht University Press, 2006.

Dabashi, Hamid. *Authority in Islam: From the Rise of Muhammad to the Establishment of the Umayyads*. New Brunswick, N.J.: Transaction, 1989.

Donner, Fred. "Piety and Eschatology in Early Kharijite Poetry." In *Fī Miḥrāb al-Ma'rifah: Festschrift for Iḥsān 'Abbās*, ed. Ibrāhīm As-Sa'āfin, 13–19. Beirut: Dār Sader, 1997.

Ennami, 'Amr K. "Description of New Ibadi Manuscripts from North Africa." *Journal of Semitic Studies* 15 (1970): 63–87.

———. *Studies in Ibadism (al-Ibāḍīyah)*. Tripoli, Libya: Publications of the University of Libya Faculty of Arts, 1972.

Fierro, Maribel. "Al-Aṣfar." *Studia Islamica* 77 (1993): 169–181.

Flathman, Richard E. *The Practice of Political Authority: Authority and the Authoritative*. Chicago: University of Chicago Press, 1980.

Francesca, Ersilia. "Early Ibāḍī Jurisprudence: Sources and Case Law." *Jerusalem Studies in Arabic and Islam* 30 (2005): 231–263.

———. "The Formation and Early Development of the Ibāḍī Madhhab." *Jerusalem Studies in Arabic and Islam* 28 (2003): 260–277.

Gaiser, Adam. "The Ibāḍī 'Stages of Religion' Re-examined: Tracing the History of the *Masālik al-Dīn*." *BSOAS* 73/2 (2010): 207–222.

———. "Source Critical Methodologies in Recent Scholarship on the Khārijites." *Historical Compass* 7/5 (2009): 1376–1390.

Ghubash, Hussein. *Oman—The Islamic Democratic Tradition*, tr. Mary Turton. London: Routledge, 2006.

Gibb, Hamilton A. R. *Studies on the Civilization of Islam*. Lahore: Islamic Book Service, 1987.

Goldziher, Ignaz. *Muslim Studies*. 2 vols. Chicago: Aldine, 1967.

Guillaume, Alfred. *The Life of Muhammad*. London: Oxford University Press, 1970.

Hawting, G. R. "The Significance of the Slogan *Lā Hukm Illā Lillāh* and the References to the *Hudūd* in the Traditions about the Fitna and the Murder of 'Uthmān." *BSOAS* 41 (1978): 451–463.

Henderson, John B. *The Construction of Orthodoxy and Heresy*. Albany: State University of New York Press, 1998.

Higgins, Annie C., "Faces of Exchangers, Facets of Exchange in Early *Shurāt* (Khārijī) Poetry." *Bulletin of the Royal Institute for Inter-Faith Studies* 7 (2005): 7–38.

Hinds, Martin. "Kufan Political Alignments and Their Background in the Mid-Seventh Century A.D." *IJMES* 2/4 (1971): 346–367.

———. "The Siffin Arbitration Agreement." *Journal of Semitic Studies* 17 (1972): 93–129.

———. "The Murder of the Caliph 'Uthman." *IJMES* 3/4 (1972): 450–469.

Hobsbawm, Eric J. *Bandits*. New York: Pantheon, 1969.

Hodgson, Marshall G. S. *The Venture of Islam*. 3 vols. Chicago: University of Chicago Press, 1977.

Hoffman, Valerie J. "The Articulation of Ibādī Identity in Modern Oman and Zanzibar." *Muslim World* 14/2 (2004): 201–216.

Hrbek, Ivan., ed. *Africa from the Seventh to the Eleventh Century*. Paris: UNESCO, 1992.

Humphreys, R. Stephen. *Islamic History: A Framework for Inquiry*. Princeton: Princeton University Press, 1991.

Izutsu, Toshihiko. *The Concept of Belief in Islamic Theology*. New York: Books for Libraries, 1980.

———. *God and Man in the Koran*. Kuala Lumpur: Islamic Book Trust, 2002.

Jafri, Syed Husain Mohammad. *The Origins and Early Development of Shi'a Islam*. Oxford: Oxford University Press, 2000.

Johnson, James T., and John Kelsay, eds. *Cross, Crescent and Sword*. Westport, Conn.: Greenwood, 1990.

Juynboll, G.H.A. "The Qur'ān Reciter on the Battlefield and Concomitant Issues." *Zeitschrift der Deutschen Morganlandischen Gesellschaft* 125 (1975): 11–27.

———. "The Qurrā' in Early Islamic History." *Journal of the Economic and Social History of the Orient* 26 (1973): 113–129.

———, ed. *Studies in the First Century of Islamic Society*. Carbondale: Southwestern Illinois Press, 1982.

Kaylani, Nabil. "Politics and Religion in 'Umān: A Historical Overview." *IJMES* 10 (1979): 567–579.

Kenney, Jeffrey T. "The Emergence of the Khawārij: Religion and the Social Order in Early Islam." *Jusūr* 5 (1989): 1–29.

———. *Muslim Rebels: Kharijites and the Politics of Extremism in Egypt*. Oxford: Oxford University Press, 2006.

Khalidi, Tarif. *Arabic Historical Thought in the Classical Period*. Cambridge: Cambridge University Press, 1994.

———. "The Poetry of the Khawārij: Violence and Salvation." In *Religion between Violence and Reconciliation*, ed. T. Scheffler, 110–122. Wurtzburg: Ergon- Vertag, 2002.

al-Kharusi, Kahlan. "An Overview of Ibāḍī *Tafsīr*." In *Islamic Reflections, Arabic Musings: Studies in Honour of Professor Alan Jones*, ed. Robert Hoyland and Philip Kennedy, 268–278. Oxford: E.J.W. Gibb Memorial Trust, 2004.

Khuri, Fuad I. *Imams and Emirs: State, Religion and Sects in Islam*. London: Saqi Books, 1990.

Lambton, Ann K. S. *State and Government in Medieval Islam*. Oxford: Oxford University Press, 1981.

Lazarus-Yafeh, Hava. *Some Religious Aspects of Islam*. Leiden: Brill, 1981.

Levtzion, Nehemia, and J.F.P. Hopkins. *Corpus of Early Arabic Sources for West African History*. Cambridge: Cambridge University Press, 1981.

Levy, Reuben. *The Social Structure of Islam*. Cambridge: Cambridge University Press, 1957.

Lewicki, Tadeusz. "The Ibādi Community at Basra in the Seventh to Ninth Centuries and the Origins of the Ibādite States in Arabia and North Africa" (part one). *Journal of World History* 13 (1971): 51–130.

———. "The Ibādites in North Africa and the Sudan to the Fourteenth Century" (part two). *Journal of World History* 13 (1971): 83–130.

———. "Les Subdivisions de l'Ibāḍiyya." *SI* 9 (1958): 71–82.

Lewinstein, Keith. "The Azāriqa in Islamic Heresiography." *BSOAS* 54 (1991): 251–268.

———. "Making and Unmaking a Sect: The Heresiographers and the Ṣufriyya." *SI* 76 (1992): 75–96.

———. "Notes on Eastern Ḥanafite Heresiography." *JAOS* 114 (1994): 583–598.

———. "The Revaluation of Martyrdom in Early Islam." In *Sacrificing the Self: Perspectives on Martyrdom and Religion*, ed. Margaret Cormack, 78–91. New York: Oxford University Press, 2001.

Lewis, Bernard. *The Arabs in History*. New York: Harper and Row, 1966.

Lings, Martin. *Muhammad: His Life Based on the Earliest Sources*. Rochester: Inner Traditions International, 1983.

Little, David, and Sumner B. Twiss. *Comparative Religious Ethics*. San Francisco: Harper and Row, 1978.

al-Maamiry, Ahmed Hamoud. *Oman and Ibadhism*. New Delhi: Lancers Books, 1989.

al-Mad'aj, 'Abd al-Muhsin Mad'aj M. *The Yemen in Early Islam, 9–233/630–847: A Political History*. London: Ithaca, 1988.

Madelung, Wilferd. "Abd Allāh Ibn Ibāḍ and the Origins of the Ibāḍiyya." In *Authority, Privacy and Public Order in Islam: Proceedings of the 22nd Congress of L'Union Européenne des Arabisants et Islamisants*, ed. Barbara Michalak-Pikulska and Andrzej Pikulski, 51–57. Leuven: Dudley, 2006.

———. "The Origins of the Controversy Concerning the Creation of the Koran." In *Orientalia Hispanica sive studia F.M. Pareja octogenario dictate*, ed. J. M. Barral, 1: 504–525. Leiden: Brill, 1974.

———. *Religious Trends in Early Islamic Iran*. Albany: Bibliotheca Persica, 1988.

———. "The Shiite and Kharijite Contribution to Pre-Ash'arite *Kalam*." In *Islamic Philosophical Theology*, ed. Parviz Morewedge, 120–140. Albany: State University of New York Press, 1979.

———. *The Succession to Muḥammad: A Study of the Early Caliphate*. Cambridge: Cambridge University Press, 1997.

Morony, Michael. *Iraq after the Muslim Conquest*. Piscataway, N.J.: Gorgias Press, 2005.

Muammar, Ali Yahya. *Ibadhism: A Moderate Sect of Islam*. Muscat: Ministry of Justice, Awqaf and Islamic Affairs, 1979.

Nasr, Seyyed Hossein, Hamid Dabashi, and Seyyed Vali Reza Nasr, eds. *Expectation of the Millennium: Shi'ism in History*. Albany: State University of New York Press, 1989.

Nicholson, Reynold A. *A Literary History of the Arabs*. Cambridge: Cambridge University Press, 1966.

Oseni, Zakariyau I. "The Revolt of Black Slaves in Iraq under the 'Abbasid Administration in 869–883 CE." *Hamdard Islamicus* 12/2 (1989): 57–65.

Peters, Rudolph. *Jihad in Medieval and Modern Islam*. Leiden: Brill, 1977.

Peterson, J. E. "The Revival of the Ibadi Imamate in Oman and the Threat to Muscat, 1913–20." In *Arabian Studies III*, ed. R. L. Bidwell and R. B. Serjeant, 165–188. London: C. Hurst, 1976.

al-Qadi, Widad. "The Development of the Term *Ghulāt* in Muslim Literature." In *Akten des VII. Kongresses fur Arabstik und Islamwissenschaft*, 295–319. Gottingen: Vandenhoeck und Ruprecht in Gottingen, 1974.

al-Qadi, Widad. "The Limitations of Qur'ānic Usage in Early Arabic Poetry: The Example of a Khārijite Poem." In *Festschrift Ewald Wagner zum 65. Geburtstag*, vol. 2: *Studien zur arabischen Dichtung*, ed. W. Heinrichs and G. Schoeler, 168–181. Beirut: Kommission bei Franz Steiner Verlag Stuttgart, 1994.

Rahman, Fazlur. *Major Themes of the Qur'ān*. Minneapolis: Bibliotheca Islamica, 1994.

Rahnema, Ali. *An Islamic Utopian: A Political Biography of 'Ali Shari'ati*. New York: I. B. Tauris, 1998.

al-Rawas, Isam. *Oman in Early Islamic History*. Reading: Ithaca Press, 2000.

Retso, Jan. *The Arabs in Antiquity: Their History from the Assyrians to the Umayyads*. London: Routledge Curzon, 2003.

Robinson, Chase F. *Empire and Elites after the Muslim Conquest: The Transformation of Northern Mesopotamia*. Cambridge: Cambridge University Press, 2000.

Sachedina, Abdulaziz Abdulhussein. *The Just Ruler in Shi'ite Islam*. Oxford: Oxford University Press, 1988.

Salem, Elie Adib. *Political Theory and Institutions of the Khawarij*. Baltimore: Johns Hopkins University Press, 1956.

al-Salimi, Abdulrahman. "Identifying the Ibāḍī/Omani *Siyar*." *Journal of Semitic Studies* 55/1 (2010): 115–162.

———. "Themes of the Ibāḍī/Omani *Siyar*." *Journal of Semitic Studies* 54/2 (2009): 475–514.

Savage, Elizabeth. "Berbers and Blacks: Ibadi Slave Traffic in Eighth-Century North Africa." *Journal of African History* 33/3 (1992): 351–368.

———. *A Gateway to Hell, A Gateway to Paradise: The North African Response to the Arab Conquest*. Princeton: Princeton University Press, 1997.

———. "Survival through Alliance: The Establishment of the Ibāḍiyya." *Bulletin of the British Society for Middle East Studies* 17/1 (1990): 5–15.

Schimmel, Annemarie. *And Muhammad Is His Messenger: The Veneration of the Prophet in Islamic Piety*. Chapel Hill: University of North Carolina Press, 1985.

———. *Mystical Dimensions of Islam*. Chapel Hill: University of North Carolina Press, 1975.

Sears, Stuart. "Umayyad Partisan or Khārijite Rebel?: The Issue of 'Abd al-'Azīz b. MDWL?" *Studia Iranica* 31/1 (2002): 71–78.

Shaban, M. A. *Islamic History: A New Approach*, 2 vols. Cambridge: Cambridge University Press, 1971.

Sizgorich, Thomas. *Violence and Belief in Late Antiquity: Militant Devotion in Christianity and Islam*. Philadelphia: University of Pennsylvania Press, 2009.

Skeet, Ian. *Muskat and Oman: The End of an Era*. London: Faber and Faber, 1974.

Skladanek, B. "Elements of Chronology of the Khārijite Insurrection of Ḥamziyya in Sīstān (8th–9th Century): Its Outbreak and Fall." *Folia Orientalia* 22 (1981): 81–95.

———. "The Khārijites in Iran. I: Division into Sects." *Rocznik Orientalistyczny* 44/1 (1985): 65–92.

———. "The Khārijites in Iran. II: The Achievement of Political Goals." *Rocznik Orientalistyczny* 44/2 (1985): 89–101.

Talhami, Ghada Hashem. "The Zanj Rebellion Reconsidered." *International Journal of African Historical Studies* 10/3 (1977): 443–461.

Tayob, Abdulkader. "Fitnah: The Ideology of Conservative Islam." *Journal of Theology for Southern Africa* 69 (1989): 65–71.

Thomson, William. "Kharijitism and the Kharijites." In *The MacDonald Presentation Volume*, 373–389. Princeton: Princeton University Press, 1933.

Timani, Hussam S. *Modern Intellectual Readings of the Kharijites*. New York: Peter Lang, 2008.

Von Grunebaum, Gustav E. *Classical Islam: A History 600–1258*. New York: Barnes and Noble Books, 1970.

Walker, John. *A Catalogue of the Arab-Byzantine and Post Reform Umaiyad Coins*. London: Trustees of the British Museum, 1956.

———. *A Catalogue of the Arab-Sassanian Coins*. London: Trustees of the British Museum, 1941.

Walker, Paul. "An Isma'ili Version of the Heresiography of the Seventy-Two Erring Sects." In *Mediaeval Isma'ili History and Thought*, ed. Farhad Daftary, 161–177. Cambridge: Cambridge University Press, 1996.

Wansbrough, John. *The Sectarian Milieu*. Oxford: Oxford University Press, 1978.

Watt, Montgomery W. "The Conception of the Charismatic Community in Islam." *Numen* 7 (1960): 77–90.

———. *The Formative Period of Islamic Thought*. Oxford: Oneword Press, 1998.

———. *Islamic Political Thought*. Edinburgh: Edinburgh University Press, 1968.

———. "Kharijite Thought in the Umayyad Period." *Der Islam* 36 (1961): 215–231.

———. *Muhammad at Mecca*. Oxford: Oxford University Press, 1953.

———. *Muhammad at Medina*. Oxford: Oxford University Press, 1955.

———. *Muhammad's Mecca*. Edinburgh: Edinburgh University Press, 1988.

———. "The Signifigance of Kharijism under the Abbasids." In *Recherches d'Islamologie*, ed. S. A. Ali, 381–387. Louvain: Editions Peeters, 1977.

———. "Was Wasil a Kharijite?" In *Early Islam*, ed. Montgomery Watt, 129–139. Edinburgh: Edinburgh University Press, 1990.

Wellhausen, Julius. *The Religio-Political Factions of Early Islam*. New York: American Elsevier, 1975.

Wensinck, A.J. *The Muslim Creed: Its Genesis and Historical Development*. London: Frank Cass, 1965.

Wilkinson, John C. "Bayāsira and Bayādir." *Arabian Studies* 1 (1974): 75–85.

———. "Bio-Bibliographical Background to the Crisis Period in the Ibāḍi Imamate of Oman (End of 9th to End of 14th Century)." In *Arabian Studies III*, ed. R. L. Bidwell and R. B. Serjeant, 137–163. London: C. Hurst, 1976.

———. "The Early Development of the Ibāḍi Movement in Basra." In *Studies on the First Century of Islamic Society*, ed. G.H.A. Juynboll, 125–144; 241–249. Carbondale: Southern Illinois University Press, 1982.

———. "Ibāḍi Ḥadīth: An Essay in Normalization." *Der Islam* 62/2 (1985): 231–259.

———. "The Ibāḍi *Imāma*." *BSOAS* 39/3 (1976): 535–551.

———. "Ibāḍī Theological Literature." In *Religion, Learning and Science in the 'Abbasid Period*, ed. M.J.L. Young, J. D. Latham and R. B. Serjeant, 33–39. Cambridge: Cambridge University Press, 1990.

———. *The Imamate Tradition of Oman*. Cambridge: Cambridge University Press, 1987.

———. "The Julanda of Oman." *Journal of Oman Studies* 1 (1975): 97–108.

———. "The Omani and Ibāḍī Background to the Kilwa Sīrah: The Demise of Oman as a Political and Religious Force in the Indian Ocean in the 6th/12th Century." In *A Miscellany of Middle Eastern Articles in Memoriam for Thomas Muir Johnstone*, ed. A. K. Irvine, R. B. Serjeant and G. R. Smith, 131–148. London: Longman International, 1988.

Wittgenstein, Ludwig. *Culture and Value*, tr. Peter Winch. Chicago: University of Chicago Press, 1980.

Index